The Politics of Caspian Oil

Also by Bülent Gökay

BRITISH DOCUMENTS ON FOREIGN AFFAIRS: TURKEY 1923–1939 (*seven volumes*)

A CLASH OF EMPIRES: Turkey between Russian Bolshevism and British Imperialism

KOSOVO: Myths, Conflict and War (*co-editor*)

The Politics of Caspian Oil

Edited by

Bülent Gökay
Coordinator of European Studies
Lecturer in International Relations
Keele University
Staffordshire

palgrave

First published 2001 by
PALGRAVE
Houndmills, Basingstoke, Hampshire RG21 6XS and
175 Fifth Avenue, New York, N. Y. 10010
Companies and representatives throughout the world

PALGRAVE is the new global academic imprint of St. Martin's Press LLC Scholarly and Reference Division and Palgrave Publishers Ltd (formerly Macmillan Press Ltd).

ISBN 0–333–73973–6

This book is printed on paper suitable for recycling and made from fully managed and sustained forest sources.

A catalogue record for this book is available from the British Library.

Library of Congress Cataloging-in-Publication Data
Gökay, Bülent.
The politics of Caspian oil / Bülent Gökay.
p. cm.
Includes bibliographical references and index.
ISBN 0–333–73973–6
1. Petroleum industry and trade—Political aspects—Caspian Sea Region. 2. Geopolitics—Caspian Sea Region. 3. Caspian Sea Region—Politics and government. I. Title.
HD9576.C372 G65 2000
333.8'23'09475—dc21

00–059175

10 9 8 7 6 5 4 3 2 1
10 09 08 07 06 05 04 03 02 01

Printed and bound in Great Britain by
Antony Rowe Ltd, Chippenham, Wiltshire

Contents

Acknowledgements

My thanks are due to so many friends and colleagues, who have shared my interest in the history and politics of the Caspian–Caucasus over many years, that I cannot mention them all here.

I am particularly indebted to the contributors to the volume, from whom I have learned a tremendous amount in the editing process: many thanks for their support and patience.

I appreciate the comments of David Scrivener who gave me a helpful set of critical comments on an earlier version of the 'Background' chapter. I am particularly indebted to Lily Hamourtziadou who read all parts of the text and offered numerous suggestions and comments. I would like to thank Jo North whose excellent editorial reading and efficiency added much to the manuscript in its final stages of preparation.

Bülent Gökay
Keele University
June 2000

Notes on the Contributors

Bülent Gökay is a lecturer in the Department of International Relations and the Director of the European Studies Programme at Keele University. His publications include *A Clash of Empires: Turkey between Russian Bolshevism and British Imperialism* (1997), and seven volumes of *British Documents of Foreign Affairs – Turkey, 1923–39*(1997). He is a joint editor of *Kosovo: Myths, Conflict and War* (1999).

Avedis Bedros Hadjian was born in Aleppo, Syria, in 1968. Living in Argentina since 1970, he has an MPhil in International Relations from the University of Cambridge. He is currently working in Argentina with *La Nacion* and *La Prensa*. He is also an assistant lecturer at the Faculty of Journalism, Universidad Austral, Buenos Aires.

Kamer Kasim graduated from the Faculty of Political Science at Ankara University, and finished his MA and PhD at the Government Department of Manchester University. His research interest is in the field of Turkish foreign policy and the Caucasus and Central Asia.

Jean-Christophe Peuch spent four years (1993–1997) with Reuters news agency in Moscow where he covered energy, commodities and politics in Russia and the CIS. He also worked two years with France's Total oil group in Moscow. Prior to this, he was an analyst for the Research Center for Strategic and Technological Studies (CREST), Ecole Polytechnique, Paris.

Roland Sinker is a qualified solicitor, working with the law firm Linklaters and Alliance in London, since completing his MPhil in International Relations at the University of Cambridge in 1996. During an eight-month secondment to Hong Kong he worked in project finance on energy and infrastructure projects in the developing economies of Southeast Asia. During 1998–1999 he was seconded to the UK as policy adviser to the telecommunications regulator. He is currently an assistant solicitor in the telecommunications and information technology corporate departments.

Angeliki Spatharou is a Doctoral Candidate at the Faculty of Social and Political Studies, University of Cambridge. Her research interest is in the area of oil and international politics in Eurasia.

Andrew Towner graduated from Keele University with a degree in Russian Studies and International Politics. He spent twenty months in Moscow during the Chechen war, studying at the Moscow Linguistic University. During this period he witnessed the deep-seated psychological effect the war had on all sectors of Russian society, including the political and military establishment.

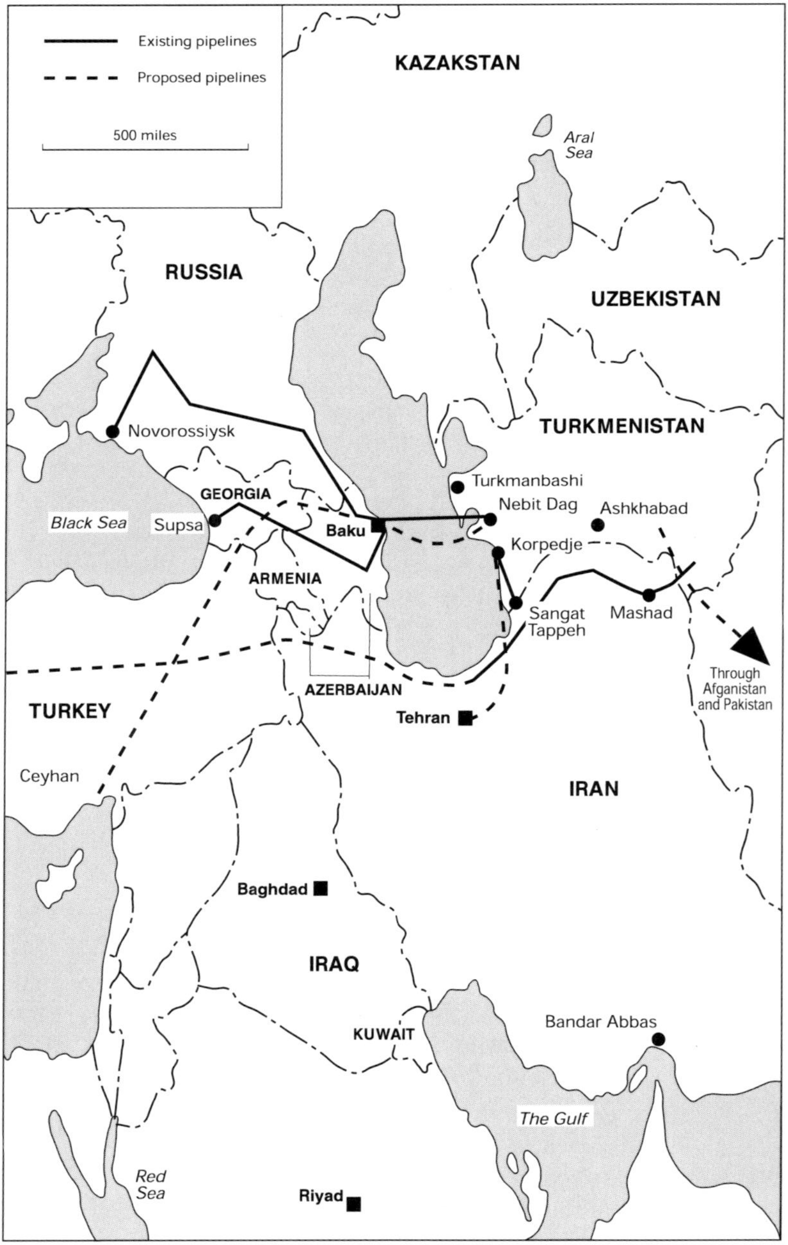

Caspian Oil Pipelines

1
The Background: History and Political Change

Bülent Gökay

The Caspian–Caucasus region has received considerable attention over the past seven years, both because of its potential as a source of oil and gas for world energy markets, and because of the environmental consequences of such development for this ecologically delicate body of water. The Caspian Sea is an enclosed body of water, roughly 700 miles from north to south and 250 miles across, lying directly between the states of Central Asia and the Transcaucasus. It is a salt-water body, connected to the Black Sea by the Volga and Don rivers, the artificial Volga–Don canal (all passing through Russian territory), and the Sea of Azov, a branch of the Black Sea.

The Caspian–Caucasus is a region of complexities, rich in the diversity of peoples, nations and language. Hardly anywhere else on the planet can one find a territory of a comparable size as heterogeneous in terms of language, religion and culture. The countries of this region are blots on the map, pimples on the backs of Russia, Turkey and Iran. They are represented in Western perceptions by equally scrappy images: genocide and earthquake in the case of Armenia, wild horsemen and smiling centenarians in the case of Georgia, utterly foreign and barbar Muslims in the case of Azerbaijan and the North Caucasus. The total inhabitants of this area are not more than 30 million. Yet their cultural and historical heritage goes back further than those of many European nations. Caspian–Caucasus has always had a romantic appeal for foreigners. Thousands of years ago the routes connecting northern and eastern Europe with Asia Minor and the Greek colonies passed through here. The Argonauts were the first 'foreign tourists', so to speak, to visit the Black Sea coast of the Caspian–Caucasus. Prometheus, who brought fire to mankind in defiance of Zeus, was said to have been chained to a cliff in the Caucasus.

Thousands of years have passed since then, but people are still attracted to the region of Caspian–Caucasus. The recent attraction of the region is related to its natural resources, especially the oil reserves of the Caspian Sea basin. Since 1991, oil has become a major symbol of the region's potential. During the Soviet period, the Caspian basin was politically closed to the world oil industry. The hydrocarbon potential of the Caspian basin states had been suspected by outsiders but remained unconfirmed during the Soviet period. Moscow had been unwilling to invest in oil and natural gas development in the region, and the resource base has remained relatively untouched. With the collapse of the Soviet power and the emergence of the new independent republics in Central Asia and the Caucasus, the Caspian Sea basin, with its vast oil and natural gas resources, has become an area of great interest as well as foreign investment. The oil industry has returned to the region after decades of Soviet isolation, hoping to rebuild the Caspian Sea basin into one of the world's great oil-exporting regions.

Current industry estimates put oil reserves under the depths of the Caspian Sea at up to 13 billion tonnes, more than any region outside the Persian Gulf.[1] The oil potential of this colossal territory is so significant that the analytical centres of the world's large oil and refining companies consider it to be more long-term than the unstable Persian Gulf. Such reserves put the region on a par with Saudi Arabia, and it is expected that the Caspian basin will become the second most important source for oil for the world's industrialised centres in the next century.

Since 1991 the oil rush to the Caspian has been underway. Large oil companies are racing one another, eager to invest billions of dollars to tap unexploited hydrocarbon resources of the Caspian Sea basin. The intensifying struggle for control of the vast oil resources of the Caspian Sea basin is often cast as a replay of the nineteenth-century 'Great Game', in which the British and Russian empires fought each other for political power and military influence in the same region.

Early history

Since ancient times, the Caspian–Caucasus has been one of those regions of the world where there is a long history of involvement with oil. Early travellers' reports attest to the historic presence of the oil in the Baku region. Oil over the centuries seemed as much a magic potion as an industrial commodity. Exploitation by collection from springs and shallow pits was well noted in the earliest historical records. Oil was being extracted and considerable commerce was carried on in the area, providing oil both for medicinal purposes and for cooking, heating and lighting in homes. The natural flow of oil and gas at Baku is one of the most spectacular in the world and has been narrated since the earliest times.

Stories of Baku's 'eternal fires' have emanated from the area for at least 2500 years, and authenticated reports since the sixth century BC. Zarathustra (Zoroaster)[2] was said to have travelled to see the fires with his own eyes.[3] The ancient literature of Greece and Rome contains many references to the oil and gas of the Baku area. Herodotus of 450 BC complained about the evil smell of north Persian oil and described the production of oil and salt from springs and wells.[4] Still, the oldest records on the 'eternal fires' of Baku are not very precise and give us little information about oil extraction and its uses.[5]

The Byzantine authors often referred to 'Median fire', meaning the fire from the north-western region of Persia (Medina). This might well mean the oil from the Baku area. When the Byzantine emperor Heraklius invaded Panthia, his troops, we are told, destroyed the temples of the fire-worshippers in the region. Some of the temples were said to be burning natural gas.[6] Yet, nothing more definite was known about the methods of exploitation of the seepages and gas-wells.

Despite numerous references, the early history of commercial exploitation of the Baku oil springs and hand-dug wells is not completely known.[7] The first records of deliberate export of oil appear during the tenth century. At this time, wells were already being dug on the Apsheron Peninsula at an average depth of about 10–12 metres.[8]

European travellers came to Baku at the end of the thirteenth century. Marco Polo, who visited northern Persia in 1271–3, while travelling along the Ancient Silk Route,[9] wrote of a spring that spouted a liquid 'good to burn'.

> On this frontier towards Georgiana, there is a spring from which flow oil in such abundance that a hundred ships at a time may be loaded with it. The oil is not good to eat, but it is good to burn and to anoint camels with, against mange and dandruff. People come from great distances to fetch this oil, and in the whole district no other oil is burnt but this.[10]

From the early seventeenth century onwards there is a great variety of records of the Baku oil, oilfields and the trade of oil. The evidence shows that petroleum was widely used as a fuel, and as a solvent for removing stains from textiles.[11]

Russian control

Although knowledge and exploitation of the oil springs of Caspian–Caucasus region dated back to ancient times, and hand-dug wells had been supplying oil for several centuries,[12] the great oilfields of Baku were too isolated from important consuming centres to play much of a role in the development of the modern oil industry. After the region came under Russian control this picture began to change. The Russian tsar was aware of the importance of the Baku oil, and had anticipated the modern petroleum industry. This awareness of the importance of oil did, indeed, drive him to wage war on Persia to wrest control of Baku, bringing its oil wealth under Russian control.

At the beginning of the Russian period, there were 82 oil wells in Baku.[13] There were other oil springs along the eastern Caspian shore. On the Cheleken island in the Caspian Sea oil was being obtained from about 3500 pits and seepages in 1838. The product was used for lighting and as a substitute for tallow.[14] The annual production of the Baku oil region was described in 1843 as 3 372 162 kilograms (28 000 barrels) of 'black naphtha' and 14 143 kilograms (106 barrels) of 'white naphtha'. All this was from common pits and surface springs.[15]

Prince Mikhail S. Vorontsov, first viceroy of the Caucasus, wrote in July 1847 to the Russian State Secretary, Vronchenko, that:

> I authorised new oil exploration in the Bibi-Eibat section, Baku District, on the Caspian Sea coast, by means of earth drills, and used 1,000 rubles allocated by you for this purpose. In consequence, the director of the Baku and Shirvan mineral fields has reported that oil was found in a well drilled at Bibi-Eibat.[16]

According to the Azerbaijan Academy of Sciences, the first well was prepared in what is now the giant Bibi-Eibat field in 1848.[17] When they drilled for water they found oil. However, mechanical drilling did not substitute digging by hand until drilling machinery was imported to Baku in 1871. The annual production of Russia increased from 41 000 barrels in 1863 to 204 000 barrels in 1870, all of which was from the Baku fields. Some attempts at refining the crude oil began in the Baku region in 1863 with the opening of a local refinery, and in ten years' time there were ten small-size refineries processing the oil successfully.[18]

Under Russian control, diverse ownerships of the tsarist government, regional authorities and private claimants complicated mineral titles. The Russian government, which owned most of the oil land, practised a lease system from 1813 to 1825, and a contractor exploited the ancient oil springs and pits under a licence from the Russian authorities. From 1825 to 1849 the Russian government operated the field on its own. The contractor system was reintroduced in 1849 and lasted to 1872.[19] The Russian government abandoned the use of a single contractor after 1871 and instituted the practice of auctioning leases in 1872. This system was designed to encourage growth in the oil industry, by opening the market to investors with substantial capital ready to engage in large-scale, mechanised production. After this, leasing for longer terms was introduced to the highest bidder at public auction. A combination of public auction and royalty system was practised from 1896 until 1917.[20]

Large flowing wells were obtained in the region of Baku in 1873. For the next twenty years, Russian output increased each year without a setback. The Baku district produced most of the Russian oil. Local conditions and the tsarist initiatives gave rise to particular Russian concepts and engineering practices. The more extensive experience of the American oil industry, however, had a significant impact on this development.

The distinguished Russian chemist Dimitri Mendeleyev, who was commissioned to analyse the situation in the Caspian–Caucasus oil region, attended the US Centennial Exposition at Philadelphia in 1876 as a member of the official Russian delegation. This offered him the opportunity to visit the Pennsylvania oil-producing region. He was impressed by the fact that the Pennsylvania oil belt and the principal axes of the Alleghany mountains bore a remarkable resemblance to the Baku fields and the Caucasus mountains.[21] Mendeleyev, together with Steinmann, the Director of Mines in the Caucasus, also played an important role in the abolishment of the four-year contract system.

The 1880s witnessed a reorganisation of the oil industry under a centralised system. In particular, the post-1873 reforms in the organisation of oil exploitation were important for preparing the way for many new entrepreneurs who were about to enter the oil business at this time. Three significant oil conferences,[22] in 1884, 1885 and 1886, became instrumental in creating the Baku Oil Producers Society, an executive body for the Caspian–Caucasus oil industry. All aspects of the oil industry, from the production of oil to its transportation, dues levied on producers, refineries and pipeline carriers came under the control of this umbrella body. The Baku Oil Producers Society exerted a stabilising influence on the oil industry, contributing to the creation of a climate of opinion, encouraging further confidence in the oil extraction, sales and trade.

The organisational skills of the Baku Oil Producers Society helped advance a more confident attitude in the Russian oil industry. The creation of the Statistical Office in 1889 was one of the significant achievements of the Society. This contributed seriously to the promotion of a more rational attitude and professional practices in the Russian oil industry. Prior to this date, precise statistical data were difficult to obtain, and based as much on estimates as on solid information. After 1889, the growth of the Russian oil industry and its expansion could be mapped in detail.[23]

The impact of the growing impulse within the tsarist empire towards industrialisation in the 1890s was significant for the further progress of the oil industry. The accession to the throne of Tsar Alexander III and the performance of his Minister of Finance, Count Sergius Witte, helped to create a more fertile ground for the industrialisation drive. Before Witte, the oil industry in Russia, despite the daring achievements of the 1870s and 1880s, was growing in an environment which had barely changed for centuries.

Count Witte was appointed as Minister of Finance in 1892. Institutional changes and new practices introduced by Witte had a profound impact both in economic and social terms, both during and after his tenure in office. Witte's currency reforms stabilised the ruble, which attracted many foreign entrepreneurs to the Baku oil business. The construction of the Trans-Siberian Railway in this period provided more practical means of transporting the fuel oil to the far corners of the empire. In 1883, the Transcaucasian railroad was completed, connecting the Black Sea port of Batumi to Baku. As a result, effective and swift access to world markets could become possible through railway tank cars to Batumi and thence by steamship to Western Europe.[24]

There were impressive developments in the field of exploration and exploitation. Successful wells were completed at Balakhany, and the productive area spread eastward through Surakhany, Sabunchy and Zabrat. Significant increase in production was achieved when Binagady field was discovered in 1896, and the large Surakhany field was opened in 1907. A pipeline from Baku to the ports on the Black Sea was constructed in 1901. Russia became the largest oil-producing country in 1898, and held that position until 1902. The peak year was 1901. Half of the world's petroleum in 1901 came from about 1900 wells in the Caucasus, in an area of less than six square miles. The oilfields of the Baku district on Apsheron peninsula – the giant Bibi Eibat, and Balakhany–Sabunchy–Ramany fields – supplied 95 per cent of the total.[25]

Foreign companies in the Caspian basin

The most important achievement of the Russian oil industry in the 1880s and 1890s was to foster a more confident attitude amongst the foreign investors. The Russian oil industry began to inspire foreign buyers, who found themselves impressed by the new vigour and modern climate within which the Russian oil industry was now run. The entrance of foreign capital began with the arrival of the Swedish Nobel brothers, Robert and Ludwig Nobel, who more than anybody else deserve the credit for bringing the Russian oil industry to world prominence in the late ninetenth century.

Robert was the first Nobel who visited Baku. When he arrived in Baku in March 1873, the boasting optimism and passion of a boomtown fascinated Robert. He spent a few days in Baku, mostly investigating oil refineries and listening the tales of oilmen, and spent 25 000 rubles to buy a small refinery and several parcels of oil-rich land in Baku. Starting with this small enterprise, Robert Nobel improved and modernised the refinery process, and, in two years, proved that he was the most competent refiner in Baku. His modernised refinery produced the highest quality kerosene that had ever come out of Russia.[26]

In 1875, the Nobel family purchased the giant Balakhany field and built their first modernised refinery. In 1877, they built the first tanker in Russia, *Zoroaster.* A pipeline was laid during the same year from the Balakhany field to the refinery. They supplied a substantial market for illuminating oil in northern Europe by tank steamers on the Caspian to Astrakhan. At Astrakhan the cargo was transferred to Volga River barges. During the next twenty-five years, the Nobel interests drilled more than 500 wells, employed as many as 12 000 men in their petroleum business, and produced about 150 million barrels of petroleum.[27]

Following the Nobels, the international Rothschild company came and contributed further to the expansion of the oil industry in the Caspian–Caucasus region. The Rothschilds came to the region in 1892 and founded a company called the *Société Commerciale et Industrielle de Napthe Caspienne et de la Mer Noire.*[28] The Rothschild interests were more concentrated on developing markets than in exploring. Together with the Nobels, they built small tank steamers to carry petroleum across the Caspian Sea for transfer to Volga River barges, and they were largely responsible for the construction of a railroad from Baku to Batumi. They also built an oil pipeline, which was built part way in 1901 and finished in 1905.

The Nobel company was one of the world's earliest big integrated oil operators. It was the largest producer in Russia before the First World

War. The Rothschilds' was the second largest Russian producing enterprise. At the beginning of 1911, the Royal Dutch-Shell group acquired the Rothschilds' company.[29] Until the First World War, large, assertive, well-financed, well-managed and technically competent companies maintained principal control of the oil industry in the Caspian–Caucasus region. When the war started the oil business was in strong hands and seemingly on the verge of a period of more orderly progress.

Caspian oil under Soviet control

When the Bolsheviks came to power in 1917, Russia had 28 oil and gas fields, mostly in the Caspian–Caucasus region. The Revolution confiscated private holdings and practically isolated the immense crude resources of the country from the rest of the world. The petroleum industry remained in chaos for the next ten years.[30] During the period of the Russian Civil War, 1918–21, the Caspian–Caucasus region entered a phase of complete economic catastrophe and political disorder. At the beginning of the Civil War, Azerbaijan, together with Georgia and Armenia, declared independence in April 1918. In September of the same year, the Ottoman forces occupied Baku. When the First World War was concluded in two months' time, this time the British forces replaced the Turks as the occupying power in Baku. They imposed martial law and maintained control on the Baku–Batumi railway line, mainly to secure the oil transport.[31]

The oil industry was in the control of the new government of independent Azerbaijan. During this period, Standard Oil of New Jersey signed a contract worth a third of a million dollars with the Azerbaijani government for the purchase of eleven plots in Baku, and purchased half of the shares of the Nobel interests.[32] When the Bolsheviks overthrew the independent Azerbaijani regime and established the Soviet Azerbaijan in April 1920, all these came to an end.[33]

Oil production, however, increased consistently from 1920 to 1928. Bibi Eibat was extended into the Caspian Sea by dirt fill in 1922–3, and the construction of steel pilings in 1924. During 1925 the first well was completed by the Soviet engineers in the Caspian offshore area from a ramp of steel pilings and boards.[34] Oil production surpassed the former 1901 peak in 1928. The resumption of drilling in 1924, which had completed extensions and deeper sands in the Baku fields, and the development of better methods of operation were the main reasons for this.[35]

With the adoption of Stalin's First Five-Year Plan in April 1929, the central government maintained control over every detail of petroleum exploration and exploitation. During the years of successive Five-Year Plans, a new geography of raw materials and fuel was created, which brought the industry closer to the sources of raw materials and the regions of consumption.

The late 1920s and 1930s were notable for significant technological accomplishments in the Soviet oil industry. Electrical prospecting began in 1928 and was used more extensively than in other oil-producing countries. It was employed effectively in basement studies and also for mapping sedimentary intersects with large resistivity divergences.[36]

Despite the new discoveries in the Volga–Ural region, during the period up to the Second World War, the Baku–North Caucasus region continued to provide an average of 80 per cent of the Soviet Union's crude oil output. In 1940, out of the 227 030 000 barrels of oil produced in the whole country, 62 060 000 barrels came from Baku, 16 060 000 barrels from the North Caucasus, and 49 910 000 barrels from the other regions.[37]

The Second World War, particularly the German military threat to the oilfields of the Caucasus, influenced the Soviet planners to focus drilling activities in the interior, especially in the newly thriving Volga–Urals district. As a result, in the post-war era, the Caspian–Caucasus oil region's importance declined in the Soviet oil industry. By 1949, the expanding Volga–Urals production had compensated for the wartime decline.[38] During the Fourth (1946–50), Fifth (1951–6), and Sixth (1956–7) Five-Year Plans, outstanding discoveries were made in the Volga–Urals. In this way, the focus of Soviet oil development shifted from the Caspian–Caucasus to a strategically crucial area between the Volga River and the Ural mountains. Other major discoveries were made in the Dnepr–Donets in the Ukraine, in the South Caspian, on the Bukhara–Khiva platform further east, and in the West Siberian basin. It took the Soviets time to recover from the damage done to their oilfields during the Second World War. But once the recovery was complete, achievements were notable: oil production in 1958 was more than five times greater than that of 1946.[39]

Following the death of Stalin in 1953, Soviet oil exports increased substantially and in 1954 the Soviet Union became a net exporter and remained one until the late 1970s. Soviet oil production was on the rise, and this greater production, coupled with limited refinery capacity, was an important reason for this export drive. The Soviet oil industry was faced with a shortage of pipes suitable for oil and gas line construction. One of the objectives of the oil export campaign was to secure pipe in return for oil. Italy, many other European states and Japan were willing to enter into such an arrangement.[40]

The Sixth Five-Year Plan was abandoned in 1959 and a Seven-Year Plan was introduced instead. The Seven-Year Plan reorganised the managing system of economy on a territorial basis with an emphasis on decentralisation. A territorial pattern of governance for the petroleum industry replaced the centralised organisation. The Ministry of Oil Industry was broken up and its functions were given out to the regional economic councils. In the new structure, the local trusts were responsible for operations and they were directly subordinate to regional economic councils.

The period of the Seven-Year Plan (1959–65) was remarkable for achievements in the oil industry.[41] Soviet oil production increased from 949 million barrels to 1770 million barrels. Trunk lines were laid from remote oilfields to leading industrial centres and new industries in underdeveloped areas. The COMECON oil line was completed from the Volga–Urals to Poland, East Germany, Czechoslovakia and Hungary in 1964. The first Soviet well drilled from a mobile self-elevating platform, the *Apsheron*, was completed in the Caspian Sea in 1966.[42] This massive development greatly advanced industrial growth, and fuel certainly contributed to whatever improvements had taken place.[43]

The Soviet oil industry developed substantially in this period. Yet there remained significant problems. Petroleum exploration was energetic and greatly successful. However, it lacked much of the modern instrumentation. Efforts were held back by the inappropriateness, on occasion, of Soviet technology and lack of an incentive system. Complaints of inefficiency were especially prevalent near the close of the Seven-Year Plan, when partial decentralisation had further increased the red tape. Many organisational and methodological difficulties remained in the oil industry. There was often enormous waste. There were ill-advised practices in operating the pressure-maintenance installations, inadequate use of available geological data concerning reservoir-rock characteristics, lack of intelligent planning for a drilling programme suitable to each reservoir, conflicting exploration goals, and scarcity of large capital expenditures for pumping equipment and drilling more wells.[44]

Still, great progress was recorded during the period of Economic Plan 1966–70. Annual production increased visibly and extensive pipeline construction continued. By the early 1970s, the number of proven fields increased enormously, and extensive pipeline construction made large supplies of oil and gas available to new industrial centres throughout the Soviet empire. Increasing regularisation and better facilities helped to create a more constructive environment for the Soviet oil industry.

However, compared to the West, many of the technical advances were still at an early stage of application in the Soviet Union. The equipment was bulky and difficult to transport. Recording equipment was poor, and depth penetration rarely exceeded 1500 to 3000 m.[45] Digital recording was still experimental. Data processing was done by old-style analog computers. Common-depth-point shooting was largely experimental in most regions. The Soviet oil researchers were far short of having the amount of sophisticated equipment that they needed for detailed deep-penetration studies of the geological structure. As a whole, the Soviet oil industry was 10 to 25 years behind US technology. Soviet gestures of détente in the 1970s seemed directed primarily to acquisition of high-tech machinery and know-how from the more advanced Western states.

During the late 1960s and 1970s, a combination of various problems – inadequate capacity to manufacture sufficient quantities of such indispensable equipment as compressors, large pipe, and electronic equipment; laggard technology; and bureaucratic inflexibility – was slowing down the development of the Soviet oil development. Still, production achieved such high levels despite material deficiencies and major mistakes. In 1974, Soviet oil production became the largest in the world. The Soviet Union was the only country on earth that was practically independent in energy. During the decade of détente, 1972–9, the unprecedented increase in the price of oil and gas created a chance to import Western know-how and technologies and made it possible to modernise some sections of the oil industry. Yet, the drop in the oil and gas prices at the end of 1979 slowed down this process.

In the 1980s, the Soviet Union was still the world's largest producer of energy and managed to achieve further industrial development. Yet the economic structure of the country was absolutely unprepared for the technological reorientation that was happening in the Western world. At the beginning of the same period, the microprocessor was invented in Silicon Valley, which opened the road to further and further miniaturisation and an increase in capacity. All this started the age of computerisation, which opened the road to an emerging new high-technology industry. Eventually, modern communications and computers penetrated virtually every sphere of the modern world economy. As this new age of high technology was emerging in the West in the 1970s, the Soviet Union and its satellites in eastern Europe were not prepared and not able to follow. The rigid model of modernisation was absolutely unprepared for technological re-orientation. Consequently, the technological gap broadened.

The problems in the Soviet petroleum industry were many, and for the most part conditions seemed to be worsening. The main structural factor was related to the perversity of the Soviet incentive system. Many of the older petroleum fields had been exhausted. But most Soviet officials commonly accepted that the depleted fields were working poorly in any case. Advanced recovery procedures were applied badly or not at all. There were numerous examples of poor or unused equipment imported for use in petroleum production and distribution.[46]

The rise in the cost of oil exploration and extraction was certainly a factor. However, the most pressing aspect of the petroleum industry in the Soviet Union in the late 1980s was the fact that Soviet technology seriously lagged behind that of the West. The oil extraction technology was underdeveloped. Soviet drill pipes and bits were of such poor quality that the drilling process often had to be stopped for repairs. Most steel goods did not meet minimum Western requirements for quality and construction standards. The drill pipe was too weak to withstand the torque for rotary drilling.[47] Equipment inadequacies hampered the efforts in offshore drilling and further geological exploration.[48]

When the Soviet Union was approaching its historic end in the late 1980s, the economy was faced with an interrelated set of mutually reinforcing problems. In virtually every sector of the Soviet economy growth rates were falling steadily. There was a serious shortage of much-needed investment funds. Labour productivity was about 40 per cent of the US level. And there was an extremely backward and inflexible infrastructure in industry.[49]

Within this gloomy picture, the Soviet oil industry was faced with deep structural problems to contend with. Soviet as well as Western sources indicated that oil production in the Soviet Union was in decline since 1984. As a result of the steady depletion of the oilfields through over-exploitation and under-investment in exploration efforts, the petroleum industry was deteriorating.[50]

Most of the problems had arisen not because the country lacked indigenous oil resources, but because the Soviet leaders, planners and the managers of the petroleum industry made poor use of what they had. This contradiction was one of the major characteristics of the oil industry in the Soviet Union: nature's exceptional bounty and man's inefficiency. The self-assured and complacent leaders simply refused to acknowledge the mounting signs of the growing crisis. What was at stake was 'the ability of the Soviet Union to enter the new millennium in a manner worthy of a great and prosperous power'.[51] The vast lands, controlled by the Soviet Union, were noted for the richness of their natural resources. Raw materials were for many years regarded as a limitless resource. In a sense the country's vast size, one of its most decisive potentials, was also one of its major handicaps.

Caspian Sea basin in the post-Soviet era

The collapse of the former Soviet Union has opened a new era in the history of oil production in the Caspian–Caucasus region. Despite long-standing problems, the post-Soviet Caspian–Caucasus is still considered as having enormous oil potential. The region provides one of the largest unexploited sources of oil in the world. The resource potential of the Caspian basin remains huge. If properly exploited, the oil resources in the region could become the driving force behind a broad economic development.

The largest reserves of explored oil in the region are concentrated near the shores of Azerbaijan and Kazakhstan. Almost all of Azerbaijan's oil reserves are located in the Caspian Sea shelf. Deposits on the Russian part of the shelf are not fully developed and will need further exploration in order to verify their worth. The coast of Turkmenistan is the least explored of all. Among the nations of the Caspian Sea basin, Iran possesses the largest total oil reserves. It is, however, least interested in the immediate development of the Caspian oil deposits. Russia has a large oil complex with a powerful export sector and a well-established system of pipelines. Turkmenistan is less concerned with oil than natural gas deposits. It has large reserves of natural gas, and at present is more concerned with exploring this gas potential and establishing an infrastructure that would allow this to take place.

As in fairy tales, where a series of problems have to be resolved before the reward can be claimed, the arrival of benefits following exploration, extraction, exploitation and the transportation to world markets of the hydrocarbon riches of the Caspian Sea basin is complicated by a number of serious problems and flammable pitfalls.

Working in the Caspian Sea basin has been a difficult task for international companies. The demise of the Soviet Union has opened up vast and hitherto unexplored hydrocarbon fields to outside investment, but it did not make the new independent republics that surround the Caspian Sea easy places to work in. The area is riddled with ethnic tension and has witnessed a number of nasty little civil wars and cross-border conflicts break out over the last eight years. The Caspian Sea region's crumbling and inadequate infrastructure has made exploration, development, exploitation and export of oil reserves a logistically difficult proposition.

There are increasing dangers of collision and miscalculation basically at three mutually inter-related and overlapping levels. First, the legal confusion over the definition of the Caspian Sea's status and the inability to obtain agreement by all the five riparian states. A considerable amount of oil is concentrated in the shallow shelf of the Caspian. It is important to craft the basic legal and commercial framework that the riparian states and private companies need to negotiate more detailed commercial agreements. There has been disagreement over the jurisdiction of the Caspian Sea and control of its economic zones. The Caspian's ambivalent status poses questions for preservation of regional stability.

Secondly, the issue of oil and gas transportation from the Caspian basin has now become an issue relating to the tight knot of regional rivalries, especially between Russia, Turkey and Iran. Political symbols come in many forms in the Caspian, but few are quite so compelling as oil and gas pipelines. The choice of an export route is fraught with political and economic problems. The project has been stymied by long-term ethnic hatreds, massive cost overruns and lasting Cold War rivalries. The question of which route to use for the Caspian's considerable reserves has inspired a high-stakes tug-of-war among the countries of the region. At present, the only operational oil export route follows the line Baku–Groznyi–Tikhoretsk–Novorrossisk, with a possibility of bypassing Chechnia to the east and joining the Atyray–Novorrossisk pipeline at Komsomolsky. Oil exports from this route are dependent on tanker transportation via the Turkish Straits. As the main alternative to the Russian pipeline, Turkey is actively promoting its own pipeline option, the Caspian–Mediterranean pipeline. Many in the West, however, now have the opinion that because of the many tensions in the region, instead of concentrating on building one pipeline, several pipelines should be built, including a route through Iran. Currently, US–Iranian antagonism makes the Iranian route seem like a long shot, yet given commercial realities, any political opening could shift the terms of the pipeline question very quickly.

And finally, serious questions arise with regard to environmental and ecological issues. There is a danger of ruining the Caspian's unique ecosystem, which could soon lead to an irreversible environmental catastrophe. Present environmental problems are attributed to the violation of the former well-understood, accepted and practised norms in the regulation of the Caspian, and the present lack of control in oil exploration operations by some of the newly independent Caspian riparian states. The general ecological situation in the region is on the verge of catastrophe. In addition to the rising sea level and the flooding of coastal zones in the Republic of Kalmykia in the Russian federation, and the independent Republic of Azerbaijan, the problem of increasing saturation and greasiness of the soil further exacerbates the situation. In the danger zone of serious flooding there are towns and population centres with an overall population of 700 000 people who need urgent evacuation. There is also a need to move 200 000 km of electricity power lines from this zone. Another aspect of ecological danger is the threat of the complete destruction of sturgeon and other aquatic forms of life, fish and plants. As a result of the development of offshore oilfields, sturgeon stocks along the coast of Azerbaijan face the threat of extinction. The development work of the Azeri, Chirag and Guneshli oilfields has produced a concentration of hydrocarbon waste in an area where large shoals of sturgeon spend the winter months. The recent developments in the oil industry affect the 10 million people living around the Caspian basin, whose life is bound up in the fishing industry. Over-hasty exploitation of the Caspian's oil reserves, at the cost of its ecosystem, could well bring disaster to the people of this region. There is an urgent need to accept responsibility and implement measures devoted to preserving the ecosystem.[52]

The new states of the Caucasus and Central Asia are in a tough neighbourhood. Wedged between Russia to the north and Iran and Afghanistan to the south, these countries have been dominated by outside powers and plagued by political instability and economic dependency for centuries. Today, for the first time ever, these states have a chance to seize their own destinies and develop into a region of stable and prosperous states. The massive scale of investment and activity related to the oil extraction in and around the Caspian Sea will definitely have a noticeable effect on social and economic life in the region. There is great potential for and variety of investment oportunities in the region. Because the oil economy requires an immense infrastructure, many service industries will be involved. This means major capital expenditure in houses, roads, railroads, hotels, telecommunications, warehouses and services. However, the very factors that might promote regional stability and development, ironically, could also sow the seeds of instability. The same potential development in Caspian oil and pipelines could provide the fuel for further political conflict and environmental damage. With a rapid growth in revenue, the rulers' positions could be bolstered, and oil revenues will enable them to modify their military establishments dramatically. For the leaders of Georgia and Azerbaijan, a torrent of oil money might increase the temptation to reconquer the territories they lost in the aftermath of the collapse of the Soviet Union.

The potential for regional instability is not restricted to interstate competition, but could also be the result of challenges by global competition. The interrelationship of geopolitics, economics and technology, which is the basis of the oil industry, is a complex one. The recent competition between Amoco, Pennzoil, British Petroleum, Statoil and Lukoil as to how the oil from the region would be exported and brought to the world markets is an example of the explosive nature of geo-economics. Extra-regional competition, when linked to the traditional and contemporary sources of conflict within the region, may form the basis of a dangerous system of alliances with catalytic effects.

The Politics of Caspian Oil is a collection of essays aiming to present the results of recent research, and in this way to serve as a reference book for the politics of Caspian oil. The integration of the Caspian region into the world economy, and the interconnection of oil, politics and regional stability are analysed by Angeliki Spatharou in an interesting essay which sets the scene for other articles in the collection. Roland Sinker covers many legal aspects of the management of this transboundary energy resource. Through an analysis of the oil and gas of the Caspian, Sinker's essay aims to investigate the ways to develop effective approaches to the management of transboundary resources. Azerbaijan's energy policy and its implications for Russian security are the subject of Avedis Hadjian's essay. The essay investigates the process through which Azerbaijan has sought to escape Russian influence in the development and export of Azeri oil during the last seven years. Jean-Christophe Peuch's essay deals with the role of private corporations in the development of Caspian Sea resources, and analyses the complex and sometimes contradictory relationship between the economic motives of private enterprise and official policies of their governments. Kamer Kasim's chapter explores the Nagorno-Karabakh conflict in the context of Caspian oil and regional power rivalries. Finally, a cogent assessment of the 'oil factor' in Russian policies in Chechnya is presented by Andrew Towner. Towner attempts to answer the question of whether the war in Chechnya may be interpreted as a continuation of the varied policies implemented to protect Russia's most economically prized natural resource.

Notes

1 Kamilzhan Kalandarov, *Nezavisimaya Gazeta*, 4 June 1997, p. 5.
2 Zoroaster, the founder of a religion called Zoroastrianism, was reputed to date from about 1000 BC. His ideas are said to have been inspired by the eternal fires to be found in Baku, now known to be underground gas emissions.
3 John McLaurin, *Sketches in Crude Oil*, Harrisburg, 1896, p. 8.
4 Given in Edgar Wesley Owen, *Trek of the Oil Finders: a History of Exploration for Petroleum*, Tulsa, Oklahama: American Association of Petroleum Geologists, 1975, p. 1.
5 J. Mitzakis, *The Russian Oil Fields and Petroleum Industry*, London: Pall Mall Press, 1911, pp. 21–2.
6 Given in R. J. Forbes, *Studies in Early Petroleum History*, Leiden: E.J. Brill, 1958, p. 154.
7 Ibid. The rise of Islam in the seventh century saw the whole of the Caucasus region fall to Arab invasions. For 300 years Azerbaijan was under the sway of Arab caliphs.
8 Ibid., pp. 154–5.
9 The Silk Road passed just a few hundred kilometres to the south of Azerbaijan, providing commercial opportunities to merchants.
10 *The Travels of Marco Polo*, translated into English by A. Ricci, George Routledge and Sons, 1931, pp. 21–2.
11 Forbes, *Studies in Early Petroleum History*, pp. 157–9.
12 At least 52 hand-dug wells were active on the site of the present-day giant Balakhany field in 1734 (given in Edgar Wesley Owen, *Trek of the Oil Finders: a History of Exploration for Petroleum*, Tulsa, Oklahoma: American Association of Petroleum Geologists, 1975, p. 1354).
13 Forbes, *Studies in Early Petroleum History*, pp. 161–2.
14 Owen, *Trek of the Oil Finders*, p. 3.
15 Ibid.
16 Frank Garaber, 'Watching the World', *Oil and Gas Journal*, 6 February 1967, p. 75.
17 The *Azerbaijani International* claims that it was 1844 when this first oil well was drilled (*Azerbaijani International*, 4.2, summer 1996, p. 50).
18 Owen, *Trek of the Oil Finders*, p. 4. Marcel Mitzakis, *The Oil Encyclopaedia*, New York: John Wiley and Sons, 1922, pp. 35–6.
19 Owen, *Trek of the Oil Finders*, pp. 90–1.
20 Owen, *Trek of the Oil Finders*, p. 149. Tadeusz Swietochowski, *Russian Azerbaijan, 1905–1920*, Cambridge University Press, 1985, p. 20. M. I. Goldman, *The Enigma of Soviet Petroleum*, George Allen and Unwin, 1980, pp. 14–17.
21 Owen, *Trek of the Oil Finders*, p. 149.
22 Conferences were sponsored by the Ministry of Public Works, the Imperial Department of Mines, the military governor of Kutais commanding the port of Batum, the Baku branch of the Imperial Technical Society, and the individual oil producers. (Robert W. Tolf, *The Russian Rockefellers: the Saga of the Nobel Family and the Russian Oil Industry*, Stanford, California: Hoover Institution Press, 1976, p. 141.)
23 Tolf, *The Russian Rockefellers*, p. 141.
24 Owen, *Trek of the Oil Finders*, p. 101.

25 Owen, *Trek of the Oil Finders*, pp. 257–61. M. I. Goldman, *The Enigma of Soviet Petroleum*, George Allen and Unwin, 1980, pp. 18–19. *The Oil and Gas Guide to the Former Soviet Union*, London and Moscow: CIS Technical Publishing Institute, 1995, p. 11.
26 Tolf, *The Russian Rockefellers*, pp. 36–47.
27 In 1901, the Nobel Prize was established from Alfred Nobel's will after his death (1833–96) by consolidating the wealth from sales of explosives and from shares in the oilfields in Baku. Alfred was the largest single stockholder (12 per cent) in the Nobel brothers' oil-producing company in Baku. The Nobel family's decision to allow the withdrawal of Alfred's money was the decisive factor that enabled the Nobel Prize to be established.
28 Herbert R. Lottman, *Return of the Rothschilds*, I. B. Tauris, 1995, p. 100.
29 Owen, *Trek of the Oil Finders*, p. 383.
30 M. I. Goldman, *The Enigma of Soviet Petroleum*, George Allen and Unwin, 1980, p. 21. A. A. Meyerhoff, 'Soviet Petroleum: History, Technology, Geology, Reserves, Potential and Policy', in R. G. Jensen, T. Shabad and A. W. Wright (eds), *Soviet Natural Resources in the World Economy*, University of Chicago Press, 1983, p. 306. Nikolai Baibakov, *The Cause of My Life*, Moscow: Progress Publishers, 1986, pp. 15, 21.
31 Tadeusz Swietochowski, *Russian Azerbaijan, 1905–1920*, Cambridge University Press, 1985, p. 143.
32 Tolf, *The Russian Rockefellers*, p. 214.
33 Owen, *Trek of the Oil Finders*, p. 1358. Goldman, *The Enigma of Soviet Petroleum*, pp. 23–4.
34 Owen, *Trek of the Oil Finders*, p. 1359.
35 Ibid., p. 1361.
36 Ibid., p. 1385.
37 Ibid., p. 1371. Meyerhoff, 'Soviet Petroleum', pp. 309–10.
38 Owen, *Trek of the Oil Finders*, p. 1371.
39 Marshall I. Goldman, 'Soviet Economic Trends, with Special Emphasis on Investment and Energy Policies', in Kinya Niiseki (ed.), *The Soviet Union in Transition*, Westview Press, 1987, p. 74.
40 Arthur Jay Klinghoffer, *The Soviet Union and International Oil Politics*, Columbia University Press, 1977, p. 65.
41 Meyerhoff, 'Soviet Petroleum', p. 310.
42 Owen, *Trek of the Oil Finders*, p. 1393.
43 Ibid., p. 1381.
44 Goldman, *The Enigma of Soviet Petroleum*, pp 35–54.
45 In contrast, in the West, depth penetration of 5000 to 10 000 m was commonplace (Meyerhoff, 'Soviet Petroleum', p. 316).
46 Goldman, 'Soviet Economic Trends', p. 79.
47 Meyerhoff, 'Soviet Petroleum' p. 317.
48 Ibid., p. 316.
49 *The Oil and Gas Guide to the Former Soviet Union*, p. 11.
50 Susan J. Linz, 'Gorbachev's Master Plan for Economic Recovery', in Jane Shapiro Zacek (ed.), *The Gorbachev Generation*, Paragon House, 1989, pp. 42–3. Many Soviet publications mentioned the technical problems facing the petroleum industry. They stressed the need for much scientific and

technical improvement in geophysics and in drilling. (Cited in Meyerhoff, 'Soviet Petroleum', pp. 348–9.)

51 Gorbachev, cited in Seweryn Bialer and Joan Afferica, 'The Genesis of Gorbachev's World', *Foreign Affairs*, No. 64–3, 1986, p. 605.

52 BBC Monitoring Inside Central Asia, issue 171, 12–18 May 1997, p. 6, 'Azeri sturgeon stocks under threat from oil extraction'.

2

Geopolitics of Caspian Oil: the Role of the Integration of the Caspian Region into World Economy in Maintaining Stability in the Caucasus

Angeliki Spatharou[1]

In the last eight years, the Caspian Sea, the Caucasus region, as well as the entire geographic area commencing at the Black Sea coast and extending to the inner depths of Central Asia, have become the focus of international attention. The region is thought to contain some of the largest unexploited oil and gas reserves in the world, situated strategically in the heart of Eurasia.

For more than two centuries, Russian rule, either under Imperial Russia, or under the successor state-structure of the Soviet Union, cast the administration of this immense natural wealth to the embrace of a power with clearly defined geopolitical interests.

The collapse of this rule, in 1991, and its replacement by the Newly Independent States,[2] initiated a fierce economic and political competition, ultimately aiming to secure unrestricted access to Caspian energy reserves and control over the commercial routes that will be established to market them. The new state authorities, albeit mostly consisting of former Soviet officials, were less experienced in foreign affairs management and more vulnerable to external pressures, while facing increasing demands of a volatile international setting. Major world powers – including the USA, the Russian Federation, the European Union and China – and colossal international economic interests sought to establish their presence in the region. At the same time, ancient ethnic rivalries and historic conflicts intermingled with regional economic development, thus perpetuating the pattern of local instability.

Therefore, the strategic geographic location of Caspian reserves and their magnitude have created a power game over their control, involving the world's major economic and political interests. The interconnection between them is indeed narrow, in order to attempt to set a dividing line between the two – especially when it involves the role of the oil industry in a region like Transcaucasia. Yet, in order to clarify the phrase *Geopolitics of Caspian Oil*, we will risk the following classification, based on the predominantly political or economic dimension of the issues involved.

The (mostly) political issues involved in modern Caspian oil development are:

1 the definition of the role of Russia in the post-Soviet world;
2 the establishment of a new power balance in Eurasia;
3 the re-appearance of regional actors with diachronic, rivalling interests and conflicting agendas;
4 the national awakening of the former Soviet south peoples and the emergence of an economic nationalism based on oil, further triggering ethnic confrontations.

The (mostly) economic issues are:

1 the competition of giant multinational corporations for a share in the exploitation of the reserves;
2 the effort of the oil industry to reduce import dependence on Gulf oil – and at the same time to keep the price of oil stable;
3 the preoccupation of the Western states to secure access to the prospective energy supply sources, against the emerging South-East Asian economies;
4 the intense efforts of all interested parties to control the huge projected pipeline networks that will be used to supply oil and gas to the global markets.

These pipeline proposals involve geographically, one way or another, countries such as Russia, Georgia, Turkey, Iran, Armenia and Azerbaijan, the Central Asian producers (at the time Kazakhstan and Turkmenistan), also Pakistan, Afghanistan, India and China. Around them an intense geopolitical struggle has begun, since the power in control of trade and communication routes in Eurasia will be in the position to control the entire region.

Naturally, projects concerning Caspian oil refer not only to the reserves that lie in the Azerbaijani part of the Caspian, but also to the significant reserves of Kazakhstan, Russia, Turkmenistan, even Iran. Yet in none of former Soviet territories were the interests of the outcoming superpower, Russia, questioned so actively as in the Caucasus.[3] And as all three Caucasian republics demonstrated early their desire for independence, Azerbaijan became the only Caspian riparian state where oil has been in the centre of such a clash of interests between the local government (e.g. the Popular Front in 1992) and Moscow, becoming a tool used by the small republic to express its wish for emancipation. As Azerbaijan became militarily involved in Nagorno-Karabakh, oil development became intermingled with a war that for a long time, along with the conflict in Chechnya, was the main source of instability for the Caucasus. Therefore, under the circumstances, in order to relate Caspian oil, as a means of international economic integration, to regional stability in the Caucasus, we have to focus on oil developments in Azerbaijan. Even more so, since Azerbaijan remains the only oil-affluent state in the Caspian that has actually been threatened with dismemberment due to ethnic instability.

Chronologically, the focal point will be the four-year-long negotiations (1990–4), for the signing of the first Production Sharing Agreement (PSA) with a foreign consortium, and the process towards the adoption of an export pipeline route for the first – 'early' – oil, in the years following the agreement (1994–6).

To reiterate the problem of the integration of the Caspian region into world economy, it is necessary to deliberate upon the following. As mentioned, over the *tsarist* and the Soviet period, the region was integrated into the world economy, through Russia. For more than two centuries, Russia cast its shadow on the Caucasus and fully exploited its natural wealth. The cornerstone of the system was a thick network of inter-regional (and inter-republican, within the Soviet Union) trade and a vertical transactions structure: to deal with the rest of the world, all goods had to pass through Moscow, the only international gate to the non-Russian world.

When the Union was dissolved, trade links with other countries were temporarily severed and production, agricultural and industrial, was disrupted. At this point the Caspian oil appeared like a *deus ex machina*, being the only commodity that was highly revered and needed by the rest of the world, easily accessible by means of an already existing infrastructure and practically immediately exportable, through the Soviet pipeline network.[4] Oil brought the war-torn Transcaucasian republics into the focus of international attention, both politically and economically.

The unlocking of Caspian reserves through the planned oil and gas pipeline networks creates today the foundation for a united economic area, from Europe to Central Asia and China. Hence, after Communism, oil becomes the new connecting tissue, providing the new, united structure, through which the region reintegrates itself into the world economy. And oil affluence in Trancaucasia is traditionally associated with Azerbaijan.

The Azerbaijani oil industry at the eve of independence

The oil potential of Azerbaijan was, indeed, the factor that brought immediately the war-torn republic into the focus of international capital interest. The importance of the local oil industry was never underestimated. Its extent is such that, according to the current President of the State Oil Company of Azerbaijan (SOCAR), Natiq Aliev, half of the 87 000 sq km territory of the republic is related to oil one way or another.[5] This exaggerated statement points to the enormous infrastructure accumulated in more than a hundred years of oil exploitation: onshore and offshore reserves, storing and processing facilities, refineries, pipelines, oilwells and platforms, offices, technical institutions, roads and railways; everything was constructed to serve an economic development woven around oil.

Azerbaijan was seriously affected by the economic decline of the period 1980–90. The crisis hit Azerbaijan with a greater emphasis than other Soviet oil production areas. Its production share in the annual USSR volume shrank. Azerbaijan was for the first time forced to import oil from Russia and natural gas from Turkmenistan and Iran. We should note that the gas-producing potential of the republic's oilfields was never exploited, although it was easily accessible and sufficient to cover Azerbaijan's needs at minimum cost. As a result, millions of cubic feet of natural gas were daily released in the air by offshore fields. The underperformance of the Baku oil and gas industry came as a result of the decision by central Soviet authorities to develop fields in other areas[6] that required less investment and could be developed using available technology.

In fact, most of the onshore fields around Baku were by 1990 in their latest stages of operation. The advantageous geological structure and the shallowness of the deposits that had rendered exploitation so profitable seemed to belong to the past. Estimates of onshore hidden reserves referred to 178 million tons,[7] but their recovery was now only possible at great depths.

The offshore reserves were, on the other hand, more promising. Almost 60 per cent of the Azeri production in the last decade came from the Guneshli oilfield, which lies 120 kilometres east of Baku. Soviet Azerbaijan were the first to develop offshore drilling and extraction technologies, in the 1960s. However, in the last years production had decreased at a rate of 9 per cent, because of the maturity of the wells and the outdated equipment, part of which dated back to 1950.[8] There were technical problems too, mainly a complex sea-bed with mud volcanoes, shallow gas and high seismic activity. Significant structures in deeper parts of the Caspian remained undeveloped, because of the lack of funds.

Similar circumstances prevailed in the entire Soviet energy sector, in the period before 1991. The need for investment overcame traditional objections of the central authorities, and by the late 1980s Moscow sought for the first time negotiations with Western firms over joint energy developments, and the international circumstances were favourable. Global energy demand forecasts demonstrated unprecedented growth for the next two decades, with new energy markets developing in several parts of the world, but mainly in the 'Pacific Rim' – South-East Asian economies. On the other hand, dependence of the Western world on the volatile Middle East, made both the USA and its European partners seek alternative oil supply sources.

When Communism collapsed in 1991, most agreements between Western firms and Moscow federal authorities froze. The political instability and inter-ethnic turmoil that prevailed created an unstable business environment. In Russia, a perpetuated struggle for power between rival groups and lobbies began and the future of democratic reforms was on several occasions seriously tested. Then the nationalities question posed a serious threat to the cohesion of the Federation as a state and to the agreements reached with foreign companies. Most importantly, areas rich in oil and gas and more than one-third of the USSR's processing facilities lay outside the boundaries of the Russian Federation. This meant that all agreements had to be renegotiated with new state authorities, and a new balance of interests had to be established.

These were two major agreements of that sort and both involved the Caspian region. The first one was the agreement with the American oil company Chevron for the development of the giant Tenghiz oilfield, in the territory now comprised by the independent Republic of Kazakhstan. The second involved the oil company of Soviet Azerbaijan, Azerineft, the republic's offshore oil company, Kaspmorneftgas, and the

British Ramco Energy, that had previously been associated with the North Sea oil exploration projects.

We can conclude that, at the eve of its independence, Azerbaijan was in a qualitatively different position with regard to both its Transcaucasian neighbours, Armenia and Georgia. The declared interest of Western companies and the existence of an important, though antiquated, oil industry infrastructure, would theoretically enable the republic to maintain its independence and to sustain a protracted fight against Armenia. In the early post-Soviet period, as economic structures in Transcaucasia were totally disrupted and the demands of the war economy were significant, the oil factor emerged as panacea to all problems. It boosted the Azeri ethnic pride and their intransigence over Nagorno–Karabakh and it transformed domestic politics into oil politics. An emerging oil nationalism was the response of Azerbaijan to economic and geopolitical challenges of the post-Soviet years and also the Trojan horse of foreign intervention.

Examining the events connected to Azerbaijani oil development in the first two years of independence (1991–3), we will see that these years are marked by the collapse of the geopolitical balance that commanded the region and its energy reserves in the past. We will, then, investigate the roots of events that consecutively marked the area and how the Transcaucasian enigma unfolded and its parameters became clear; how new factors emerged and old interests reappeared: and how, after a 'trial and error' period for all powers involved, came an understanding of the geopolitical dynamics that allowed the reaching of a mutually acceptable status quo, woven around Caspian oil and its unlocking through ancient market routes. The 1991–3 period will be examined separately, since after the advent of the former Communist H. Aliev to power, the resulting change in dynamics within and outside Azerbaijan was such that one might use the terms 'before Aliev' and 'after Aliev' to describe these turbulent years.

Oil and domestic politics: Mutalibov and the Azerbaijan Popular Front

In May 1989, soon after the rise to power of the technocrat Ayaz Mutalibov as the First Secretary of the Azerbaijani Communist Party, the first representative of a Western oil company visited Baku.[9] The bilateral discussions that followed examined the possibility of a cooperation with Kaspmorneftgas, the republic's offshore oil company. Mutalibov was more liberal than his predecessors and supported economic reforms.

An oil engineer and a technocrat himself, he had in the past accused Moscow administration of 'economic colonialism',[10] referring to the unwillingness of the central ministry to invest capital in order to reboost the declining Azerbaijani oil industry.

After 1991, the government continued negotiations with several Western companies, partly in an attempt to appease the opposition.[11] Although no agreement was reached, developments were speeded up. The government created the State Oil Company of Azerbaijan (SOCAR), that replaced the Soviet companies Azerineft and Kaspmorneftgas. The company was under the direct control of the state, which affirmed Mutalibov's determination to consolidate central command over the affluent oil sector. SOCAR inherited a significant infrastructure (by 1996 it employed more than 80 000 people).

However, oil developments in Azerbaijan were held back. In contrast with Georgia and Armenia, where anti-Communist, nationalistic governments had guided their countries to independence from the very early days, Azerbaijan needed a longer period of de-lactation from Moscow. The former Communist President Mutalibov was rather hesitant to undertake agreements that would induce the fury of hard-liners in the Kremlin. He also avoided declaring the republic's independence until the 1991 coup against Gorbachev, and only after all other republics had become independent.

Mutalibov could not ignore the importance of the oil factor in domestic politics. The political opposition, namely the Azerbaijan Popular Front (AzPF), adopted strong views on the issue. Oil was perceived as the key to Azerbaijan's independence and to a desirable solution in the Nagorno-Karabakh conflict. As AzPF was gaining power, it consistently invoked the issue in mass rallies organised in the *Azadlig* – 'Freedom' Square in Baku. It was commonly known that the Soviet state used to sell Azerbaijani oil it had bought from Baku at a fraction of the international price in the world markets. It would then pay the republic in rubles and would keep hard currency revenues for itself. Contemporary comments in the Western press reported that the 'Moscow government has been paying Azerbaijan 4.60 rubles per barrel of oil – about 7 cents at the widely accepted market rate of 6 rubles to the dollar. It then sells the oil at the world market price, which has reached $28.60 . . .'[12]

The AzPF was created in 1989 by intellectuals, originally to support Mikhail Gorbachev's newly introduced policies and to promote among other things the political and economic sovereignty of Azerbaijan, within the framework of the Soviet Union.[13] Quite soon, it was transformed into a radical nationalistic political group, particularly after the ex-dissident Abulfaz Elchibey was chosen to become its leader. The Front started challenging the stance of the Communist Party of Azerbaijan in the sensitive issues of Nagorno-Karabakh and of the republic's relations with neighbouring Armenia. Accordingly it emphasised the importance of economic sovereignty, as a form of independence and emancipation from Moscow. Oil revenues were seen as the major force behind a future military victory in Nagorno-Karabakh, since they would provide the means for a protracted struggle against an economically weaker Armenia. Also, oil would be an important element of Azerbaijani foreign relations with neighbouring states (Iran, Turkey, Georgia) and especially with the West. The policy that Abulfaz Elchibey adopted, once in office, was based on these exact principles.

As in many oil-producing countries that were formerly colonies,[14] the continuity of foreign control over the most important national resource was seen as the continuation of the colonial relation by other means.[15] It was perceived that, if Azerbaijan was not in position to control and dispose of its oil at will, after all these years of Soviet dominance and colonial exploitation independence would, indeed, be merely a word.

The deep conviction of most Azerbaijanis was that the republic had contributed disproportionately through its oil to the wealth and might of the Soviet state, and that other republics had benefited from that. The Transcaucasian neighbours, Armenia and Georgia especially, were envied as the beneficiaries of an economic spring based solely on geographic proximity with Baku. Not surprisingly, since the 1991 declaration of independence, the issue of oil development became inextricably intertwined with national sovereignty, with foreign policy, with domestic developments and, above all, with Nagorno-Karabakh. Every government in Baku, regardless of political background and international affiliations, played the oil card to the end, to serve Azeri national interests.

The stance of the West

Over the chaotic first post-Soviet period, Western states, including the US, sought to prescribe their involvement in the region in primarily economic terms. It was estimated that no other interests could be vested until Russian intentions for the FSU republics were crystallised; on the other hand, Western investment capital would be more than welcome. By 1991, the straightforward economic interests of the West in

Transcaucasia were focused on Caspian oil; yet developments in negotiations were painfully slow.

Given the amount of public reaction in Baku to any stalling of the unlocking of the republic's oil resources, the delay in concluding an agreement with the West cannot be attributed solely to Mutalibov's reluctance. One other possible explanation for the perpetuation of negotiations must have been the political instability in the whole FSU area. Foreign investors were hesitant to proceed in agreements with an authority that might eventually be overthrown. The major stake of the period was whether centrifugal tendencies of the Union republics would take the form of political independence, or whether the republics would re-succumb to the central power. For a long period, even after the dissolution of the USSR, the Russian Federation did not recognise the right of other republics to exploit their resources unilaterally. Consequently, most major oil companies which even before 1991 had come to an understanding with the central authorities in Moscow, e.g. Exxon and Mobil, avoided any participation in agreements with the new republics until the situation stabilised.

Not all companies maintained the same stance towards the breakaway republics. British Petroleum and the Norwegian Statoil, for instance, had negotiated the joint development of the offshore Azeri oilfield in Azerbaijan with the Soviet Ministry of Oil and Gas, and with the local authorities, before the country's independence.[16] The field was estimated to contain more than one billion barrels and it lay 120–130 metres under water. After 1991, the agreement was re-evaluated. Smaller, flexible competitors, like British Ramco and Turkish Petroleum (TPAO), had the opportunity also to bid for the project. Quite soon, other major companies opted to join the Caspian development, following the example set by BP in Azerbaijan and the American Chevron in Kazakhstan. They represented a wide range of nationalities and geo-economic interests: from the US to the Russian Federation, from Europe to Japan, and from Saudi Arabia to Turkey.

The question then remains why so many investors rushed into Azerbaijan, right after the country's independence. A combination of factors made investment in Azerbaijan attractive, although at the time, the country risked becoming the first FSU republic whose borders were about to change as a result of warfare. One reason has to do with the general appeal of the Caspian region to Western oil companies. The Caspian is, after all, 'the most sought after new oil province in the world; [. . .] although many risks remain, there are few areas in the world with such a considerable long-term upside', according to the Chairman of

Ramco Energy, one of the first companies that became actively involved in the country's oil development.[17] The region's proven reserves are approximately 10.8 billion barrels, with a strong possibility of further discoveries,[18] although other estimates raise the proven reserves of the south Caspian basin alone to 17.5 billion barrels.[19] The specific reserves in the Azerbaijani section of the Caspian Sea are conservatively estimated at 4 billion barrels. The possibility of joining the vast Caspian oil and gas reserves with those of Turkmenistan and Central Asia, in a unified pipeline mega-structure destined for European markets, put additional focus on the region for the major industrial powers.

The main considerations were geopolitical: first, whether it was safe to invest in such a 'complex political and commercial environment' (to quote the BP official and President of the Azerbaijan International Operating Company, Terry Adams[20]) and, second, how this oil would reach the markets. Azerbaijan was one of the fragile new republics emerging from the ashes of the Soviet Union. In the aftermath of its independence, its domestic political developments and its problematic relations with neighbouring states (especially with Armenia, over the Nagorno-Karabakh enclave) did not point to a promising future. The religious affiliation with Iran, that shares the same (*Shia*) Islamic faith and an Azeri population of 15 million in its northern provinces, stimulated fears of Islamic fundamentalism crossing the Iranian border with Azerbaijan.

On the other hand, the land shared a Soviet secular tradition of 70 years. Perhaps the Turkish, also secular, model could fill the ideology vacuum created by the collapse of Communism. Turkey was seen as a pivotal state for an increasing Western influence in Azerbaijan and the Central Asian republics. Its ethnic kinship with Muslim peoples of the Former Soviet Union and its pro-Western secularism were hoped to set a role model for the new republics to follow. Hence, the Bush administration in Washington was supportive of the expansion of Turkish influence in the area, as an antidote to that of Iran.[21] Also, Russia was not seen as a threat at the time. The new Russian authority was rather introverted in its effort to deal with economic problems and radical reforms. Azerbaijan was far away from Moscow – further than Kazakhstan, anyway[22] – although the Russian interest and ability to influence developments in the region were underestimated. A peaceful solution to the problem of Nagorno-Karabakh was seen as a matter of time, in the logic of the appeal of Western economic aid for reconstruction and development, versus the eminent financial bankruptcy of both warring parties.

Old and new regional actors: Iran, Turkey and Russia

The first years of Azerbaijan's statehood were marked by the appearance of new actors who also sought to influence regional developments, with varying results in each case.[23] The first one was Iran. Although Iran and the Former Soviet Union never shared common views about systems of political government, it appears that they had reached an understanding concerning the Soviet Muslim south and Central Asia in general. The northern part of Iran, that used to be called Azerbaijan, is inhabited by 17 million ethnic Azeris. This population has been traditionally well integrated within the multi-ethnic Iranian state. Yet the efforts of the Soviets to establish the Tebriz Communist Republic in northern-Iran Azeri provinces, right after the Second World War, demonstrated the destabilising potential that competitive policies of the two neighbouring powers could have for the region. In the late 1970s, the imposition of theocracy by the Shia fundamentalists in Teheran did not alter the established balance. Since both regimes were opposing the regional presence of Western interests, relations between them were furthered.[24] Iran was actually supplying the FSU with gas via Azerbaijan at the end of the 1980s[25] and bilateral relations comprised border crossing points and customs posts, as well as an agreement for the delivery of military aircraft to Teheran, characterising relations with Moscow as 'strategic'.[26]

In 1991, the connecting tissue for the Soviet Muslim population, Communism, was no more. Iran approached the new republics with caution. President Rafsanjani feared 'unrest, clashes and quarrels along [the] long border'.[27] Although under pressure to recognise the independence of Azerbaijan, Teheran delicately avoided the issue, in the name of good relations with Moscow. At the same time, radical circles in Iran and the significant Iranian-Azeri population demanded a substantial Iranian presence in Azerbaijan, fearing competition by Saudi Arabia and Turkey. Both these pro-Western and Sunni states had officially recognised the new republic. They had also participated in negotiations concerning the Caspian oil projects: Saudi Arabia, through its company Delta, and Turkey, through its national oil company, TPAO. In September 1991, pressure in Teheran culminated:

> Any hesitation or delay in recognising the independence of Soviet Azerbaijan [...] would give Turkey, i.e. NATO, a free hand on our northern borders and might lead to bitter consequences[...].[28]

Iran realised early the benefits of promoting relations with Azerbaijan and the other Muslim republics, and not only as a rival influence to Turkish policies in the region. After a destructive eight-year war with Iraq, the Islamic republic faced an economic embargo imposed by the US and a profound marginalisation by the international community. The opening of the former Soviet south offered a new market outlet, consisting of approximately 60 million Muslims, some of whom were also Shiites (the Azeris), and some of Iranian origin (the Tajiks). On the issue of oil, a close cooperation with Azerbaijan would be in the interest of Iran. Ideally, a swap agreement would provide for Iranian exports to Azerbaijan (and through that, to the other southern Commonwealth countries), while Azerbaijan would be free to direct the bulk of its production to Western markets. Iran hoped for a share in lucrative exploitation of the Azerbaijani offshore reserves, that would provide hard currency and contact with Western partners, new technologies and international finance. The republic was facing the problem that the Soviet Union faced in the last decade of its existence: lack of funds and technology to develop extensive new deposits.[29] In order to guarantee a share in Azerbaijan's competitive oil projects, Iran needed to increase its political, cultural and commercial presence in the country. During Mutalibov's administration, Iran inaugurated political and commercial relations with Baku and avoided fanatic religious preaching that could awake reactionary reflexes to its presence in Azerbaijan.

Turkey was the second new actor and for the West a counter-weight to Iran. The US welcomed the model that Turkey sought to promote in Azerbaijan and the other Muslim republics. Initially, the break-up of the Soviet Union drove Turkish politicians to a 'state of euphoria'.[30] The country possessed an enviable geographical position, as a natural link between Europe and the Central Asian republics and Azerbaijan was an obvious gate to the latter. Apart from Western support, Turkey shared with the new states a historic and cultural heritage, a common Sunni faith (with the exception of Shia Azerbaijan) and an ethnic bond. Turkey handled these nations as lost brothers, envisioning the creation of a Turkic common market of 60 million people, comprising all lands of the ancient *Turan*,[31] from the Aegean Sea to China.

Azerbaijan was exceptionally important within this pattern: it lies in the geographical proximity of Turkey (more than the other Muslim republics), it shares an ethnic and linguistic kinship with the Turks and yields a promising, oil-related future. We should note that since the 1980s, Turkey has swapped goods and services for natural gas and oil from Azerbaijan. The fast-growing Turkish economy depends on energy imports for 85 per cent of its needs, that are currently estimated to increase by 30 per cent by 2010.[32] Additionally, becoming a transit point for the export of Azeri oil to the West, would increase Turkey's geopolitical importance. Aware of these considerations, high Azeri officials pressed their Turkish counterparts for military support in the war with Armenia and for diplomatic recognition: 'If Turkey does not recognise us, the world will not recognise us.'[33]

For all these reasons, in November 1991, the Prime Minister Mesut Yilmaz made Turkey the first state to recognise the independence of Azerbaijan. High-level government contacts and economic relations with Baku were initiated, although Turkey mainly emphasised cooperation on educational and television broadcast projects that would solidify the cultural links between the two countries. Azerbaijan was viewed as an economic *hinterland*, a vital economic zone for Turkish products and an answer to the country's oil needs.

At the eve of the break-up of the Union, the stance of the Russian Federation was puzzling. Russia sought to re-establish its position as a pivotal state in a more loose, but still Russian-dominated form of federation with the other NIS, the Commonwealth of Independent States (CIS). Russia undertook several mediation efforts concerning Nagorno-Karabakh, although Baku reacted to this external interference in a 'domestic' matter, since the area was officially part of the Republic of Azerbaijan. Yet Mutalibov was sympathetic to a Russian-sponsored solution and eventually accepted negotiations in Moscow with the Armenian President, Ter-Petrosyan, although the outcome was merely a long-lived ceasefire. Russia soon gave up the effort, among problems concerning its domestic economic and political reform and the future of the Commonwealth. Over this first period, Russia lacked a clear vision of its interests in Transcaucasia and especially in Azerbaijan.

After presenting the old and new influences and actors that shaped developments in the years to follow (the West, the Russian Federation, Iran and Turkey, new trends in domestic politics), it is time to proceed with events that led to the governmental changes in 1992 and in 1993, and to examine any potential correlation of politics with the oil development projects.

1991–2: the fall of Mutalibov

Responding to accusations of deliberately stalling oil negotiations, the government of Mutalibov offered, in spring 1991, the two biggest offshore fields (Azeri and Chirag) to an open bid. The American company

Amoco was selected in June 1991 to develop the project, among offers from companies including British Petroleum and Ramco Energy. In September of the same year, Amoco signed an Area of Mutual Interest (AMI) agreement with the other Western companies interested in participating in the exploitation of the oilfield, notably the BP/Ramco/Statoil alliance and the American companies Unocal and McDermott.[34] At this point, the companies' motivation in forming a united front was to control the increasing demands of local officials, who were allegedly involved in widespread corruption.

Considering that only 20 per cent of the total foreign (non-Azeri) interest was controlled by non-American companies (the BP/Ramco/Statoil Group), the American stake in the project was important. Amoco had a lion's share of 45 per cent, while Unocal and McDermott followed with 25 per cent and 10 per cent respectively. After a period of fierce competition, Western interests in Azerbaijan seemed to coincide for the first time. A wave of optimism overtook Baku: with major foreign capital vested in the country, active Western political involvement in Transcaucasia was becoming a tangible reality.

Not only did Azerbaijan attempt to use its energy as a diplomatic and political weapon in international relations, but it also used it as a tactical weapon, in the real war, with Armenia. One of the first things that the government in Baku did was to cut off gas supplies to Armenia in September 1991. Previously, it had long been blockading the passage of food and consumer goods along the Baku–Yerevan railway line.[35] The pipeline blockade, although not unexpected, had devastating results for Armenia: the republic covered 90 per cent of its energy needs through imports from Azerbaijan.[36] The industry was totally paralysed and the population was threatened by serious food shortages. Azerbaijan used the blockade card each time a ceasefire was to be brokered. Azeri officials in Moscow declared: 'It is definite that the pipeline will not be reopened unless the Armenians comply with our political demands.'[37]

Oxymoron as it might sound, Armenia managed to use the oil affluence of its opponent to its own benefit. An efficient publicity mechanism was mobilised to bring to the West images of lengthy queues in front of bakeries and people in dark, cold houses, during electricity cuts in Yerevan. Headlines like 'Energy Crunch Slows Armenia',[38] 'Azerbaijan Cuts Gas Line, Plans Attack Armenia', or 'Fuel Blockade of Armenia Creates Bread Shortages',[39] flooded the Western press and international newswires. The enclavement of Christian Armenia among Muslim neighbours was also emphasised, especially as the pro-Turkish turn of the Elchibey government was being referred to in combination with the fate of Armenians under the Ottomans, at the beginning of the century.[40]

In the US, where the Armenian diaspora is more numerous, public opinion was openly sympathetic. In November 1991, the Armenian President Levon Ter-Petrosyan was invited for bilateral talks with US President George Bush in Washington, where he secured American material and moral support in this seemingly unlevelled war effort. The natural wealth of Azerbaijan functioned like a boomerang for Azeri political goals. Although American companies were about to secure an 80 per cent stake in the country's oil development, making the US the state with the largest vested interests in Azerbaijan, the US refused to recognise its independent statehood or to conclude diplomatic relations with Baku, until the latter's stance over Nagorno-Karabakh was re-evaluated and its human rights record was improved.[41]

Another side-effect of Azerbaijan's oil affluence was the emergence of a harsher stance in Armenian domestic politics, through nationalist factions. Up to a certain degree, Armenians did feel that the conflict was a matter of survival towards a mighty opponent; memories of their victimisation in the past accounted for that to some extent. Nationalism grew stronger in Baku, too, where people felt that victory was imminent.

In the end, the failure of Azerbaijani foreign policy to attract international support over Nagorno-Karabakh was attributed to President Mutalibov, who became the scapegoat and lost power in February 1992. The main reason for unrest was the massive military defeats at the war front, especially after the loss of the Azeri-populated Xodjali, an enclave among Armenian territories in Nagorno-Karabakh.[42]

Mutalibov's ex-Communist government was never particularly popular. Its victory in the September 1991 elections was mostly the result of inertia of the opposition in the period following the traumatic 1990 'Black January' events.[43] Mutalibov's denouncement of his Communist Party membership, after the Moscow coup against Gorbachev, and the subsequent dissolution of the Party in Azerbaijan were not perceived as sincere: he, after all, was one of the few leaders of FSU republics who did not condemn the coup at its heyday.

One of the factors that eroded public support for the government over this period was foreign oil policy. The AzPF accused Mutalibov of trying to maintain ties with Moscow by perpetuating the oil negotiations and also, of not wanting Azerbaijan to become really independent and of being a frontman for a Russified central command. With the war effort at its peak, the logic of the days was that landlocked Armenia, formerly depending on Azerbaijan for energy supplies and currently under embargo, was in no financial position to sustain protracted warfare. By not resolving the oil issue, Mutalibov was promoting the interests of Moscow to deprive Azerbaijan of its most critical asset, at the most critical stage. The feeling of isolation from the international community was critically accentuated when Turkey, at the time considering a weapons supply request from Baku, chose in the end a neutral position towards the warring parties, by opening diplomatic and trade relations with Armenia. This, along with the embargo from the US and the inability of the government to enlist foreign companies' cooperation to further Azerbaijan's incorporation into world economy, as expected, were used by the AzPF opposition in its effort to overthrow Mutalibov. Once in power, the Front adopted a different oil policy, in accordance with its nationalistic aspirations.

The Azerbaijani Popular Front government (June 1992–June 1993)

The Front came to power in June 1992, after a period of instability. One of the new administration's major concerns was to conclude the oil agreement. In November 1992, Azerbaijan signed five Memoranda of Understanding (MOU) with foreign companies. Their object was the establishment of working groups to study and plan the development of a joint infrastructure for the three biggest offshore oilfields, notably Azeri, Chirag and Guneshli. As reports about the vastness of the reserves reached Western markets, the struggle for concessions among foreign companies intensified. In March 1993, BP and the Norwegian Statoil purchased the right to exploit the major Chirag oilfield. In June of the same year, SOCAR announced its decision to proceed into an agreement with the Western companies, for a joint exploitation of the three oilfields. By that time, one more company became involved, expressing the international affiliations of the current Baku leadership: it was the Turkish national petroleum company, TPAO.

The project involved the three most promising undeveloped structures. They were discovered in the last twenty years, but their exploitation was hampered by underfinancing of the Baku oil industry. All three lay a significant distance offshore and at a great depth. Gunashli was discovered in 1979, 82 km east from the coast of Baku; its deep-water portion, that was included in the agreement, lay deeper than 200 metres. Chirag, at 94 km offshore, and Azeri, discovered in 1988 at 113 km, were also important, by international standards. The three fields combined possess estimated reserves of approximately four billion barrels (511 million tons).[44]

There was only one problem. The Russian Federation questioned the right of Azerbaijan, and every other former Soviet republic in the Caspian for that matter, to exploit unilaterally natural resources offshore. The Russian argument was that the Caspian is a closed water system with a fragile ecological balance and all decisions concerning its economic exploitation have to be taken jointly by all states participating in the Caspian littoral. Russia demonstrated a 'proprietary attitude' towards the Caspian oil deposits and energy ventures in the Commonwealth.[45] This factor complicated economic arrangements, given the extent of the influence that Russia still exercised in the international affairs and the domestic political scene of former Soviet republics – even in areas like Azerbaijan, where the government was not sympathetic to Russian policies.

This government, led by the Orientalist and former Soviet dissident Abulfaz Elchibey, never concealed its nationalist orientation. The Front seized power capitalising on the anti-Armenian and anti-Russian reflexes of the Azeri people. Elchibey made clear from the beginning that his government and the Azerbaijani Parliament would not ratify the agreement signed by former president Mutalibov, for the adherence of Azerbaijan to the Commonwealth of Independent States. Instead, he concluded an agreement providing for the withdrawal of Russian troops from the republic's territory. In foreign policy, he made a pro-Turkish, pro-Western turn and he sought to exclude Russia from Caspian oil developments.

The AzPF and the war

The new government based all hopes for a resolution of the Karabakh conflict and the establishment of the republic's sovereignty on relations with the West. The oil partnership was seen as a means to gain diplomatic and political support from the respective countries involved: the UK, Norway, Turkey and the US.

The support of the latter was considered critical. The end of the Cold War and the dissolution of the Soviet Union lifted the US to the status of the only global power, and the only power that could influence developments in the Caspian, apart from Russia. The numerous Armenian community, concentrated in big cities of the US, had lobbied effectively to gain American support over Nagorno-Karabakh. In 1992, for instance, the US Congress voted the 'Freedom Support Act', that determined the assistance to be given by the US to the former Soviet republics in their transition to democracy and to market economy. Azerbaijan was the only state not deemed worthy of receiving such support, on the basis of energy and food blockades imposed on Armenia and what was referred to as 'offensive uses of force' in the Karabakh battlefield.[46]

The government of Azerbaijan considered the unique opportunity to balance the influence of the Armenian–American lobby in the US, via another mighty pressure group: the oil companies. The prevailing attitude in Baku was revealed by the Azeri Vice-Premier. He was quoted characteristically as saying

> Houston [meaning the headquarters of Amoco] may become Azerbaijan's gateway to America. Washington is strategically interested in good business contacts with the oil-rich former Soviet republics, fearing that the Arabs might 'turn off the oil tap' anytime. If American companies start investing in Azerbaijan's economy, the United States will have to defend its economic interests and maintain stability in the Transcaucasia, stimulating Azerbaijan's higher political weight. All the more so, as Armenia is clearly oriented towards the CIS. American oil companies are ready to lobby for Azerbaijan.[47]

Besides, the political support of the UK, also a party to the negotiations through the state company BP, has been constant. Britain was one of the most active Western states to establish and maintain diplomatic contact with Azerbaijan. As early as 1992, significant bilateral contacts and official visits had been made, that corresponded to the extent of British commercial interests in the republic – e.g. the visits of the Deputy Foreign Minister, Douglas Hogg, the Trade Minister, Michael Heseltine,[48] and even the former Prime Minister, Margaret Thatcher. An important aspect of the British interest in Azerbaijan was 'to involve British industry in helping unlock these [meaning oil] resources'.[49]

The Turkish involvement in Azerbaijan in 1992–93

One of the reasons the US saluted the advent of the AzPF to power was the belief that Elchibey's nationalism would attach the country to the pro-Western model of Turkey. Indeed, the participation of the TPAO – the Turkish national company – in the negotiations indicated an important policy shift in the international relations of Azerbaijan.

The pro-Turkish affiliations of the leaders of the Popular Front were never concealed. Azerbaijanis have always been conscious of their Turkic past; they call themselves Azeri Turks and speak a language similar to Turkish. Yet, their Shiite religion and a distinct historic past, first within the Russian empire and then in the Soviet state, have created a separate sense of national identity. When Elchibey came to power, he sought to strengthen ties with Ankara: diplomatic, political and economic. A series of bilateral contacts, commercial agreements, cultural and educational programmes and official visits was inaugurated. Elchibey's visit to Ankara was reciprocated by consecutive visits to Baku from prominent Turkish politicians, like Süleiman Demirel and Turgut Özal. The Turkish leadership had developed a vision of a Turkic market, spreading from the Balkans through Central Asia, to the Muslim populations of western China. Turkey would naturally assume a protagonistic role, on the basis of its cultural influence over these populations. Azerbaijan participated in the discussions for the formation of this market, along with the Central Asian republics (except Kazakhstan). In a demonstration of the shared cultural bond with Ankara, it adopted the Latin alphabet that had been introduced in Turkey by Kemal Atatürk.

Elchibey's acts could be seen as an attempt to assure access to global community and international institutions, by means of Turkish political sponsoring. Turkey was a potential neutraliser of the impact of the Armenian lobby and a 'gateway to the West'[50] for the Azerbaijani economy. The declared wish to be part of the Azerbaijani oil development points to the fact that the greatest part of the energy requirements of the Turkish economy are being covered by oil imports. In order to participate in the Azeri–Chirag–Guneshli project, Turkey offered to finance a pipeline through its territory, that would bring the oil to the Mediterranean terminal of Ceyhan – a proposal that Azerbaijan accepted.

Iran, Russia and the 1993 coup

By June 1993, the first major oil agreement with the foreign companies was about to be signed in Baku. Russia and Iran, both important regional actors, were excluded from the Caspian oil development. In the case of Iran, exclusion reflected the deterioration of bilateral relations, after the advent of the AzPF to power. The fervent nationalism of the new Baku leadership extended to relations with its southern neighbour. For instance, before becoming President of Azerbaijan, Abulfaz Elchibey referred on various occasions to the reunification of the Azeris of northern Iran with Azerbaijan, as a natural process in historical evolution. He pointed to the 1828 agreement (signed in the city Gülistan) between Russia and Iran, that divided Azerbaijan into a northern and a southern part, as the beginning of colonisation of Azeri land. He also accused Teheran of attempting to export religious fundamentalism through the Iranian–Azeri frontier and of trying to keep Azerbaijan in the sphere of Russian political influence. The mutual mistrust of the two leaderships was based, on the one hand, on the aspirations of Baku for a unification with the Azeris of northern Iran and on the other, on Iranian neutrality in the Armenian–Azeri conflict, that was perceived by President Elchibey as pro-Armenian. Iran had even offered humanitarian assistance to Armenians; in May 1992, Teheran had also hosted an Armenian–Azeri conference, in one of the many mediation efforts undertaken during that period.

Initially, Iran attempted to promote relations with the new authorities in Baku. In the summer following the election of Elchibey, Iran agreed to resume transboundary deliveries of natural gas that had been disrupted in 1991. There was also talk of reopening the common frontier that was closed because of the fighting within the territory of Azerbaijan, and of resuming the rail and road traffic that was stopped.[51] The AzPF soon made any cooperation unfeasible. Its fear of ideological infiltration from Iranian radicals was such that only one month after the bilateral agreement it deployed significant troops along the common border.[52] Bilateral relations deteriorated further. Soon the Islamic government realised that Elchibey's option for secularism was modelled after Turkey, whose interests in the broader former Soviet south region did not coincide with those of Iran.

At that point, Iran reaffirmed the traditional alliance with the Russian Federation and adopted readily the latter's views on the status of the Caspian. The two countries invoked as binding an agreement signed between the Soviet Union and Iran in 1921, according to which states with no territorial waters in the Caspian had no right to participate in its economic exploitation. That practically gave them the 'upper hand' in Caspian oil development, excluding from it the American and Western-based companies, as well as Saudi Arabia and Turkey. Instrumental in this effort was the Caspian Sea Cooperation Council, a regional organisation initiated by Russia and Iran, with geographic presence on the Caspian littoral being the sole criterion of eligibility. Azerbaijan joined the Council in 1992, when it also joined the Black Sea Cooperation Council (BSCC), a rival institution sponsored by Turkey.[53]

The other great absentee from the agreement was Russia. Officially, Russia criticised the unilateral exploitation of the Caspian reserves, even on environmental grounds. However, Russian companies sought a share in all energy projects in the FSU. The basic characteristic of Moscow's foreign policy over this period is the lack of clear objectives. One trend in the Russian Ministry of Foreign Affairs (MFA) was arguing that Russia should adopt a Euro-Atlanticist perspective and cooperate with the West and with the other CIS countries on an equal basis. The opposite view eventually became more influential. It argued that, since Russia had subsidised the economies of the other constituent republics all over the Soviet period, through underpriced energy supplies, it now had a rightful share in all energy ventures in the Commonwealth. The concern was partly economic, and partly related to the Russian great power/anti-Western reflexes. The FSU was an area of Russian influence. The monopolisation of natural resources by the republics and their single-handed cooperation with the West, while excluding Russia, would create an irreversible precedent.

The only ventures vividly questioning Russian supremacy in the CIS were the Tenghiz project in Kazakhstan and the agreement to be signed in Azerbaijan, but Tenghiz presented for a long time minimal activity, due to internal problems. In June 1993, the Azerbaijani State Oil Company (SOCAR) announced the imminent signing of a final agreement with the selected foreign oil companies. The projected pipeline would pass through Turkish territory. For the first time, a former Soviet republic would market its oil directly to Western consumers, without being controlled by Moscow.

Meanwhile, Azerbaijan had also turned to Turkey for mediation in the Nagorno-Karabakh conflict and Armenia had accepted the neutrality of Turkey as a mediator. There was widespread optimism in Baku that the conflict would be finally resolved, thanks to the oil factor. The international community had for the first time cast light on the Azeri side of the conflict: the drama of thousands of Azeri and Kurd refugees who were forced to evacuate Kelbajar, an Azeri city that does not lie in Nagorno-Karabakh and that had been seized by the Armenian army. The UN Security Council passed a first resolution condemning the Armenian occupation of Azerbaijan's territory[54] and the interest of the West culminated in a proposed US–Russian–Turkish peace plan. Promising contacts with Armenia took place within the framework of the CSCE 'Minsk Group'. Nine countries, including the US, Russia, the UK, Turkey, as well as Germany and other European states, demonstrated their intention to help resolve the dispute.

Then Elchibey was invited by the British Prime Minister, John Major, to discuss the oil agreement and other bilateral issues in London, on 30

June 1993. This was the first official visit of an Azeri politician to a major Western power, a first break in the international isolation imposed on Azerbaijan by the West because of the war and a definite indication of an increasing diplomatic, political and economic allegiance.

At this point, Russian troops stationed in the city of Ganja, in Azerbaijan, announced their withdrawal from the republic's territory. Azerbaijan was to become the first former Soviet state to have the Union troops removed from its territory one year ahead of their scheduled departure. A number of volunteers with a significant volume of Russian weapons remained in Ganja, where they joined a militia group, under the command of the owner of a local factory, Surat Husseinov. Refusing to subordinate his forces to the central command in Baku, and after a military defeat in the war front in Karabakh that was attributed to him personally, Husseinov marched with his troops towards Baku. It was June 1993, just before the scheduled presidential departure for London. The insurgency ended in the flight of Elchibey, the rightful President, from Baku, after the army announced that it would not interfere with political disputes, nor defend the capital.

The dawn of independence was a critical period for future developments in the region, both political and economic. We saw the appearance of new actors Iran and Turkey, the conflict of their historic legacies with those of Russia, the major foreign economic and geopolitical interests involved in Caspian oil development and the impact of oil in domestic and external policies of Azerbaijan.

In retrospect, 1991–2 seems like a period during which every actor was testing the ground for future moves, while checking the reactions of others. Re-establishing a balance of powers and interests was a particularly difficult task under the circumstances.

First of all, the goals and deliberations of the Russian Federation were unclear. The lack of consistency and orientation in its foreign policy, partly due to the impact of rival groupings in Russian political and economic life, confused the other interesting parties: the West, the neighbouring countries and the newly independent republics themselves. Still, Russia managed to emerge from this period as a dominant player. Many saw the domestic turmoil in Azerbaijan as Russian-triggered, since the signing of the oil contract with the West would signal the economic and political detachment of Baku from the Federation and from the Commonwealth (CIS). The fact that the successor situation was introduced by a former high-level Communist official, Heidar Aliev, who immediately froze[55] the signing of the oil agreement, points to the importance of the latter for Moscow. As we will see, when Russia crystallised its priorities and perceptions with regard to Transcaucasia, it emerged as the main actor capable of pulling the strings.

The United States lacked a definite understanding of Caucasian politics and of the limitations of their own interference in the region. Although the primary American interest was economic, an impulsive response to the collapse of Communism brought a rush to extend American political influence and affect future developments, in a way that led to conflict between economic and political strategies. An illustration of this is the case of the Freedom Support Act of 1992. The US Congress imposed a financial embargo on Azerbaijan, over its policy in Nagorno-Karabakh, while American companies were pioneering the oil development of Baku, investing some 7.8 billion US dollars in the region.[56]

With greater experience in the Middle East region and representing British interests, BP was more pragmatic in its approach. From the early days it sought to ascertain the cooperation of the Russian factor through a share in the oil project and mobilised all available forces, political and economic, with the active support of the British political elite.

In any case, the active – even military – engagement of Turkey and the West that Baku was aiming for did not occur for some time. The oil companies did not initially overstep the mark between their commercial involvement and political developments in Azerbaijan. They did not enlist full support of their respective governments in the international scene and acted 'as if the conflict was none of their business'.[57]

On the other hand, Azerbaijan tried to use its oil potential as an asset in the exercise of foreign policy and in relations with neighbouring countries and the West, with emphasis on the Karabakh conflict. Both the first two governments, of the technocrat Mutalibov and of the historian/dissident Elchibey, did the same, but with various results and with distinctive deliberations. Mutalibov tried to gain international support through the oil negotiations yet without committing the country's potential to the West, in fear of a Russian reaction. Elchibey, ignoring regional dynamics, relied heavily on Western support. Both were accused of stalling the negotiations with foreign companies, in order to secure concrete advantages in the warfield, while Armenia benefited by presenting the dispute as a disproportional battle for survival of a small nation versus an affluent neighbour.

In conclusion, during this period oil destabilised regional politics, by accentuating the intransigence of the parties and the domestic political pressure towards a harsher attitude, and without balancing this effect by international support towards the resolution of the conflict. Yet, when this support came, it was to a great extent due to the important energy resources. According to former US ambassador to the OSCE and a key representative of the US policy in the Caucasus, John J. Maresca, the unlocking of the Caspian reserves had a great impact on the decision to form the 'Minsk Group':

> There has been a gradual process of realisation in the US and in the West in general that the Caucasus and the Caspian Basin are important for Western interests, largely, though not entirely, due to the energy resources to the region. This has led to an increased interest in the various conflicts in the region – Nagorno-Karabakh, Georgia and Chechnya.[58]

The new balance

The contract

In July 1993, after Aliev came to power, negotiations with Western oil companies ceased. Over the summer, the situation in the war front deteriorated and the UN Security Council condemned the seizure of Azerbaijani territory from Armenia.[59] Aliev tried to arouse neighbouring support, by pointing to the possibility of an oil pipeline passing through Iran and Turkey. As the war escalated, thousands of Azeri refugees gathered in the border with Iran, and Turkey implied that any attack against Nakchichevan would provide a *casus belli*. Then, Aliev decided an open turn towards Russia: he visited Moscow[60] and agreed to join the CIS.

Relative stability followed, only to be interrupted in 1994, when the previously stalled contacts of the government with the foreign oil companies restarted. The most interesting period was during the summer before the contract was signed. Trying to secure international support for the agreement, Aliev made contacts in the West and even among Karabakhi-Armenians for the first time, while the domestic situation in Azerbaijan was unclear. In September, martial law was imposed.[61]

The signing

The contract was signed on 20 September 1994. In the opening speech, Aliev emphasised the confirmation of friendship bonds 'with the US, Russia, Turkey, Great Britain and other countries'.[62] He had previously offered the Russian company Lukoil a part of SOCAR's stake in the Production Sharing Agreement (PSA). The companies involved in the agreement were:

Amoco, 17 per cent
BP, 17.1 per cent
Delta Nimir, 1.68 per cent
Lukoil, 10 per cent
McDermott, 2.45 per cent
Pennzoil, 9.8 per cent
Ramco, 2.08 per cent
Statoil, 8.56 per cent
TPAO, 6.75 per cent
Unocal, 9.5 per cent
SOCAR, 10 per cent[63]

The project would last 30 years and Azerbaijan's share would be half of all oil produced and a total profit of $34 billion.[64] The exact economic data were not given to the *Milli Mejlis*, the Parliament that ratified the agreement in December 1994. Whispers of selling out Baku's oil wealth in exchange for support in the war were mixed with rumours that Aliev wanted to establish diplomatic relations with the US, by having the contract signed before his official visit to Washington a few days after the ceremony. SOCAR officials secretly claimed that the terms on which Baku signed were 'two times worse than [...] a year ago'.[65]

Most importantly, the cleavage in Russian interests was openly demonstrated. While the Russian ambassador in Baku, the representative of the Russian Ministry of Fuel and Energy and Lukoil officials addressed the ceremony,[66] the Ministry of Foreign Affairs declared that 'Russia will not recognise [the agreement], with all the ensuing consequences'.[67] Just before the agreement's final validation from the *Mejlis*, a coup attempt threatened Aliev and domestic stability once more.

The pipelines

Having stated the geopolitical importance of projected pipelines in integrating the Caspian region into world economy, we should examine the political parameters in the decision-making of Azerbaijan International Operating Company (AIOC) and the effects on regional stability.

Among the numerous pipeline projects in existence,[68] those mostly connected with stability in Transcaucasia are two:

1 the northern route, from Baku to the port of Novorossisk, in the Russian Black Sea Coast, and
2 the southern option, from Baku to the Georgian Coast and then to the Turkish Mediterranean port of Ceyhan. A shorter, alternative

route could be through Iran and Armenia, or Nakchichevan, to Turkey.

While for Russia the pipelines are principally a means of political control, for the other actors they are related to regional stability, survival and economic affluence. Armenia, for example, does not reject a pipeline route through its territory. Since the long ceasefire with Azerbaijan made such a route feasible, the Armenian–Georgian relationship has become more antagonistic (as had the Russian–Georgian relation in the past). Theoretically, the Georgian route could include Armenia, but only if the ceasefire turned into a permanent peace.

The decision

The AIOC was about to announce its decision in October 1995. The President of AIOC, Terry Adams, admitted that not only economic but also political considerations would weigh heavily. The West, especially the US, supported the Turkish route through Georgia, but could not oversee the regional particularities that might render such a project unfeasible. The long-established interests of Russia would not disappear. Therefore, the dual pipeline route for the early production was a Solomonic solution, reducing dependence on one state and accommodating most of the actors involved.[69]

What these two connected incidents indicate is a process towards the establishment of a new geopolitical balance in Transcaucasia, that will accommodate various interests, but principally those of Russia, the traditionally dominant power in the region. This balance evolved around the distribution of the oil affluence that springs out of the Caspian and was consolidated between 1993 and 1996,[70] through developments relative to energy production and transportation projects.

Conclusions

The aim of this paper was to address questions concerning the role of the Caspian oil development plans in promoting the integration of the region into the world economy in the post-Soviet era, and also the direct or indirect effects of these developments on regional stability. With the reminder that this paper is not a study of the modern Caspian oil projects or of the immense issue of the Caspian pipelines,[71] the research tried to combine the impact of these projects on inter-ethnic stability in Transcaucasia.[72] The main reason for focusing on the early days of independence has been that 1993 was a turning point. The coming to power of the ex-Communist Aliev signalled the crystallisation of the Russian perceptions of the strategic importance of the region and the shift in Russian priorities, through the expansionary plans of the Russian private oil sector (especially of Lukoil, the only Russian company to participate in the Consortium agreement of 1994).

My original contentions were, that behind the external influences in the region lies a gradual process of re-establishing a power balance in the FSU area, with focus on the distribution of its energy reserves, and also that the emergence of oil nationalism in Azerbaijan rendered the domestic scene intransigent in national issues and politically vulnerable at a critical point in the country's independent existence.

The geopolitics of Caspian oil offers dominance in the heart of Eurasia as a prize for actors like giant oil multinationals, traditional regional powers, Russia and the West.[73] On the basis of inter-ethnic harmony being the cornerstone of stability in Transcaucasia, it becomes apparent that oil geopolitics affected the regional stability through two distinct mechanisms. The first is associated with the influence of external actors in Transcaucasia, during the period 1990–6. The paper has indicated the existence of a similar evolution pattern between the years 1918–21 and the early days of Azerbaijani independence. The collapse of Imperial Russia and of the Soviet Union disturbed the existing power balance, initiating a change of circumstances that in the world oil history is associated with the renegotiation of interests and spheres of influence, through a gradual process resulting in the establishing of a new balance.

The process was associated with severe regional instability, since local passions were triggered by an intense antagonism of foreign powers, of political and economic interests, ancient affiliations and the Russian quest for reassertion of its presence in the FSU. The outcome in the 1920s was the absorption of the young republics by the Soviet Union. Today, in the era of economic warfare, it has taken the form of Russian control over the strategic oil reserves and their export routes.

The second mechanism through which Caspian geopolitics affected regional stability is through the emergence of oil nationalism. In the case of Azerbaijan, there were phases of evolution. Initially, there was people's pride over the affluent oil industry. It was easily transformed by resentment of the appropriation of the national wealth by other nationalities, the post-war decline, unequal wealth distribution and ethnic cleavages. Even before Azerbaijan became independent, ethnic tension and economic disarray accentuated the importance of oil as a national asset. Emphasis was put on the need for national control of the oil industry and a widespread optimism for the outcome of an eventual war with Armenia appeared. Under the Mutalibov government, oil became synonymous with intransigence and rigidity, which eventually turned against the government and lost its public support. For AzPF, the country's oil was the panacea to all its problems. Aliev, on the other hand, was practical in using it to guarantee the external support that his ambitious economic planning demanded.

The aim of this paper has been to illustrate the importance of the relationship between oil, politics, economic integration and regional stability, in the case of Transcaucasia, and in the light of the recent developments, shape its present and set the basis for its future. However, the extent of the topic is not limited to this geographic area: as world energy requirements grow and competition for oil power becomes fiercer, this case will set an example of the patterns of instability that might appear under similar circumstances in other regions, too. After all, the history of oil is universal, still relatively new, and the patterns are strikingly similar.

Notes

1 I would like to thank the Alexander S. Onassis Foundation which supported me with a scholarship during my research. I also want to express my gratitude to my father who inspired and encouraged me during my work.

2 The Former Soviet Union Republics which declared their independence in 1991.

3 Among the other Caspian states, Kazakhstan has remained under strong Russian influence, that is partly due to its proximity to the Federation and to a large Russian minority within its borders. Iran and Russia share common interests in the Caspian, while Turkmenistan is absorbed by domestic turmoil and lies far from the centre of developments in the Caucasus.

4 Of course, the Soviet downstreaming and upstreaming network necessitated a substantial injection of investment, in order to adjust to new technological requirements.

5 'From SOCAR's Perspective', *Azerbaijan International,* 3/4 (Winter 1995), p. 26.

6 Nominally, Western Siberia and the Volga Basin.

7 'From SOCAR's Perspective', p. 26.

8 M. Sparks (Kvaerner), 'Gunashli', in *Azerbaijan International*, 3/4 (Winter 1995), p. 38.

9 The company was the Scottish Ramco Energy. Ramco subsequently promised the Azeri authorities to find investment partners for joint offshore projects in the Caspian.

10 *The Economist*, 29 September 1990.

11 'Azerbaijan Invites Foreign Firms to Develop Oil', *Reuters,* 15 September 1991.

12 *The Chicago Tribune*, 20 August 1990.

13 See Elisabeth Fuller, *Azerbaijan at Crossroads,* p. 3.

14 Particularly in the Middle East and Latin America.

15 See Peter R. Odell, *Oil and World Power*, pp. 197–8.
16 'Statoil, BP, Aim to Develop Soviet Caspian Oilfield', *Reuters*, 23 October 1990.
17 'Ramco Energy Says Caspian "Most Sought After Oil Province"', *Extel Examiner*, 5 September 1995.
18 See John Roberts, *Caspian Pipelines*, RIIA, 1996.
19 These data were presented by the President of the Azerbaijan International Operating Company (AIOC), Terry Adams, addressing the Conference 'Investment Opportunities for Azerbaijan', Adam Smith Institute, London, 30 September 1995 (from *Azerbaijan International*, 3/4, Winter 1995).
20 Ibid. The AIOC was formed in 1994 by the consortium of companies participating in the Production Sharing Agreement of September 1994, as a joint administrative structure to supervise the oil development and especially the marketisation of the first 'early oil' production.
21 'Turkey Aims to Revive the Ancient Silk Road Ties', *MidEast Markets*, 18 November 1991.
22 Many observers saw the stalling in negotiations of the government of Kazakhstan with the American Chevron over the development of the giant Tenghiz oilfield as a result of the pressure exercised on the republic by Russian officials.
23 The term 're-appearance' might be more appropriate, since both these new actors, as we will see, were traditionally active in the area over the last centuries.
24 We should note that bilateral interests coincided even in the thorny issue of the Soviet involvement in Afghanistan. Shia Iran opposed the presence of the Sunni Mujahedeen fighters in Afghanistan, that were linked to neighbouring, pro-Western Pakistan.
25 *Middle East Business Weekly*, 28 August 1992.
26 *Middle East Economic Digest*, 20 September 1991.
27 Ibid.
28 Ibid. The warning came from the radical daily *Jomhuri Islami*, said to express forces within the Teheran government.
29 It should be noted that these reserves lay in Northern Iran, homeland of the Iranian Azeri population.
30 See B. Gökay and R. Langhorne, *Turkey and the New States of the Caucasus and Central Asia*, p. 2.
31 The historic Central Asian heartland, considered to be the home of the Turkic peoples.
32 'Getting Azerbaijan's Oil to the International Market: the Turkish Perspective', *Azerbaijan International*, 3/3, Autumn 1995, p. 54, article of the TPAO representative for the Oil Expert Subcommittee of the AIOC, N. Pamir.
33 Statement of Azerbaijani Prime Minister H. Hassanov during his visit in Ankara, in October 1991. See 'Turkey Aims To Revive Ancient Silk Road Ties'.
34 'Amoco Subsidiary Names Five Western Partners in Azeri Oilfield Project in Azerbaijan Sector of Caspian Sea, USSR', *PR Newswire*, 27 September 1991.
35 *Reuters*, 15 November 1991.
36 Ibid.
37 Ibid.
38 *Wall Street Journal*, 11 November 1991.

39 *Reuters*, 5 and 15 November 1991.

40 It is necessary to add here that Armenians and Azeris had lived together in Transcaucasia for centuries. Any disputes that might have existed focused on the possession of land, as in Nagorno-Karabakh, or were covert social clashes against the better-off Armenians, as in the beginning of the century, but seldom, if ever, were about religion. Proof is the fact that in most cases, the also Christian, but relatively underprivileged Georgians were in conflict with Armenians, too. See T. Swietochowski, *Russian Azerbaijan*.

41 Congress of the United States of America, 'Freedom Support Act', Section 907, October 1992.

42 The loss of Xodjali, among allegations of an Armenian massacre of Azeri population, was attributed to the inefficiency of the government's military tactics in the enclave. The opposition claimed that Mutalibov was serving the interest of Moscow.

43 In January 1991, there was widespread popular dissatisfaction in Azerbaijan against the authorities in Moscow, mainly because of economic reasons and the issue of Karabakh, triggered by the determination of Armenians. Nationalist circles attempted to capitalise on these negative feelings, organising mass rallies and demonstrations, that culminated in the famous 1990 events of 'Black January' in Baku. On 15 January, Michael Gorbachev demonstrated for the first time a rigid intention to control centrifugal tendencies in the Union republics. Soviet troops entered Baku and imposed a state of emergency and martial law, in order to stop inter-ethnic clashes between Armenians and Azeris, although riots had by that time already ceased. The real aim was to control nationalist attempts to gain power – the result was the death of at least a hundred civilians. See *The Economist*, 20 September 1990.

44 'Azerbaijan's *Contract of the Century* Finally Signed with Western Oil Consortium', SOCAR Section, *Azerbaijani International*, 2/4 (Autumn 1994), p. 26. Also, Dr K. Yusifzade, SOCAR's Vice President, 'The Development of the Oil and Gas Industry in Azerbaijan', *Azerbaijan International*, 4/2 (Summer 1996), p. 53.

45 'Moscow Pressures its Neighbors to Share their Oil, Gas Revenues', *The Washington Post*, 18 March 1994, p. A24.

46 Congress of the United States of America, 'Freedom Support Act', Section 907, October 1992.

47 *Megapolis-Express*, No. 38, p. 22; *Russian Press Digest*, 23 September 1992.

48 *The Times*, 1 October 1992.

49 Interview of the British Ambassador in Azerbaijan, Thomas Young, in *Azerbaijan International*, 2/2 (Spring 1994).

50 See Elisabeth Fuller, *Azerbaijan at Crossroads*, p. 16.

51 'Azerbaijan Wants Gas; Azerbaijan's Natural Gas Supplies; News', *Middle East Business Weekly*, 28 August 1992.

52 *Radio Free Europe/Radio Liberty Research Report*, 1/42, p. 63.

53 Both organisations were instruments in a fierce competition for supremacy in the new Muslim republics, after the failure of efforts to coordinate geopolitical interests through the Economic Cooperation Organisation (ECO). This last organisation was re-activated in 1990 and had Iran, Turkey and Pakistan as founding members. Azerbaijan joined ECO too in 1992.

54 UN Security Council Resolution (822) 1993.

55 In July 1993.
56 'The Development of the Oil and Gas Industry in Azerbaijan', *Azerbaijan International*, 4/2, 1996.
57 Interview of the Former US Ambassador to the OSCE, J. J. Maresca, *Azerbaijan International*, 4/1, Spring 1996.
58 Ibid.
59 UN Security Resolution 853 (1993).
60 September 1993.
61 *Yerevan SNARK* (FBIS), 16 September.
62 Baku *Turan* (FBIS), 20 September.
63 Official Data, AIOC Baku, *A New Oil Era*, 1994.
64 *Interfax*, 16 September.
65 *Turan*, 21 September.
66 Baku *Azerbaycan Radio*, news conference of H. Aliev, 20 September.
67 *Interfax*, 20 September.
68 See Roberts, *Caspian Pipelines*.
69 Given the geopolitical importance of the issue, the American oil lobby did not need to exercise all its persuasion, in order to convince the US President, Bill Clinton, to telephone the Azeri leader in Baku and express his concerns over a Russian-controlled route. After six years, Azerbaijan was being admitted and integrated into the international world community, on the basis of its oil.
70 When oil production was commenced and a decision on the 'Early Oil' pipeline route was reached.
71 A brief presentation of the topic can be found in Chapter 1 and in Chapter 5.
72 The use of primary sources was also original in its approach of digging into new material from the region, e.g. from Baku, Yerevan and Moscow, and official documents (agreements, news releases and publications) that illustrate the central argument. When the sources are not new or primary, the originality lies in the approach according to which they were used, in order to cast light on the main question: the effect of oil on politics and vice versa.
73 D. Yergin, *The Prize*, p. 13.

3
The Management of a Transboundary Energy Resource: the Oil and Gas of the Caspian Sea

Roland Sinker

The management of transboundary energy resources is extremely important to international relations. Poor or ineffective management can have damaging consequences. This was seen most recently in the Middle East in 1991. The lack of an effective regime for the management of the oilfields straddling the boundary between Iraq and Kuwait allowed Kuwait to develop more oil than was perhaps equitable. This led in part to Baghdad's decision to invade. The resulting destabilisation of both states, the region, and indeed the international community, is well documented.

However, this need not have been the case. An effective regime for the management of such resources can greatly improve the stability of relations between states in the wider international community. In the same unstable Middle East that witnessed Desert Storm, Saudi Arabia and Kuwait accept that there is disagreement over the precise delimitation of the boundary between them, but concentrate on fair and efficient development of straddling hydrocarbons, through their 'neutral zone agreement' with improved relations and stability between the two.

This chapter examines the energy resources of a similarly unstable and hydrocarbon region: the Caspian Sea. It will discuss the management of this transboundary energy resource in four stages. This will include an appraisal of its 'transboundary resource' characteristics and its contribution to our understanding of such a phenomenon. Secondly, there will be a detailed examination of the regime that is managing this resource. This will necessitate a detailed analysis of the regime governing the legal status of the Caspian Sea as a whole, discussing whether it is under condominium or joint sovereignty, subject to delimitation into sovereign blocks between the littoral states, or indeed whether there is a 'neutral zone' type agreement in place. Two regimes will be examined: the legal regime governing the status of the Caspian at present, arising from the treaty history and practice of the littoral states, followed by discussion of the regime most likely to emerge in the future. In this section I will claim that the regime governing the legal status of the Sea is, and will remain, one based on delimitation into five sovereign independent blocks.

So, with no 'neutral zone', 'Timor Gap' or 'Gulf of Thailand' agreement governing the management of this resource, the third section will investigate exactly how this resource, straddling seven boundaries, is being managed. This will demonstrate that the hydrocarbons of the Caspian are being managed under five regimes, each very different, under the five riparian states. Each of these will be examined, dealing with the extent of resource development and management. This will include discussion of the factors influential to these developments and will demonstrate that resource development has been highly uneven between the sectors.

From this, the fourth section will conclude that whilst the oil and gas resources of the Caspian Sea are being managed under five different regimes, that have produced five very different levels of development, this may not represent 'poor' management. Indeed, this uncoordinated management may develop into five very similar regimes as all sectors move towards 'user friendly' systems, to ensure development. This organic growth to such an endgame is arguably far more stable than any imposed regional regime where tensions and *realpolitik* are not accorded due influence. Moreover, the complexities of the Caspian Sea, its hydrocarbons and players are almost certainly too intricate for the capacity of the model 'neutral zone' agreement. Nonetheless, there is scope for greater cooperation in development.

There are many important aspects to the Caspian Sea. However, this chapter focuses on the regime managing the Caspian as a transboundary resource. Considerations of these other aspects, such as pipeline issues, are not intended to be comprehensive.

The resource

'Since the collapse of the Soviet Union, the Caspian Sea region has become the focus of considerable international attention, primarily because it is one of the oldest and potentially richest oil and gas producing areas in the world.'[1] The oil and gas resources of the Caspian Sea are unique. The Caspian basin contains large proven reserves of oil and natural gas, which are recoverable under the right political conditions. If these resources are properly developed, they could provide world markets with some million barrels of oil a day.[2] It is with good reason that the Sea's estimated production of 60–80 billion barrels of oil is seen as being equal to, if not surpassing, the resources of the Persian Gulf.[3] This resource has the potential to supply global markets well into the next century and the Caspian is now the world's most sought-after new oil province.

A number of other factors characterise this resource and make it important. Firstly, despite its physical isolation, the Caspian Sea sits at the very heart of one of the world's geopolitically most significant and sensitive areas. The turbulent Caucasus lies to the west, Iran and the Middle East to the south, the unpredictable republics of Central Asia to the east and the Russian Federation to the north. As such, strategic control of the Caspian Sea has been, and always will be, an issue. This was demonstrated as far back as the 1813 Treaty of Golestan, by which Russia refused to allow Persian naval vessels in the Caspian.[4]

Secondly, the implications of this resource for economic development make it very important – especially since the break-up of the Soviet Union in 1991. This increased the number of the littoral states from two, Iran and the Soviet Union, to five: Azerbaijan, Iran, Kazakhstan, Russia and Turkmenistan. All five states are desperate to develop their economies and maximise their foreign currency earning potential. The resource offers them the chance to do so. Such is its significance, that Pratt and Schofield note the 'desperate scramble by both the littoral states and a wide range of multinational corporations and external interests to secure access to as large a slice of the Caspian pie as possible'.[5]

Thus, a large number of players see the resource as important, making the Caspian region the subject of a second 'Great Game'. A brief overview of such geopolitical, strategic and economic facets of the resource is illuminating.

The littoral states view the resource in different ways. For example, Azerbaijan, Kazakhstan and Turkmenistan, as young states with fledgling economies, see the resource as the key to their economic development and political independence from Russia, in part through the investment of Western oil companies. As Kazakh Deputy Foreign Minister Gizzatov notes, 'for Kazakhstan, exploration of the Caspian mineral resources will determine how quickly the country will be able to stand on its feet'.[6] However, all three have used the resource to maintain peaceful relations with Russia and Iran through allowing access to development and transport projects.

Iran also sees the development potential of the resource. However 'the major Iranian concern in the Caspian is not economic but strategic'[7] and its main objective is to expand its influence, for historic, economic and political reasons. In this way, the resource is a means of ending Iranian isolation and ensuring the development of a strong Central Asian community, headed by Iran, and without the involvement of Western non-littoral states, namely the US.

Similarly, whilst Russia sees the economic value of the resource, this is secondary to its geopolitical value as a means of maintaining control over its 'near abroad', and ensuring only nominal independence for the republics of the former Soviet Union. This policy is most clearly evidenced in their 'Monrovski Doctrine' leading to intervention in the former republics.[8] Moreover, as Russia seems unable to control the development of the resource, it has moved to dominate the region through resource transportation, in what officials from the new republics call 'Russian dictatorship in the area of oil pipeline transport'.[9] It has attempted to block pipeline routes other than its own by encouraging the war in Armenia, destabilising Georgia and publicly invading Chechnia, the route of its own pipeline. Moreover, like Iran, Russia envisages this resource as developing the Caspian into the energy hub of a non-Western energy zone.

Such is the importance of this resource that its influence stretches beyond the immediacy of the littoral states. Turkey, Greece, Bulgaria, Armenia and Georgia have all been involved as potential pipeline routes – all hoping for lucrative pipeline tariffs.[10] Turkey is refusing to allow large quantities of Caspian oil to pass from the Russian Black Sea port of Novorrossisk to the Mediterranean, through the Bosphorus. It validly claims environmental protection, but is also keen to host a pipeline from the Black Sea to the Mediterranean Turkish port of Ceyhan. As a result, a frustrated Russia has proposed piping the resource through Bulgaria and Greece, bypassing troublesome Turkey altogether.

Similarly, this resource is vitally important to the 'great powers' of the West, both in terms of energy provision and also through its geopolitical significance. In this way, Glen Rase, Director of the US Office of International Energy Policy, notes that 'the US interests in the Caspian are fairly simple: we have important commercial interests and we see long-term benefits for the global energy balance. In addition, we support the sovereignty of the new states in the region'.[11] This resource also represents a strategic alternative to the hydrocarbons of the volatile Middle East and a means of emphasising the continued isolation of Iran and the limitation of Russian influence.

Caspian oil and gas as a 'transboundary resource'

This oil and gas resource of the Caspian Sea may be viewed as a single geological 'whole'. However, this resource is not under the jurisdiction of a single state. It is subject to the jurisdiction of the five littoral states, either under joint sovereignty or divided between them. In any event this may be termed a 'transboundary' resource.

Transboundary resources such as this have been managed in a number of ways. For example, resources in the Gulf of Thailand and Timor Gap are subject to regimes of proactive cooperation by the interested parties. Conversely, such resources may be subject to a striking lack of cooperation or management. The approach to Caspian oil and gas is unique and offers further evidence of how such resources are managed in practice. Moreover, this may indicate principles of more or less effective management.

The legal status of the resource

In considering the legal regime for the management of the oil and gas of the Caspian Sea it is necessary to look at the legal status of the Caspian as a whole. This necessitates investigation of the legal regime in aspects other than oil and gas – for example, fishing and navigation, which in turn are a consequence and thus evidence of the legal regime for the Sea as a whole.

The legal status of the Caspian is in a state of confusion. Prior to the break-up of the Soviet Union, the Caspian was managed by the two littoral states, Russia (or the Soviet Union) and Persia (or Iran). The break-up of the Soviet Union in 1991 increased the number of the littoral states to five: Azerbaijan, Kazakhstan, Turkmenistan, Russia and Iran. This, combined with proposals to develop the vast energy resources of the Sea, has highlighted the issue of jurisdiction, sovereignty and the legal regime of the Caspian.

The question of legal regime is controversial. At one extreme lie proposals for delimitation into five sectors, each giving full sovereignty rights to the respective states. At the other are claims for a regime of joint sovereignty or condominium where all five littoral states share sovereignty and resources equally. Within this framework lie a number of approaches, with varying degrees of cooperation and exclusive rights, for different aspects of the Caspian.

This chapter will examine two legal regimes relevant to the status of the Caspian Sea. Firstly, there will be an examination of the current legal status. This regime has arisen from a combination of both treaties between the littoral states and the conduct and attitude of the littoral states – the customary law of the region. This necessitates an investigation of the treaty history of the Caspian. The only relevant treaties were concluded between the two original littoral states and it is sensible to include reference to their conduct prior to the break-up of the Soviet Union in this section. This will be followed by assessment of the customary law of the region since the break-up of the Soviet Union. The conduct and attitude of the five littoral states is greatly contributing to the further development of the current legal regime. Moreover, this latter section provides useful evidence of a possible future legal regime.

Secondly, there will be discussion of the future legal status of the Caspian. It is widely accepted that there is a need for a codification of a new legal regime to manage the Caspian, since the present treaties are not sufficient to regulate the increasingly complex ecological, political, economic and resource environment of the region. This future regime will probably evolve from the emerging trends of the current regime. However, this section will examine the future status of the Caspian, as suggested by rules of international law, focusing on the important issue of whether the Caspian might be subject to joint sovereignty or delimitation. Interestingly, the outcome of this assessment indicates the importance of the emerging trends of the current regime.

This will allow some conclusions to be drawn as to the likely nature of the future legal status of the Caspian, based on both emerging trends of the current regime and the principles of international law. For over 250 years the legal regime of the Caspian Sea has been the subject of a series of bilateral treaties between Tsarist Russia and Persia. However, the legal regime established by these treaties has been further developed by conduct and business practice between the two states. The core of these treaties and the state conduct focuses on the regulation of navigation and fishing by the two riparian states. For example the Treaty of Resht (13 February 1729) between Persia and Russia provided in Article 8 for the freedom of commerce and navigation in the Caspian Sea.

The early nineteenth century saw two rounds of the Russo-Persian War. Defeat for Persia on the first occasion gave rise to the Golestan Treaty (12 October 1813), Article V of which ruled that, whilst both states enjoyed freedom of navigation for commercial purposes and the right to each other's assistance in case of difficulty, only Russia had the right to maintain a naval fleet on the Caspian Sea.[12]

Similar circumstances on the second occasion were followed by the Turkmenchai Treaty (28 February 1828). Article VIII reiterates the conditions of Article V of the Golestan Treaty.[13] Both indicate a clear imbalance of sovereign rights between the two parties which, as Bundy notes, is 'incompatible with any notion of condominium'.[14] It is interesting to note that, having carried out a detailed delimitation of the land boundary between the two states, Article IV defines this land boundary as ending at the Caspian Sea, showing no intention to delimit the Sea at that time.[15]

These treaties remained in force until the Treaty of Friendship (26 February 1921) between Soviet Russia and Persia.[16] Soviet Russia, keen to maintain peace with its neighbour and reverse the imperialist policies of the former Tsars, changed the regime to abrogate any imbalanced provisions. Article III stipulated that both states shall have equal rights in using frontier waters and that a commission should be established to 'make definite arrangements with respect to the question of using the frontier waters', such as the Caspian.[17]

Article XI was similarly conciliatory and cooperative, revoking provisions of the Turkmenchai Treaty which gave Russia exclusive rights to a naval presence in the Caspian, and giving both states equal rights in this respect.[18] Moreover, both states agreed to offer assistance to each other's vessels in case of need. However, Article VII did prevent the Persian navy from employing subjects of a third government which might have unfriendly intentions towards Russia[19] – this was most likely intended to keep British nationals out of the region.

Interestingly, Article XIV recognises the importance of the fisheries of the southern Caspian to Russia and makes provision for agreement between the two states for Russian access to these resources.[20] An Agreement regarding the exploitation of the fisheries on the southern shore of the Caspian Sea (1 October 1927) was eventually finalised between the two governments.[21] In this, Persia granted a 25-year concession in the southern Caspian to a joint Soviet–Persian fishing company, in which both states had equal shares. This might suggest a degree of cooperation between the two littoral states in the management of the Caspian and its fish resources. However, the fact that Persia 'granted' this concession implies that it had some form of exclusive right to a sector of the Sea, and this in turn might suggest some form of division.

Interestingly, Iran appears to have claimed rights to these fishery resources of the southern Caspian since 1942, when Iran granted fishing rights to an Iranian, Mr Moustafi. Similar rights were granted to other Iranians, but in 1969, a Russian subject, Martinovich Lianazif, was granted leave by Iran to fish off the Iranian coasts of the Caspian. Four similar concessions were purchased from Iran by Russian nationals up until 1993.[22]

The 1930s saw further developments in the management of the legal regime of the Caspian. The Convention of Establishment and Commerce (27 October 1931)[23] first set the principles that were confirmed in the Treaty of Establishment, Commerce and Navigation (27 August 1935) between Iran and the Soviet Union.[24] Article XIV of this treaty makes clear that the Caspian is only open to the vessels of the two states, their nationals or their commercial and transport operations. This confirms the exclusivity and equality of rights of the two coastal states to the Caspian, and that the Sea was effectively closed to all third states and their nationals, including the crew members of Iranian or Soviet vessels.[25]

Article XV does, however, reserve a ten-mile zone along the coast of each state, for the exclusive fishing rights of that state's vessels.[26] Despite this apparent 'division', there is no attempt to delimit any official sea boundary between the two states. Indeed, an exchange of letters of 27 August 1935 refers to the Caspian as being 'regarded by the two governments as a Soviet and Iranian Sea'.[27] It should be stressed that the mischief that this statement is intended to remedy is that of excluding potentially subversive third-state nationals from the Caspian, rather than attempting to create a regime of condominium or joint sovereignty.

The Treaty of Commerce and Navigation (25 March 1940), reiterates the provisions of Articles XIV and XV of the 1935 Treaty in Articles XII and XIII respectively.[28] Similarly, there is an identical exchange of letters to those of 27 August 1935, on 25 March 1940.[29] Interestingly, a more recent boundary commission in the 1950s chose not to delimit any boundary across the Sea.[30] Similarly, the 1964 Aerial Agreement between Iran and the Soviet Union makes no attempt to delimit an international boundary in the Caspian. It does not refer to flights over the Sea. This agreement does, however, use an imaginary 'Astara–Husseinqoli line which directly links the two countries' land boundaries on both sides of the Sea, as a means for determining the Flight Information Region'.[31] However, Dabiri notes that this 'division' is solely to ensure safe flights and flight control facilities and does not provide any delimitation or the basis for a claim of sovereignty. Nonetheless, it is interesting to note that Baku controlled the Flight Information Region to the north, and Bahrain the one to the south of this line.[32]

However, Bundy notes that in the late 1970s, the Soviet Union did 'propose' a boundary line to the Iranians, who rejected it. Similarly, Azerbaijan 'claims' that in 1975 the Soviet sector of the Sea was divided into economic zones, related to the land boundaries of the republics. At the same time, there was evidence of cooperation in 1974, through the Soviet–Iranian Working Group of Scientists for the Prevention of Pollution of the Caspian Sea, which carried out an extensive programme of joint research into the degree and nature of pollution in individual sections of the Caspian Sea.[33]

There is evidence of an implicit legal regime for the resources of the seabed. The implications correspond well with the regime arising from the fishing agreements discussed earlier: cooperation in the development of resources, but some form of exclusive right to sectors of the Sea. Primary evidence is the agreement between the Iranian National Oil Company (NIOC) and the Russian company, Machinoimport (September 1987).[34] This came into force in May 1990, with a 20–month duration. In essence, this was a drilling contract, whereby the Russian company agreed to carry out drilling works for NIOC, in accordance with their wishes. Machinoimport was subject to various conditions, such as meeting international norms of pollution control, keeping NIOC informed of developments and following Iranian law. As a result, the first well was established 27 kilometres to the north-west of Anzali port.

This contract is important. As Pournouri notes, the Russian company did not acquire a share of the oil or gas resources. Moreover, this Russian–Iranian contract effectively endorsed Iranian rights of exploration and exploitation of sea-bed resources at least up to the location of the drilling site, 27 kilometres from its coast. Whilst there was no boundary delimitation, it might be argued that, as with fishery resources, the two littoral states did recognise each other's exclusive rights in their coastal zones. As such, the Sea was not a fully shared zone and was subject to some form of division. However, Pournouri does claim that the contract is evidence of a regime of cooperation between the two states in the management of the Sea. It is interesting to note that this contract would have remained in force after the break-up of the Soviet Union – whether it did or not is unclear.[35]

From this it is possible to draw some conclusions as to the status of the Caspian at this time, based on these treaties and the conduct between the two littoral states – not general norms of international law relating to the high seas. All that may really be inferred is that the Sea was exclusively the domain of the two littoral states and that there was no boundary delimitation. There was cooperation in the exploitation of fish and sea-bed resources, navigation, the study of pollution and the exclusion of third parties. However, the central issue is whether or not this amounts to sufficient evidence of a condominium or regime of joint sovereignty. The answer is almost certainly not.

Moreover, there is evidence of exclusive zones for both fish and sub-sea resources in the Caspian – possibly inconsistent with condominium claims. These resources were not divided equally between the parties. Finally, there is no concrete evidence of any intention to create a regime of joint sovereignty, for as Bundy notes, 'terms such as condominium or sovereignty simply do not appear'.[36] Under this regime, the legal status of the Caspian is best described as 'sui generis'. It cannot be classified as either condominium or delimitation.

These treaties will remain the basis for the legal regime for the Caspian until they are replaced. The law of state succession ensured that they were not invalidated by the break-up of the Soviet Union. Moreover, whilst not specifically confirming these treaties, the Commonwealth of Independent States undertook to meet the obligations of treaties and agreements concluded by the former Soviet Union, by signing the Alma Ata Declaration of 21 December 1991.

Attitude and conduct of the five littoral states since 1991

Following the break-up of the Soviet Union, the attitude and conduct of the five littoral states has contributed to the further development of the current legal regime. What is clear from multilateral and bilateral negotiations between these five is the great diversity of opinion as to the legal regime in force: from condominium to delimitation between the coastal states. This diversity of opinion has been accentuated by state conduct as some have unilaterally extended their sovereignty over parts of the Caspian.

In some cases this has been more than a nominal extension with the commencement of resource exploitation within claimed 'sectors' of the Sea. Azerbaijan is basing its approach to the legal regime of the Caspian Sea on delimitation into five sovereign sectors, one for each of the littoral states. This is based on the claim that the Sea is already subject to division, under the present legal regime, and all that remains is the delimitation of boundaries. This does not have the same implications as a claim that, whilst not presently subject to division, the Sea should be divisible in the future.

Within this, Azerbaijani policy focuses on the sovereign right to exploit the oil and gas of the sea-bed. Other aspects of the status issue are secondary, although the issue as a whole must be decided before other agreements can be reached. Koshbakht Yusifade, a Vice President of the State Oil Company of Azerbaijan Republic (SOCAR), maintains that the Caspian is subject to delimitation, at least into some form of 'economic zones'.[37] Speaking about the regime for oil and gas, he notes that regimes for governing fishery resources, such as those from the treaties above, are rarely applicable to sea-bed resources. Thus there is no reason why limitations on sovereign fishing rights are applicable to rights to oil and gas. He points to the management of the sea-bed resources of the North Sea, by 'delimitation into sovereign blocks', as a helpful precedent for the division of the Caspian. It should be noted, however, that one of the main characteristics of most economic zones is that they apply both to mineral and to living resources and, as such, limitations on fishing rights might well be applicable to sub-sea resources.

Moreover, Azerbaijan claims that in 1975 'the sea had been divided into economical regions among the neighbouring republics by the leadership of the Soviet Oil Industry and the relating republics'.[38] This delimitation was apparently carried out under principles of equidistance and 'no republic, including Russia, had criticised this division'. Similarly, Yusifade claims that recent negotiations in Moscow between President Aliyev of Azerbaijan and the Russian Prime Minister Chernomyrdin and Foreign Minister Kozyrev confirmed the division of the Caspian into economic zones.

Yusifade looks to the history of oil and gas management in the Caspian for further support. This suggests that Azerbaijani specialists carried out most of the work in oil and gas, in all parts of the Sea. Azerbaijan claims a right to a sole share of the oil and gas of the Sea, not accepting the need for some form of joint management for the regional ecology and ecosystem. Similarly, it proposes continuing negotiations on the management of some aspects of the Sea, after it has been divided up.[39]

The Azeris reject Russian arguments in favour of condominium or joint sovereignty. They do not recognise the treaties made by the former Soviet Union and assert their position as a sovereign republic. In any event, they claim that the treaties are not relevant to the modern environment facing the Caspian. However, it should be noted that this is not consistent with their signing of the Alma Ata Declaration.[40]

Azerbaijan has been involved in a number of the initiatives aimed at cooperation between the Caspian states. It supported, for instance, 'adherence to the principles of international law and the recognition of the ecological unity of the Caspian Sea'. This was expressed in the Communiqué of 14 October 1993, adopted by the 'Conference on the Problems of the Caspian Sea'. The four parties agreed that 'the comprehensive solution of the problems of the rational utilisation of the Caspian Sea requires the participation of all the Caspian States' and pointed to areas of joint activities such as control of sea level, the environment, navigation, natural resources and the development of mineral resources.[41]

However, whilst Azerbaijan clearly supported these initiatives, its position was less cooperative concerning the legal status of the Sea. In 1992, Iran organised the Teheran Conference of Caspian States which hoped to create the Treaty on Regional Cooperation in the Caspian Sea. This aimed to govern the Caspian through a regional organisation of the littoral states, without any division of the Sea. Decisions were to be based on consensus between the littoral states. However, whilst this 'consensus' appears equitable, in practice it would have given each littoral state the power to veto any Caspian development. By February 1993, Azerbaijan had announced that it would not take part in such an organisation until the international status of the Caspian was determined. By December, the Azeris had prepared their own draft convention based on dividing the Caspian into sovereign sectors, under a regime similar to those of internal waters.[42]

In October 1994, the five littoral states met in Moscow to finalise the draft work on the Treaty – this was expected to be an easy task following preliminary bilateral consultations by Iran with the other coastal states. However, it became clear that the Azeris would not accept any provisions in the draft treaty that implied a regime of 'joint sovereignty' or 'resource sharing'. For example, statements that 'the Caspian Sea is a subject of joint utilisation of the Caspian State', or calling for 'coordination of approaches to the various aspects of activities in the Caspian Sea', were not acceptable. Whilst the draft treaty was agreed in principle by the other four states, Azeri objections on the status issue ensured that no decision on the signing of the treaty was taken. Bilateral negotiations are continuing in an attempt to resolve this issue.[43]

Similarly, multilateral negotiations in early 1995 in Ashkhabad, Turkmenistan, considered a draft Agreement on the Conservation and Utilisation of Biological Resources in the Caspian Sea. Extended discussion on the extent of exclusive fishing zones eventually led to agreement on 20 miles. Again, Azerbaijan was the only state to refuse to accept the Agreement, so preventing it coming into force. It claimed that it predetermined the legal regime of the Sea and should thus be considered under the general treaty.

The position of Azerbaijan is more than nominal. Its conduct has been consistent with and has emphasised its approach to the management of the legal regime – making sectoral claims very clear. On 20 September 1994, after three years of negotiations, the Azeri government signed the

30-year-long, 8 billion dollar 'Contract of the Century' with an international consortium of oil companies headed by British Petroleum. This contract was for the development of three oil and gas fields in the Caspian: Azeri, Chirag and Guneshli. The fields, exceeding 500 million tonnes, are to be developed in conjunction with LUKoil, Turkish oil companies and SOCAR. The fields are located some 70 miles off the Azeri coast.

Azerbaijan has granted a similar licence for the development of the Karabakh oilfield. This Agreement was followed by the signing in June 1996 of a contract for a Western consortium, Russia and Iran to exploit the 1.8 billion barrels of the Shakh Deniz oilfield – also in the Azeri sector of the Sea. Such conduct clearly emphasises the Azeri position. Oil rigs are being renovated, surveys have been carried out, staff are being trained and deals for the transport of the fuel are being finalised. The investment is enormous. The implications of these activities are obvious. The longer this activity continues, the harder it is to envisage an arbitration tribunal on the status of the Caspian ignoring the fiscal realities of this investment and the agreements leading to it. In this way, Azerbaijan's attitude and conduct are effectively endorsing the current legal regime for the Caspian as one based on delimitation. It remains to be seen whether this will be the final outcome, although the activities of the other littoral states support this outcome.

Kazakhstan's approach to the management of the legal regime of the Caspian has been similar to that of Azerbaijan – the Sea should be divided between the littoral states. However, the emphasis is slightly different. It should be noted that, whilst the Kazakh arguments represent a position, they are not always based correctly on law or fact. Deputy Foreign Minister Gizzatov indicates that Kazakhstan sees three legal problems as issues that must be resolved in the Caspian:

1 the method and process of delimiting the littoral states, borders in the Sea;
2 the right of the Caspian states to have access to the high seas through Russia's Volga River, Volga–Baltic and Volga–Don Channels;
3 the establishment of a legal framework in which the Caspian states can cooperate in exploiting the Sea's resources.[44]

Kazakhstan accepts that the current regime of the Sea is governed by the treaties discussed earlier. However, it considers them unsuitable both for the present maintenance of the Sea and as a basis for regime management in the future. Thus, there is an urgent need to develop a new legal status for the Caspian. Gizzatov defends this position by arguing that one party to these treaties, the Soviet Union, no longer exists and that the status of the Caspian should therefore be decided by a new treaty between the new states. Moreover, these original treaties are incomplete. They did not delimit international boundaries on the Sea and did not give the republics the power to do so. In addition, they only cover fishing and navigation and this is not sufficient to fully determine the status of the Sea. Zones such as continental shelf and exclusive economic zones first codified in the 1958 and 1982 UNCLOS respectively post-date these treaties. Thus, they should be replaced with a more up-to-date approach.[45]

Kazakhstan believes that the new status of the Caspian should be decided under rules of current international law. Firstly, the principle of the sovereign equality of states is relevant, whereby each state may play a part in resolving issues that impinge upon its legal interests. Secondly, the principles of international law relating to both enclosed sea and international lakes might be relevant. However, as Gizzatov notes, Kazakhstan is of the opinion that the most appropriate legal status for the Caspian is that of 'enclosed sea' – whether this is 'most appropriate' in terms of meeting the UNCLOS definition or in terms of what might be the 'best' approach is not clear.[46] In any event, Gizzatov argues, perhaps tenuously, that the Caspian is not excluded from the UNCLOS because the Convention does not contain a list of the seas to which the provisions are applicable and 'in our opinion the Convention is valid for all seas and oceans because the terms "seas" and "oceans" are not defined by it'. Also 'since ancient times the Caspian Sea was referred to as a sea'.[47]

So Kazakhstan suggests that the Caspian should be delimited under the principles of UNCLOS. The Kazakhs define the Caspian as a 'sea' to ensure access to the high seas, an integral part of their management of the legal regime. They claim that since the Caspian is an 'enclosed sea', and thus covered by UNCLOS, the Volga–Don and Volga–Baltic Channels should be recognised as international waterways.[48] Kazakhstan also claims that customary International Law of the Sea and Article 3 of the 1958 Convention on the High Seas indicate that states such as Kazakhstan, without a sea shore, should have access to the high seas. Anyway, the Volga–Don and Volga–Baltic were constructed with the assistance of all the former Soviet republics – thus they should all have access now. Finally, the Akhtuba River, in the Volga River's delta area and system, flows through Kazakhstan and thus represents an international river. Under the UNCLOS 1982, Kazakhstan claims the right to use all of this channel, to the Baltic, through its participation in the Akhtuba/Volga section.

In addition, Kazakhstan views the Sea as a demilitarised zone; it proposes wrongly that the Caspian was delimited between the Soviet Union and Iran by the Treaty of 1940, along the Astara–Gassan–Qoli line, and so there is no valid claim to an undivided sea. It envisages a series of treaties to govern different regimes of the sea, such as fishing, hydrocarbons or navigation.[49]

Kazakhstan, like Azerbaijan, supported the principle of delimitation at the post-Soviet Conferences on Co-operation discussed earlier. It too presented a draft Convention on the Legal Status of the Caspian Sea in August 1994, suggesting delimitation as an alternative to proposals for joint sovereignty seen in the draft Treaty on Regional Cooperation from the Teheran Conference of 1992.

Unlike Azerbaijan, Kazakhstan has demonstrated a fairly positive attitude towards cooperation. At the Moscow meeting in 1994 to finalise the draft treaty, Kazakhstan was prepared to participate in its drafting and agreement, even though it did share the Azeri position. Similarly, the Kazakhs did accept the 1995 Agreement on the Conservation and Utilisation of Biological Resources of the Caspian Sea.[50] Moreover, in May 1995, the Kazakh government hosted representatives of the littoral states, in a session aimed at settling differences over the legal allocation of oil resources. From this, the Kazakh ambassador to Iran noted that 'Kazakhstan, Iran and Russia share identical views on this issue and believe that the Sea's legal status should be determined first in order to avoid any misunderstanding among the neighbouring countries.'[51]

A more recent example of this cooperative approach to managing the legal regime of the Sea was seen on 27 April 1996, when the presidents of the Russian Federation and Kazakhstan signed an agreement 'on issues connected with legal status of the Caspian Sea and the development of cooperation between the littoral states'.[52] This document is ambiguous enough to cover many positions on the status of the Caspian, but it does indicate that the legal status of the Caspian must be determined on the basis of consensus between the littoral states, and that nobody may tackle the issue unilaterally. However, it also notes that both states recognise each other's rights to develop resources of the Caspian.[53] This might suggest that Kazakhstan is moving towards viewing the management of the legal regime of the Caspian in terms of delimitation, but with considerable agreement and cooperation between the littoral states.

Despite this nominal position, the conduct of Kazakhstan, like Azerbaijan, strongly confirms unilateral delimitation. In December 1993, the

Kazakh government signed an agreement with the Kazakhstankaspishelf consortium of Western oil companies to explore for oil in the Kazakh sector of the Sea. This followed the development of the Tengiz oilfield by TengizChevroil, a joint venture between Chevron and Kazakhstan. This unilateral development of a sector of the Caspian raises the same issues discussed in connection with Azerbaijan – a regime based on delimitation.

Turkmenistan's management of the legal regime of the Caspian Sea is not always consistent. It appears to centre around delimitation, but with cooperation between the coastal states. However, Turkmen conduct, as with the two states discussed so far, offers a clearer picture – a unilateral claim to its sector of the Sea. 1n 1993, Turkmenistan codified its position exactly by enacting the Law on the State Border. This established, according to the rules of the Law of the Sea, a territorial sea and exclusive economic zone over the Turkmen 'sector' of the Caspian.[54] The implications of such a position have already been discussed.

However, this conflicts with the Turkmen position as expressed to the other littoral states and at regional meetings. For example, Turkmenistan was the first state to support Iran's 1992 proposals for cooperation in the Caspian, indicating the need for consensus in deciding the legal status of the Sea and rejecting any proposals for partition or unilaterally asserted claims. Similarly, Turkmenistan, like Kazakhstan, agreed to the draft Treaty on Regional Co-operation in Moscow in 1994 and also to the 'Agreement on Biological Resources 1995',[55] the implications of which have been discussed elsewhere. In addition, Turkmenistan was in accord with the 1993 'Communiqué of the Conference on the Problems of the Caspian Sea' between the four republics of the former Soviet Union.

In July 1995, prior to a visit by Turkmenistan's President Niyazov to Iran, the two states announced that 'as exploitation of the Sea's resources is not possible without the compilation of a legal order, the littoral states should continue their negotiations in order to reach a complete legal order'.[56] Then, in August of 1995, Russian–Turkmen talks resulted in a statement that the two sides were 'in basic accord on all their positions regarding the legal status of the Caspian'. This 'position' was clarified on 16 and 21 August by statements from the Russian Foreign Ministry that laws for the Caspian should be established 'with the participation of all Caspian states and that one-sided decisions by the Caspian littoral states will no longer be valid'.[57]

Whilst there are inconsistencies in the Turkmen position, conduct in the exploitation of hydrocarbons within its sector presents a much clearer position. Turkmenistan, like Azerbaijan and Kazakhstan, has completed deals with Western oil companies. For example, in August 1993, Larmag Energy Associates signed a joint venture agreement to develop Caspian fields off Turkmenistan with the Turkmen company Chelekeneft. Similarly, in 1995, International Petroleum Corp and Larmag agreed with Turkmenistan to develop further offshore fields and, in 1996, the Irish oil company Dragon was actively involved in joint ventures in oilfields in the Turkmen sector of the Sea.[58] Also, Granmayeh reports of plans in late 1994 for cooperation between Turkmenistan, Iran and Russia over exploration of oil in the 'Turkmen section' of the Caspian Sea, without any reference to the approval of other littoral states.[59]

The Russian position on the legal status of the Caspian Sea is similarly inconsistent. On the one hand, the Foreign Ministry and Russian participation in regional cooperation organisations indicates a regime based upon a form of condominium, cooperation and consensus. On the other, the Ministry for Fuel and Energy points to delimitation – an approach supported by the conduct of LUKoil.

Alexander Khodakov notes that Russia views three issue areas that must be resolved for effective management of the legal regime of the Caspian:

1. the implications of the change in the number of littoral states in 1991, for the status of the Caspian;
2. the 'rules of conduct' that the Caspian states must now follow;
3. how the lawful rights and interests of the Caspian states can be protected.[60]

In determining these issues, Russia has a very clear view of the current legal regime of the Caspian. Firstly, the Russians believe that the legal status of the Caspian is governed by the treaties agreed between Iran and the Soviet Union. Russia summarises these provisions as indicating 'very clearly that both the USSR and Iran regarded the Caspian Sea as an object of common use by the Caspian countries, which was open for exploitation by them on an equal basis throughout its waters.'[61]

In support of this they point to many of the provisions discussed earlier, including references in letters to a 'Soviet and Iranian Sea'. Moreover, they state that the rights of a Caspian coastal state could only be acquired by international agreement, and that the Sea was never delimited between the two. It is interesting to note that Russia does not actually claim that the Caspian was under 'condominium' or 'joint sovereignty', doubtless because it recognises the difficulties in reaching the required burden of proof for such a defined term. Rather it notes that 'it seems therefore more accurate to use the term, "object of common use"'[62] – although the differences in practice are hard to see.

Secondly, the Russians state that the Caspian is not a 'sea' in legal terms. It is a landlocked or inner continental water reservoir and as such its status and management should be different. Moreover, whilst the treaties governing the current regime were concluded before the 1958 and 1982 UNCLOS, there is no validity in the argument that Iran and the Soviet Union would have followed Convention norms had they already been in place. Indeed the principles of law enshrined in UNCLOS existed as customary law already and might have been followed, had that been desired. In any event, the two states could have chosen to revise the treaties in accordance with the Convention had they wished to do so.[63]

Khodakov develops this position a stage further as he claims that the regime developed by the treaties is still in force, regardless of the emergence of new members of the Caspian club. This is supported by both customary international law and the Alma Ata Declaration. As such, the Caspian remains 'as territory beyond national jurisdiction, the legal regime of which has to be decided by all of them, proceeding from the premise that they have equal rights to its utilisation'.[64]

Nonetheless, Russia does have a clear approach to the future management of the legal regime of the Sea. Firstly, it claims that international law contains no mandatory obligation that lakes must be divided – indeed it claims two examples of 'undivided lakes'. Furthermore, Russia is of the opinion that such delimitation and the unilateral development of oil and gas are not compatible with effective environmental management of the Caspian as a whole.

Thus Russia favours a regime of 'cooperation amongst all the Caspian States, based on the existing legal regime of the Caspian, in the utilisation of its resources'. For this reason, Russia has proposed fishing agreements since 1991 based closely on those codified in the treaties – namely an exclusive coastal fishing zone and, beyond this, a free fishing zone with national quotas and fishing regulations.

Russia has been a primary proponent and supporter of the initiatives towards regional cooperation discussed earlier – for example, work in 1992 and 1994 on the Treaty on Regional Cooperation in the Caspian Sea; the 1993 Conference on the Problems of the Caspian Sea; and the 1995 Biological Resources Agreement.[65] Similarly, a draft agreement was produced by Russia in late 1994, proposing a 20-mile 'zone of influence' extending out from the coastline of each Caspian state, within which states would be free to develop resources. Development of the central part would be regulated by a regional cooperation organisation. However, none of these proposals has been implemented.

Russia indicates that, unlike Azerbaijan, it does not believe that the question of legal status of the Caspian needs to be decided before legal regimes for conservation and resource management are developed. It expresses the fear that extended 'status debate' could prevent the conclusion of agreements that are needed immediately. However, it does recognise that such agreements might assure 'the rights of coastal states to the exploitation of mineral resources but without any national appropriation of the Caspian Sea'.[66]

Whilst recognising this right, Russia does not accept that unilateral acts by the littoral states are lawful – in particular the activities and statements of the three republics in relation to their deals with Western oil companies. The Caspian is not a legal vacuum, and there must be agreement on the legal regime between all the littoral states, if development is to occur.[67]

This position has been made clear on a number of occasions. This continues in a much stronger vein, indicating that unilateral actions are not considered lawful and are not recognised by Russia. Moreover, Russia 'reserves the right to take such measures as it deems necessary and whenever it deems appropriate, to restore the legal order and overcome the consequences of unilateral actions'. Indeed, on 7 November 1995, Khodakov stated that 'Russia may legally prospect for and explore Caspian offshore oil fields 10 miles away from Baku even tomorrow'.[68]

The strength of this position has been reiterated on a number of occasions and in a number of forms, be it in the 'Note to the Ministry of Foreign Affairs of Azerbaijan' of 14 January 1994 or the Russian statements of August 1995 discussed earlier in connection with Turkmenistan.[69]

However, the Russian Foreign Ministry may recognise that some form of delimitation of the Caspian is a possible solution, within the framework discussed above. For example, Russian Deputy Foreign Minister Chemyshev stated in April 1995 that 'when the shares of the littoral states are specified they could freely exercise their own rights without violating the interests of others'.[70] This position of cooperation in individual exploitation was seen most recently in the joint Turkmen–Russian statement of 27 April 1996.[71] Nonetheless, this does not really change the essence of the Foreign Ministry position that there must be cooperation and no unilateral actions.

This attitude is supported neither by the Ministry for Fuel and Energy nor by LUKoil. Indeed, there is evidence of a rift between the two, with the latter insistent that Russia cannot afford to be left behind in the scramble for Caspian resources. This leads to an implicit recognition of the legitimacy of national 'sectors' in the Caspian. Indeed, Bundy notes that the Ministry for Fuel and Energy has made delimitation proposals for the Caspian Sea as a whole.[72]

The activities of LUKoil have supported this position. In the November 1993 agreement, Russia and Azerbaijan ratified LUKoil's 10 per cent participation in the development of oilfields 'located in the Azeri sector of the Caspian Sea'. This confirmed LUKoil as a member of the consortium of Western companies signing the 'Contract of the Century'.[73] LUKoil also has a massive 35 per cent share in the Azeri 'Karabakh' field, some 10 kilometres from the Azeri coast – and the right to operate and run the project.[74] The president of LUKoil, Mr Alekperov said in April 1996 that he was keen to increase LUKoil's share in the development of a third Azeri project – the $4 billion Shakh Deniz project. LUKoil, already owning 10 per cent of this project, was 'ready' to take another 10 per cent.[75] It has also been increasingly involved in the development of Kazakh fields in the Caspian. It has been in negotiation to take part of both Chevron and the Kazakh government's share of TengizChevroil, giving it a share of the Tengiz field. Similarly, LUKoil is negotiating for shares in Kazakhstan's energy holdings and enterprises, opening access to further Kazakh Caspian oilfields. LUKoil has been involved in the Turkmen sector as well.[76]

Most importantly, Russia itself has granted licences to exploit energy resources in its sector of the Caspian. The first of these was granted to Caspian Oil Development (Caspoil), a subsidiary of the UK independent JKX oil and gas. This licence gives Caspoil the right to exploit oil and gas reserves in the InchkeMore field off Dagestan, a member of the Russian Federation.[77] This demonstrates the inconsistencies in the Russian approach to the management of the legal regime of the Caspian. It would appear that the Foreign Ministry regards the Caspian as an 'object of common use' but does accept some form of division. Above all, it insists that activities develop on the basis of consensus between the Caspian states. Unilateral actions are unlawful. However, LUKoil and the Ministry for Fuel and Energy are endorsing the sectoral claims of the republics, even endorsing a claim to a Russian sector.

Iran, as the second original littoral state, demonstrates a position similar to that of Russia. The last five years have seen a number of different policies and some inconsistencies between position and conduct. Iran's management of the current legal regime, as elucidated by the former Iranian diplomat Granmayeh, is based on the premise that the status of the Caspian is sui generis – as such it should be governed by a regime tailored to the specific requirements of the Sea.[78] Such a regime is based upon two principles:

1 that the Soviet–Iranian agreement of 1940 should be observed as the legal basis for defining the rights and obligations of littoral states in the Caspian Sea;
2 that a regional organisation of the Caspian Sea littoral states should be established to coordinate all activities in the fields of fisheries, exploration of oil and gas, transport and prevention of pollution.[79]

Within this, Iran proposes that there should be a limited exclusion zone in coastal waters, but common access or condominium for the rest of the Sea. Iran also opposes the division of the Caspian into national sectors and supports just shares of resources, since resources would not be equally divided between the sectors of the littoral states. In support of this, Iran does not accept that the Caspian was ever divided between herself and the Soviet Union. Furthermore Iran, like Russia, does not believe that third party or non-littoral states should be involved in the development of the legal regime.

On the basis of this approach, Iran initiated the 1992 Conference in Teheran, aiming to develop the Treaty on Regional Cooperation, with decisions based on consensus of the littoral states and unilaterally asserted territorial claims unlawful, as discussed earlier. Iran, like Russia, Turkmenistan and Kazakhstan, supported the 1994 Moscow Conference on this Treaty, as well as the 1995 Biological Resources Agreement. Iran was so in favour of a regional organisation that it offered to fund and host it – a proposal that did not receive universal support, for obvious political reasons.

On the basis of this position, Iran has worked extremely closely with Russia in coordinating its approach to the status issue. Thus, Iran opposed the signing of the 'Contract of the Century' in Azerbaijan, stating on 4 October 1994 that unilateral practices by littoral states in the Caspian were 'illegal'. This opinion was emphasised at the Moscow Conference later in 1994, on the basis of the 'irreparable damage that uncoordinated exploitation is likely to cause to the fragile marine environment.'[80]

It is interesting to note the apparent reversal of this position on 12 November 1994 when Iran purchased a quarter of Azerbaijan's share in the consortium. This deal followed the conclusion of a separate bilateral agreement between the two states, whereby joint exploratory work had started along Iran's own coast. These two deals effectively endorsed Azeri sectoral claims and Iran's acceptance of a legal regime based upon delimitation.

However, Iran's share in the consortium was not ratified in March 1995, largely as a result of pressure from the US on American oil companies in the consortium. Iran immediately reversed its policy on the status issue, and returned to close cooperation with Moscow. Iran's Foreign Minister Velayati stated that 'before the legal regime of the Caspian has been determined, such agreements are not valid' and the implementation of such agreements can be completed only when the legal 'basis of the Caspian Sea is determined'.[81] Similar points have been made since, urging that the status issue must be resolved before the agreements are considered valid, and emphasising the need for a regional organisation to manage the Sea and its resources.

Meanwhile, the position regarding the role of third parties in the Caspian regime has hardened. The Deputy Chairman of the Russian State Duma, Vengrovsky, stated on 13 June 1995 that 'Iran and Russia should cooperate with regional states to prevent the presence of foreign powers in the Caspian Sea',[82] a 'presence' increasingly seen as being the Western oil companies.

This remains the nominal position of Iran. However, Iran now looks set to be a major partner in the international consortium planning the development of the Shakh Deniz oilfield in the Azeri sector. Dabiri notes that 'Iran has located 18 oil platforms in the vicinity of Anzali and, to a lesser extent, in the eastern parts of its continental shelf.'[83] This implied acceptance of both its own and other states' sectoral rights will further emphasise the emerging importance of this type of regime as the current and probable future status of the Caspian.

A number of conclusions may be drawn from this. The treaties between the two original littoral states still form the basis of the current legal regime and the status of the Caspian. This regime has been further developed by the customary international law of the region, based on both the conduct and attitude of the littoral states before and after the break-up of the Soviet Union. This recent 'custom' suggests a current legal regime based on delimitation of the Caspian Sea into five sovereign and independent sectors. There may be some cooperation, but the lure of resource development has fuelled effective division. This recent conduct and attitude most clearly represents the current, emerging legal status of the Caspian, and consequently the most likely regime for the future.

The future legal status

This section assesses the possible future legal status of the Caspian Sea, as suggested by principles and rules of international law, including the developments discussed above. This will be facilitated through examination of whether or not the Caspian might be managed under joint sovereignty or condominium, or delimitation.

Status under the Law of the Sea

The Law of the Sea relating to enclosed and semi-enclosed seas is relevant to this discussion. If a corpus of law governing such seas does exist and overrides the Caspian, it might indicate whether the Sea is to be delimited and how. Initially, legal scholars such as A. Gervais, G. Fouilloux, L. M. Alexander and Ph. Pondavon differentiated between enclosed and semi-enclosed seas on the basis of geographical criterion, such as whether the sea in question had an outlet through which it could drain. This differentiation disappeared with the 1982 United Nations Convention on the Law of the Sea, which classified both types under the same category. Article 122 of Part IX indicates that:

> enclosed or semi-enclosed sea means a gulf basin or sea surrounded by two or more States and connected to another sea or the ocean by a narrow outlet or consisting entirely or primarily of the territorial seas and exclusive economic zones of two or more coastal states.[84]

This definition covers bodies of water such as the Gulf of Mexico, the Persian Gulf and the Black Sea, all of which are connected by outlets to the sea or ocean. The Caspian, on the other hand, is totally landlocked and is thus not covered by the UNCLOS definition. Concepts of territorial sea, exclusive economic zone and continental shelf are not strictly relevant. Similarly, the UNCLOS principle that delimitation be carried out by agreement in accordance with equitable principles does not have to apply. Nonetheless, this formula has gained general acceptance as a guide to delimitation of continental shelves.[85] As such, these principles could be applied by choice.

Furthermore, since the vessels of third states cannot reach the Caspian without the permission of a littoral state, the sea may not be considered 'international waters', under the UNCLOS. Thus, such vessels do not have the same rights on the Caspian that they might have on the high seas or exclusive economic zones of other coastal states[86] – freedom of navigation for example.

In this way, both Bundy[87] and Vinogradov and Wouters[88] indicate that the status of the Caspian is that of an inland lake, internal sea or 'international lake'. However, they do note that geographical, political and historical characteristics may be sufficient to differentiate the Caspian from other international lakes. This view of the Caspian as having a sui generis legal status is further supported by the Iranian writer Mohammad Reza Dabiri.[89]

The question of condominium or joint sovereignty

The Caspian is not subject to delimitation under principles of the Law of the Sea. However, this does not necessarily imply that it may not be delimited, or that it is subject to joint sovereignty or a condominium under the littoral states. As Bundy notes, 'contemporary international law has not favoured treating landlocked seas or lakes as subject to joint sovereignty absent a compelling showing to that effect'.[90]

It is important to note that a true condominium normally implies joint sovereignty between the states concerned on the basis of equality. Whilst the parties may expressly agree to an unequal condominium, the general presumption in international law is that in the absence of such an express agreement, shared sovereignty will be equal.[91]

Condominia are created by express agreement or treaties between states and do not ordinarily arise by implication. As such it should be possible to examine any such agreement and the conduct of the states involved, to confirm whether or not a regime of shared sovereignty was really intended.[92] On this basis, examples of condominia have included the city of Maastricht after the thirteenth century or joint British–French sovereignty over the New Hebrides islands.

There is no evidence of such an express agreement in any of the treaties relating to the Caspian. As Bundy notes 'terms such as sovereignty or condominium simply do not appear'.[93] There is, however, a recent exception to this requirement of 'express agreement' for sovereignty regimes to exist. The case concerns the decision of the International Court of Justice in a boundary case between Honduras, El Salvador and Nicaragua, concerning the Gulf of Fonseca.[94] It is also the only international case that applies condominium status to an enclosed or partially enclosed area of water.

For 300 years the Gulf of Fonseca was surrounded and was under the sovereignty of one state, the Spanish crown. In 1821 the Federal Republic of Central America succeeded to these sovereign rights. A few years later, as it dissolved, Honduras, El Salvador and Nicaragua emerged as successor states. The former Spanish administrative boundaries became international boundaries, and the Gulf, which had never been subject to any division before 1821, remained as a unity thereafter. The court held that the body of law relating to succession of states was relevant. It was possible to create or imply a regime of joint sovereignty where a single, undivided maritime area passed to two or more states that continued to treat the area as a unity. In this case, the three successor states had inherited the Gulf of Fonseca, which had previously belonged to one state, and had treated it as a unity.[95]

However, this precedent is not wholly relevant. It can be distinguished from the case of the Caspian on two grounds. Firstly, when the Soviet Union broke up in 1991, the Caspian was not subject to the sovereignty of a single state. Iran had been a second littoral state for a number of years. Secondly, as discussed, the littoral states have failed to treat the Sea as a unity.

Thus, the Caspian may not be held as condominium solely on the basis of state succession. This principle would only suggest condominium status if the Sea was subject to condominium before the break-up of the Soviet Union. Even the former Soviet sector, under the sovereignty of a single state, could not be viewed as a condominium. The conduct of the republics supports delimitation, so demonstrating a failure to treat the area as a unity – a condition expressed in the judgement.

International lakes – the presumption against condominium

The Caspian is not bound to be delimited as an enclosed sea in accordance with the UNCLOS. Furthermore, it does not meet the express requirements of condominium and can be distinguished from the exception to this requirement. From this, one must consider what examples from similar international water bodies suggest as a legal regime for the Caspian.

Examples from international lakes demonstrate an overwhelming trend towards some form of delimitation, dividing the body of water into sectors of full sovereignty for the riparian states. Indeed Bundy notes that he is 'not aware of a single case where an inland body of water is currently treated as a condominium subject to the joint sovereignty of its riparian states.'[96] Examples of such delimitation by the littoral states may be seen in Lake Victoria: Kenya/ Tanzania/ Uganda; and the Great Lakes of North America: Canada/ USA.[97]

There are two caveats. Firstly, the law is not completely settled as a body of 'rules' in this area. There are examples of international lakes that have not been fully delimited—Lake Constance, for example. Similarly, delimitation methods are not uniform and rights of navigation and non-navigational uses of such waters vary greatly.[98] Secondly, it might be argued that the Caspian is sufficiently unique to avoid classification as an international lake.

Despite these two issues, these examples do not appear to support proposals for condominium. Consequently, the only remaining way in which such proposals might be valid, is through demonstration that the littoral states 'genuinely intended to create a condominium and that their conduct evidences such an intent'.[99]

Status as suggested by treaties and conduct of the states

The status suggested by the treaties, conduct and attitude of the littoral states indicates that state conduct supports delimitation, and thus, there is insufficient evidence to support a 'condominium' or 'joint sovereignty' claim under international law. As such, the presumption of delimitation suggested by rules of international law is not rebutted. As a result, rules of international law support the emerging trends of the current legal regime, towards a future status of the Caspian Sea based on delimitation into five sovereign sectors.

Two legal regimes for the Caspian Sea have been considered. Firstly, the current status of the Caspian, arising from treaties and the conduct of the littoral states. This clearly indicated that the current, and probably future, legal status is emerging from state conduct supporting delimitation of the sea into five sovereign independent blocks. Secondly, there was assessment of the future regime, as suggested by principles of international law. This further supported a regime of delimitation.

Given this evidence, delimitation seems the most likely outcome, at least as far as oil and gas resources are concerned. However, there is scope for greater cooperation and coordination in managing navigation, the environment and sea-level rise. In this way, a number of different regimes may emerge to manage different aspects of the Caspian Sea.

The five regimes managing the resource

The last section investigated the legal status of the Caspian Sea and made clear that the Sea is subject to a regime of delimitation, not joint sovereignty. Within this status of delimitation, the transboundary oil and gas resources of the Caspian are not subject to a regime of joint development. We are not looking at a transboundary energy resource managed through agreements such as those governing the 'Gulf of Thailand Joint Development Area' or the 'Australia–Indonesia Zone of

Co-operation'. Rather, the oil and gas of the Caspian is being managed by five different and independent domestic regimes. It will be useful to examine how each regime is developing differently. 'Regime' is defined broadly and will encompass an investigation of, for example, the recent history and extent of resource development and the emerging domestic legal and taxation systems. It will cover the issues of importance to each sector and regime. From this, in some cases, management of the resource will necessitate consideration of the particular regime by extending investigation into other sectors. For example, where the Caspian is seen as a shared resource, the concept of 'sectors' becomes problematic.

It is also important to consider why these regimes are emerging as they are. This is largely as a result of the combination and interaction of a number of factors, such as extent and accessibility of resources, the conduct of the littoral states, the oil companies, supranational financial institutions, regional and global powers.

The conclusion to this chapter will show that this investigation provides new evidence of transboundary resource management – specifically in an environment of new and emerging states. Moreover, under the management of these five different regimes, the development of the oil and gas of the Caspian as a whole is highly skewed and uneven.

The Azerbaijani sector

Of the five sectors, the Azerbaijani sector of the Caspian Sea has seen some of the most extensive and far advanced development of offshore oil and gas. Azerbaijan has at least 15 billion barrels in probable resources beneath the Caspian. Agreements have been reached for both production and transport of the resource and there has been enormous Western investment in this sector.

In historical overview, the development of this sector started early and was the result of initiatives from both the newly emergent state of Azerbaijan and also a number of the multinational oil companies, who recognised the potential of this sector.

As early as September 1991 the Azerbaijani President Ayaz Mutalibov made clear that 'we need to undertake a radical modernisation of this sector (oil) of the economy and, we are fully aware that we will need foreign capital to do so'.

Similarly, Steve Remp of Ramco, a Scottish oil company, had spent several years nurturing oil relationships in Azerbaijan prior to the break-up of the Soviet Union.[100] Moreover, as early as June 1991, AMOCO had reached an agreement to develop the 'Azeri' oilfield in the Azerbaijani sector of the Caspian[101] and by October 1991 AMOCO had agreed to cooperate in the evaluation and development of the field with Unocal, McDermott, British Petroleum (BP), Statoil and Ramco – this was 'the first major western involvement in the Soviet oil industry'.[102]

This developed into something of an oil rush, as BP began unilaterally negotiating its own production sharing agreement (PSA), for the Capaz offshore field with Azerineft, Azerbaijan's state oil company, in March of 1992. Similarly, by September 1992, BP and Statoil signed an agreement with Azerbaijan to develop the Dostlug field, involving an investment of $1.5 billion and October saw Ramco and Pennzoil take exclusive rights to develop the Guneshli field with Azerineft. This rush was supported by Western services – for example, the commercial law firm Nabarro Nathanson was appointed by Azerbaijan to advise on the drafting of new laws for oil and gas production.[103]

However, this rapidly developing Azerbaijani playing field became very uncertain and unstable. Firstly, early in June 1993 Azerbaijan suddenly announced that the three offshore fields – Guneshli, Chirag and Azeri – would in fact be developed under a single contract regardless of earlier commitments. This move aimed to cut costs and also designated the working shares of the Western oil companies.[104]

Secondly, in a move with breathtaking implications, the new Azeri government of late June 1993, emerging from a period of political turmoil, decided to completely cancel this contract. This came some five days after the eight foreign oil companies had confronted the political crisis in Azerbaijan, advancing $70 million in good faith to ensure the continued right to negotiate to develop these resources. The bizarre explanation for this cancellation was offered later by the new Azeri Secretary of State as, 'most of the technologies bought over the past year from foreign companies turned out to be morally obsolete'.[105]

The highly fluid nature of this sector was further demonstrated by a new President, Haydar Aliev. Having demanded two and half months to review the original contracts, he introduced a new working environment for Western oil companies. Moving away from the atmosphere of cooperation, his government continued negotiations 'with barely concealed hostility', expecting up to 80 per cent of the profits of any development. In a similar move away from the West, he immediately signed an agreement with Iran for cooperation in oil.[106]

Despite this working environment of uncertainty and animosity the oil companies, operating as a united body, persisted with negotiations. Chevron was able to sign a joint study agreement with the State Oil Company of Azerbaijan (SOCAR), for areas of the southern Caspian.

In November 1993, a consortium of eight Western oil companies reached a preliminary PSA with Azerbaijan for the Chirag and Azeri fields – paying a $500 million sweetener and accepting that Azerbaijan would take 80 per cent of the profits from extracted oil.[107] The deal, subject to the approval of the Azerbaijani government and Parliament, committed the consortium to an initial investment of some $7.5 billion.

Protracted negotiation of the details of this deal continued in Istanbul and Houston. However, rumblings of Russian dissatisfaction, in June 1994, gave fresh impetus to these negotiations. On 20 September 1994, after four long years of negotiation, the consortium of eight Western companies and Azerbaijan signed the 'Contract of the Century' – the thirty-year right to develop the Chirag and Azeri oilfields. Moreover, with this new partnership, other developments progressed as BP and Statoil signed a joint venture agreement with SOCAR, for the Shakh Deniz oilfield.[108]

Reaction to these developments of the regime were mixed, and would influence further changes. The parties to the agreement were clearly enthusiastic. For President Aliev the deal was 'the first great step forward for the country in achieving its aim of moving towards a market economy'.[109] Similarly, John Brown, BP's managing director, spoke of the 'huge opportunities' for British companies as he predicted the first oil would flow within eighteen months.[110]

Reactions further afield demonstrated the importance of the strategic nature of this deal for the regime. The home states of the oil companies demonstrated their support as Tim Eggar, UK Energy Minister, and William White, Deputy US Energy Secretary, underpinned this huge development programme. They aimed to produce economic revival in Azerbaijan, so distancing the former Soviet republic from Russia. Conversely, the Russian Foreign Ministry rejected this intrusion into its 'near abroad' sphere of influence, stating that 'we shall not officially recognise this agreement. Unilateral action, especially on resources and the Caspian Sea, contradict international law and risk damaging the ecological system of the sea.'[111]

The Azerbaijani Parliament ratified this contract but this did not bring stability to the regime for resource management. By November 1994, SOCAR was using its 20 per cent share in the contract both to raise capital, and as a strategic tool to ensure support for its unilateral development of the Azerbaijani sector. Azerbaijan proposed giving Iran 5 per cent of its 20 per cent share in exchange for political support and financial and technical assistance. Iran was expected to contribute $300–350 million to assist Azerbaijan in meeting its financing requirements under the contract.[112]

This proposal demonstrated again the influence of forces outside the region on this regime. The proposal was swiftly blocked by the American oil companies in the consortium, anxious to maintain Iranian isolation. This provoked Iran to accuse Azerbaijan of caving in to US pressure and Iran reversed its position on Caspian status, stating that 'while the Caspian Sea's legal status has not been determined, Caspian coastal states cannot unilaterally exploit its resources because the oil fields are interconnected'.[113] Nonetheless, with similar strategic and financial motives, Azerbaijan did sell a 5 per cent share to Turkey in April 1995, and raised further capital through an identical sale to Exxon, in the same month.[114]

Azerbaijan has continued to tread a knife-edge in managing its resources. This regime has ensured the involvement of both Western expertise and finance, and regional powers threatening Azerbaijan's unilateral development of this sector. For example, Azerbaijan resolved the Iranian question through a joint oil and gas drilling venture with Iran. It offered Iran the chance to join a second international consortium developing the 1.8 billion barrel Shakh Deniz field in May 1996. With similar aplomb, Azerbaijan involved the Russian state oil company, LUKoil, in both the original 'Contract of the Century' and gave it the lion's share (32.5 per cent) of the deal to develop the Karabakh field with Agip and Pennzoil.[115]

The regime also witnessed increased Western involvement. For example, Pennzoil and Ramco completed a gas utilisation project last year in the offshore Neft Dashlari field and the Mashal field has been signed over to the Denver-based Hallwood Caspian Petroleum and SOCAR, for redevelopment and further exploration. It is also worth noting Western moves out of the sector. For example, in May 1996, both McDermott and Pennzoil sold their shares in the consortium to the Japanese company Itochu.[116]

This overview of hydrocarbon development in the Azerbaijani sector of the Caspian indicates the general nature of the regime for resource management. From this some of the more specific aspects can be examined. Western oil companies and the Azerbaijani government worked to ensure that the regime offered the easiest route to oil production, creating the rapid free market development that is the hallmark of this sector.

Also, Azerbaijani negotiations for the 'Contract of the Century' were carried out at the highest level, by President Aliev. He aimed to protect Azeri interests and ensure that the contract was mutually beneficial to all the parties recognising that Azerbaijan's national interests are directly linked to the success of this extremely important and historic agreement. His generous use of the 'presidential decree' allowed crucial decisions to be made immediately. Likewise the oil companies, including SOCAR, formed themselves into a single consortium, the Azerbaijan International Operating Consortium (AIOC). This negotiated as one group for shares in the three combined fields of Azeri, Chirag and Guneshli. Both the President of SOCAR, and the President of the AIOC note that this helped speed up negotiations and also 'minimised financial risk on the part of the investors as each was responsible for less initial investment'. This approach allowed all technical, commercial, production sharing, taxation, project management and legal aspects of the regime to be covered in one series of negotiations and one contract.[117]

This approach of single contract negotiation has been repeated for all subsequent development projects in the sector. Whilst there is no single body of legislation governing the regime, this approach ensures both speed of negotiation and a greater degree of security, as all issues are confirmed at the highest level. Moreover, it is evident that since the signing of these contracts. a highly cooperative regime is emerging between Azerbaijan and the oil companies in both their individual projects and also, for some of them, through the AIOC. Chevron, for instance, has undertaken an extensive programme in computer training, exploration and seismic processing for SOCAR personnel. Chevron is 'working now to build up a solid foundation of trust and understanding'.[118]

However, whilst this regime is clearly developing to allow smoother exploitation of resources, it is not without its problems. Terry Adams, the President of the AIOC, notes that, whilst the geology of developing this sector of the sea is relatively simple, the geopolitics are providing an extremely complex political and commercial slant to this regime. Clearly the dispute over the sovereignty issue in the Caspian has created difficulties, and contractual provisions for oil production have been severely hampered by problems in transporting oil out of Azerbaijan.

This issue centres around pipeline routes. There are three potential routes: through Iran to Teheran or the Persian Gulf; through Georgia to the Black Sea and then the Turkish Mediterranean Coast at Ceyhan; and through Russia to the Black Sea port of Novorrossisk and then through the Bosphorus. In brief, the US has refused to allow a route out to the south through Iran. The Georgian route is fraught with difficulties arising from Georgian unrest and the war between Armenia and Azerbaijan. Both of these factors may well have been fuelled by Russia. The Russian route is complicated by Chechen instability and a reluctance on the part of the oil companies and Azerbaijan to give Russia control over the export route and hence over Azerbaijani independence. This reluctance is intensified by the high Russian transit fees. Turkey has further complicated this Russian route through its refusal to allow a significant increase in the number of tankers passing through the Bosphorus.[119]

Nonetheless, the AIOC resolved this issue for the regime through a decision described by *Time Magazine* as a 'judgement of Solomon' – they opted to open two routes, one through Georgia and Turkey, another through Russia and the Black Sea. Terry Adams noted that 'working within the complex geopolitical environment in the Caucasus, we decided that having two viable export solutions was clearly the most effective way of pressing forward'.[120]

At the local scale, the regime has been subject to a number of complications. The AIOC itself with six national and eleven corporate interests, each with a unique dimension and approach, has made coordination and decision-making a complex process, notwithstanding the strengths that such diversity brings to the regime. Similarly, the rapid and relatively uncontrolled development of the regime has given rise to disputes between the oil companies. For example, in October 1995, Ramco and Pennzoil were involved in a dispute over relative rights in the Karabakh field, based on bilateral agreements between the two companies – not involving Azerbaijan as a central authority.[121]

There are also difficulties in bridging the divide between East and West despite the fact that the Western oil companies are working with what Adams notes is a highly educated and cultured society, with a long history of onshore and offshore oil production. They are introducing a Western business paradigm into an entrenched Soviet system: 'what we take for granted in western business is quite new in Baku'.[122]

External financial institutions are also important. The World Bank has greatly contributed to the development of this regime, through a possible $20 million loan to provide SOCAR with technical assistance. This will assist Azerbaijan in attracting its own experts and advisers, independent of the Western oil companies. The loan must provide consultation for SOCAR on the contractual, legal and financial aspects of large resource projects. Also it must assist Azerbaijan in preparing legal documents to protect her own interests in relation to the status of the Caspian Sea and Azerbaijani oilfields. Finally, some capital must enable SOCAR to become a commercial company of international standard.[123]

The implications of this loan are clear. Not only will the very existence of the regime be strengthened, through the status protection measures, but a more definite structure looks likely to emerge. Whilst SOCAR's own development will be assisted, so a Western business paradigm looks set to influence the development of the regime.

Similarly, the partnership between the Western oil companies and Azerbaijan has ensured rapid Azerbaijani development. The AIOC predicts that within five years of full field development 90 per cent of all professionals and 95 per cent of all support staff will be Azerbaijani. Support services such as new hotels, airlines and offices are all developing the economy. This sector has also seen substantial social investment on the part of the oil companies, which have donated more than $50 million to the Government Social Fund.[124]

In conclusion, the regime managing the development of oil and gas in this sector is very advanced. The Azerbaijani economy is effectively being rebuilt around the development of its Caspian energy resources. Much of this is due to the relative ease of reaching effective agreements. Although there have been a number of problems, it would appear that the regime is stabilising, with firm roots in a Western business paradigm. The security that this offers can only draw further investment and greater development to this, the sector that has courted Western assistance to the greatest degree.

The Iranian sector

The development of the hydrocarbon regime in the Iranian sector has been very different to that of Azerbaijan. Despite the fact that seismic surveys of Iran's Caspian aquatory show oil-bearing structures similar to those of the Azerbaijani sector, Iran has carried out practically no exploration or development of its own. This is because much of Iran's Caspian resources are at considerable depth, and also because the National Iranian Oil Company, NIOC, does not have the expertise to undertake these projects. This inexperience is exacerbated by US sanctions and the Iranian political and economic system, both of which have deterred Western oil companies from making the level of investment seen in Azerbaijan.

In 1995 the US oil company Conoco was forced to pull out of a deal to develop two Gulf oil and gas fields. This was a result of Bill Clinton's ban on American firms helping Iran to exploit its oil reserves. 'Conoco has had to sacrifice the chance of becoming the first big western oil company since the overthrow of the Shah to get its hands directly on Iran's reserves.' Whilst, firstly, the French firms Elf Aquitaine and Total went on to win the contract, and, secondly, the fields in question are not in the Caspian, the problems of this regime become clear – oil companies prevented from developing the straightforward oilfields of the Persian

Gulf by the political environment are unlikely to risk the levels of investment required to develop the untried and more complex Caspian fields.[125]

Despite these problems, Iran has attempted some development of this sector. For example, in 1992, Iran was determined to lift its oil output, and called in foreign companies to explore and develop its offshore hydrocarbons in both the Gulf and the Caspian. Its success was limited in the Caspian Sea, though the Finnish Neste Corporation did discuss the possibility of a joint venture petrochemicals plant.[126]

However, there has been some recent development. There have been seismic surveys and the Iranian firm Sedra has built Iran's first Caspian platform, with the assistance of two Finnish companies. This is now installed on the Iranian shelf and has the capacity to drill some 20 000 feet below the seabed. Similarly, joint development of Iranian Caspian oil has been discussed with Moscow. As a result, a group of Russian experts is now at work off the Iranian coast, near Enzeli and Naushahr.[127]

Nonetheless, development of this sector has been very limited. This is connected to Iran's subscription to a regime of resource management based on the coordinated development of the Sea as a whole, with energy resources under some form of common ownership. Whilst its conduct does not support this position, Iran does not favour the concept of fully sovereign sectors. In this way, Iranian management has been focused on two areas: firstly, the sectors of the other littoral states where there have been greater levels of development: Azerbaijan, Turkmenistan and Kazakhstan; secondly, on projects for regional cooperation.

In the first area, Iran has interests in the Azerbaijani sector. As discussed earlier Iran has also been involved in the Turkmen sector, through proposals for increased cooperation in energy development between the two states, following an Iranian visit in 1993. Similarly, 1994 saw joint plans to develop a $7 billion gas pipeline linking the Caspian to the Black Sea, via Turkey. Iran's involvement in the Kazakh sector has centred on local transport issues, with offers to transport oil across the Caspian from Kazakhstan in 1992.[128]

Iran has had no involvement in the Russian sector other than through political cooperation over resource development and status. This increased after Iran was denied membership of the consortium in Azerbaijan. As Russian Deputy Foreign Minister Chemyshev noted 'our approaches to a new legal status of the Caspian Sea are very close or identical'.[129]

In the second area, Iran views resource management based on cooperation between the littoral states. In fact, Iran has initiated, and proposed itself as the host for, a Regional Cooperation Council to manage the Caspian. Iran is keen to exclude the West from the area, as issues 'should not be decided by strategic considerations of non regional states'. The Director of Exploration for the NIOC makes clear that the need of Caspian states for technological help 'doesn't mean the countries should be overrun with foreign companies'.[130]

Iran has also approached resource management through the 'general' transport issue. It proposes itself as the most suitable export route for all Caspian oil and gas – oil could be pumped to energy-deficient northern Iran and Teheran, and equivalent amounts of Iranian crude released into the well-developed export chain in the Persian Gulf, to the south. If this proved a success, further development could encompass a new pipeline running from the Caspian to the Kharg Island export terminal in the Persian Gulf. However, American opposition makes financing, and hence the feasibility of either project, unlikely.[131]

These projects are more than merely an attempt to secure a single pipeline route out through Iran, although this would clearly benefit Iran both in strategic and financial terms. It is part of a wider Iranian vision of energy cooperation with Central Asia. In this way, some Iranian commentators envisage an Iranian-led 'Caspian Energy Zone', based on the Caspian littoral states. This would complement, rather than compete with, similar 'CIS' and the 'Black Sea' zones. Iran would be able to offer the Caspian Energy Zone outlets to the high growth markets of Asia and the Pacific Rim, through the Persian Gulf.[132]

On a larger scale, Iran has proposed Project PEACE – Pipeline Extending from Asian Countries to Europe. This aims to create a gas network stretching from India to Europe, using Iran's existing pipeline network to link up with Central Asia, the Persian Gulf, the Caucasus and Turkey.[133]

Thus, in conclusion, the Iranian sector has enjoyed limited development, although, as available concessions in other sectors diminish, this may change. This limited development is largely due to Iran pursuing a regime for resource management at a regional level, involving itself in projects throughout the Caspian and attempting to integrate the Sea into a regional energy system.

The Kazakh sector

The Kazakh sector has more in common with Azerbaijan than Iran, although it has been more of a latecomer to exploiting sub-sea hydrocarbons. Resources estimated at 27 billion barrels of oil and untold gas reserves support the prediction that from Kazakh waters alone 'the Caspian may well be the Persian Gulf of the 21st Century'.[134]

The Kazakh regime for resource management is less developed than that of Azerbaijan, notwithstanding the fact that Chevron's development of the Tengiz field is relatively well advanced and only held back by existing pipelines able to handle only 60 000 of its potential 700 000 barrels per day, and difficulties in resolving this problem. This underdevelopment is seen in the eighteen-month seismic study of the area for the state oil company Kazakhstancaspishelf and the North Caspian Consortium, which is only just nearing completion. Whilst Production Sharing Agreements will follow, oil production will not commence until 1998, with first exports in 2003.[135]

In historical overview, early developments of the Kazakh sector, in May 1992, appeared to offer great potential. After four years of negotiations, the US Chevron Corporation signed a development protocol for the huge Tengiz oilfield, estimated to contain 2500 million barrels. Shortly afterwards, Kazakhstan laid further plans for the development through a preliminary agreement with Russia, Azerbaijan and Oman for an oil pipeline out of the landlocked Caspian region. Oman was to finance the deal while the littoral states would provide labour, materials, equipment and rights of way. Despite 'lengthy and difficult negotiations' to finalise the Tengiz deal, Kazakhstan's regime for resource development made oil companies 'feel rather secure'. Delovie Lyudi contrasts this with a Russian system making investors 'fret and fume'. This attractive business regime brought in substantial foreign investment which, when 'compared to the trickle of foreign money going into Russia's much bigger oil industry, was a flood'.[136]

Kazakhstan was also active in courting foreign investment, through President Nazarbayev's promotion of Kazakh political stability to Western oil companies. As a result, seven Western oil companies signed a preliminary three-year deal, with an investment of $200 million, to explore the Kazakh sector of the Caspian Sea, in June 1993. Similarly, service industries had become well established in the capital Alma Ata by 1994. Chase Manhattan became the first US bank to set up in the city in January 1994, following Deutsche Bank, with Citicorp arriving shortly afterwards. As Steve Wagner of Dallas-based Oryx Energy Company noted 'you get the feeling that at one point or another, everyone will at least pass through here'.[137]

However, this fairy tale was not to follow the same path as Azerbaijan. Positive development of this regime was severely damaged by the problem of transporting oil out of the region. In 1994 Kadyr Baikenov, the Kazakh Energy Minister, noted that despite huge resources he was 'having difficulty attracting capital to the country's oil and gas sector', largely because of difficulties raising finance for the pipeline of the Caspian Pipeline Consortium, or CPC. This problem was linked to the reluctance of the World Bank to get involved in a deal which provided a lucrative marketing contract to the Oman Oil Company (OOC). Problems with the OOC took a turn for the worse in May 1994, with a serious conflict between John Deuss of OOC and Chevron, concerning the financing, ownership and route of the CPC pipeline. Chevron noted wryly that 'a lot of things have happened since we started work on Tengiz 15 months ago, including some things we didn't plan on'. Chevron were still in some difficulty by 1995: 'we made our forecasts in 1992 but nobody could have known the problems you would face in the former Soviet Union'.[138]

It was not until mid-1996 that these problems diminished, when Mobil purchased a 25 per cent share in Tengiz from Kazakhstan, and the CPC underwent radical restructuring. This restructuring lead to a preliminary agreement between the US oil companies with shares in the Tengiz field: Chevron and Mobil; the new members of the CPC: Russia, Kazakhstan, Oman; and six oil companies, for the construction of a pipeline from Kazakhstan to the Russian Black Sea port of Novorrossisk. This aimed to finally unlock the energy reserves of the Kazakh sector. The $2 billion project was finalised during President Yeltsin's visit to Kazakhstan on 27 April 1996.[139]

From this overview, regime trends become clearer. Kazakhstan enthusiastically courted the Western investment seen in Azerbaijan but the lack of legal guarantees and prolonged transport difficulties slowed development. This transport problem arose from both the strategic ambition of Russia to control regional resources and the inability of the oil companies and states to reach an acceptable compromise. These difficulties dissuaded further foreign investment.

A number of specific aspects of this regime are illustrative. For example, the legal regime managing oil and gas has been recently developed, in an attempt to improve the investment environment. In 1991 there were only two pieces of legislation governing resource development. Both were inadequate for the complexities of modern Western energy projects. Firstly, the law on 'On Foreign Investments in Kazakhstan' permitted the development of Kazakh natural resources.[140] However, Article 25 stated that whilst nationalisation of foreign investments was illegal, requisitioning was legitimate in 'exceptional circumstances'. This clearly created something of an uncertain and risky regime for the levels of investment demanded by an energy project.

The 'Code on the Subsoil and the Processing of Mineral Raw Material of the Republic of Kazakhstan' offered a more useful framework, including grounds for termination of contracts and a domestic process of dispute resolution.[141] It did not, however, include attractive details such as the right to go to international arbitration, or regulation of transit and intervention.

These shortcomings in the regime slowed investor interest. What is interesting is that Kazakhstan recognised these issues, and as a result 'made significant improvements to its legislative framework for foreign investment as certain of the regulations have been streamlined and simplified'. As a result, the currency has become stable, is convertible, and now facilitates the repatriation of profits. Moreover, the new Law on Foreign Investments provides a plethora of guarantees for foreign investors, including protection against adverse changes in legislation, the political environment and expropriation. There is also provision for compensation. Similarly, the 'Tax Code' has significantly simplified the taxation system, reducing the number of taxes payable to six.[142]

Kazakhstan's 'Petroleum Law' came into force at the same time as the legislation discussed above, further developing the necessary framework for effective resource management. For example, state agencies have the authority to control oil operations, issue licences and conclude contracts with subsoil users, in a far simpler system than before. Similarly, there are provisions regulating pipeline operation and a special charter on environmental protection and liability insurance. Pursuing the successful development of the Azerbaijani sector, the government does reserve the right to negotiate directly with Western oil companies, alongside a system of tendering. The legislation also contains proposals for the development of further regulations, including unified rules for oil and gas development, on and offshore. The development of the project under the Caspian Sea Consortium and its coordinating Kazakh operator Kazakhstancaspishelf (KCS), has provided similar evidence of this regime. With the same painstaking progress that 'hallmarks' this sector, the Kazakh government determined that these organisations should carry out a huge geophysical, environmental and geological programme, before any acreage attribution.[143]

In an attempt to emulate the successes of the Azerbaijani sector, Western involvement was structured as a consortium. The seismic survey was carried out under local KCS supervision, with around 30 Western secondment positions and only when this is completed will Western companies select areas for production – to be operated as PSAs.

President Nazarbayev clearly supported this structure, believing that 'by forming a consortium of the world's largest and most experienced oil companies, Kazakhstan has again demonstrated its commitment to the development of a strong market economy and a responsible approach to the management of its natural resources'. However, it is interesting to compare it to Duval's assessment of the Western view that 'this is a tough deal, and the departure from a conventional foreign company's operatorship and the number of participants make it all the more difficult to implement'.[144]

The management of oil and gas has also been influenced by international financial institutions. They have used the 'carrot' of loans to bring about regime development. For example, in 1996, Kazakhstan reached a preliminary agreement with the International Monetary Fund for a $450 million loan. However, the conditions attached, aimed at strengthening the economy, created 'tougher taxation which may discourage new investments in the oil and gas sector'. This is because Kazakhstan will now have to boost tax revenues through improving tax collection and introducing a new taxation on natural resources – those oil companies who have yet to sign a PSA will be unable to obtain the normal tax exemptions, and so face large tax increases.[145]

The European Bank for Reconstruction and Development (EBRD) has exerted a similar influence, albeit on a different aspect of the sector's development. The EBRD has recently become involved in the financing of up to 35 per cent of the CPC pipeline project, under its aim of 'assisting the countries of central and eastern Europe and the CIS to develop into market-oriented economies'.[146]

Whilst only approving loans for commercially viable projects, through consideration in this case of the cost per tonne per kilometre of the pipeline proposals, the EBRD does attach a number of conditions influential to the development of this regime. The Bank has five criteria for involvement in pipeline financing. For example, tariffs, acceptable to shippers, should reflect the actual operating and capital costs of the pipeline and provide a normal level of return on actual equity investment in the pipeline. Similarly, taxation of pipeline income by host countries should not exceed normal income tax rates. Given the benefits of an EBRD loan, the regime is likely to develop along these lines. A further facet of this sector that has proved central to regime development is the high level of infighting and the lack of cooperation. Some of this has been alluded to earlier, in the discussion of the battle for control of the CPC. Chevron, determined to force the OOC out of the CPC, while securing a role for itself, enjoyed a victory of sorts in January 1996 – John Deuss, OOC's controversial president resigned. However, the battle has continued with Kazakhstan and Chevron working together to ensure that they and Russia are the major consortium owners; OOC on the other hand is determined that it will remain as an owner, with the two states.[147]

This conflict was further complicated by LUKoil's support for OOC proposals since these ensured that the tariff levels so vital to Russian revenues would be set by intergovernmental agreement. However, OOC proposals will only be successful if it is able to secure project financing for the pipeline – financing that will clearly not be available from Chevron.

In this way, dispute rather than cooperation has dominated the development of this regime. Although this conflict will be resolved, it has retarded the development of the Tengiz field and has prevented other projects from moving out of the planning stage.

Similarly, in April 1996, Chevron had to confront another challenge in the Kazakh sector. Workers at the Tengizchevroil (TCO) joint venture, displeased with their wages, considered a strike, and as a result, 'as the labour dispute slowly grows, worker unrest could become a major problem for Chevron in Kazakhstan'. Bulat Vemiyazov, chairman of TCO's labour committee, made clear to TCO management that: 'we demand that the management raise wages immediately. Unless this is done, extreme measures such as a strike, may be taken.' TCO responded with a 44 per cent wage increase because of its 'commitment to competitive pay' – Bisenov's response was uncompromising: 'that miserable pittance won't satisfy Tengizchevroil employees'.[148]

Russian Petroleum Investor (RPI) notes that TCO is in a Catch 22 position – if they fail to meet demands, they face strikes that will weaken both their image in Kazakhstan, and their position in negotiation with LUKoil and Mobil who are planning to purchase shares in the company. On the other hand, meeting these demands will be very expensive, and would follow the $700 million that Chevron has already sunk into a venture that is producing less oil now than it did in the Soviet era.[149]

The influence of Russia on this regime for resource management is all-pervasive. Whilst Kazakhstan may appear to offer a friendlier, less confusing business environment than Russia, it is still problematic, and Russia won't be left out of big oil and gas developments since it feels it has a historical claim to the big Kazakh fields discovered during the Soviet era. This sector offers plans for a number of pipeline routes including options through Iran and Turkey to the Mediterranean, or for oil swaps with Iran. However, Russian influence is such that its proposed route will almost certainly provide the best solution. Moreover, Russia, through LUKoil, is also keen to become involved in Chevron's Tengiz project and the Consortium's seismic survey. Russia also offers the most immediate market for Kazakh oil and gas, through the existing pipeline network.

In conclusion therefore, the issues which have dominated and retarded development of this regime are transport, adverse Russian influence and the lack of a clear and secure legal and fiscal framework for resource development. However, restructuring of the CPC, new legislation and increased positive participation by LUKoil look set to resolve these issue areas, and so allow development on the scale seen across the Caspian in Azerbaijan.

The Russian sector

Russian management of oil and gas is very similar to that of Iran. Resources do lie within this sector but Russia has done little to develop them and has focused its attention on claiming an interest in the Caspian as a whole, including the hydrocarbons of Azerbaijan, Kazakhstan and Turkmenistan.

There has been some development of the Russian sector of the Sea. The first field came on stream in May 1996, on the InchkeMore prospect off the semi-autonomous republic of Dagestan. In 1993 a tender for its development was issued to the UK independent JKX Oil and Gas, in a joint development project with Dagneft, RusCaspNeft and Krasnobarricades. JKX expects production to reach 12 000 barrels per day.

An overview of the development of resources in this sector provides indications of the nature of this regime. First signs of development came in 1992 when Premier Consolidated Oilfields reached agreement to explore and develop oilfields off Dagestan. Further developments of the sector were seen through LUKoil.[150] However, despite this early belief that Russia and the Former Soviet Union represented 'one of the last areas of the world where there are huge quantities of oil and gas to be discovered', a mutual lack of confidence retarded development. Western banks were reluctant to finance projects until government credit guarantees came on line, and were only interested in lucrative advisory contracts. This reluctance was connected to a Soviet legacy that sapped Russian efficiency in energy projects. Similarly, the large-scale investment required to revitalise this oil and gas industry, as seen in Azerbaijan, was retarded by the Russian 'lingering, deep seated suspicion of the intentions and working methods of western oilmen'.[151]

Partly as a result of this impasse, Russia, like Iran, moved to concentrate on the management of the resources of the Sea as a whole. For example, in 1992 Russia agreed to join the Caspian Pipeline Consortium in the Kazakh sector. In 1994 LUKoil pushed hard for an equity stake in the planned development of Caspian fields in the Kazakh sector, only weeks after it was allowed to participate in the Azerbaijani government's share of the consortium in the Azerbaijani sector.[152]

Despite LUKoil's involvement, Russia did attempt to disrupt resource development in the Sea, through refusing to accept that any Caspian oil deals were valid without its approval, given uncertainties over the legal status of the Sea. These statements in themselves did not disrupt developments in resource exploitation. As McDermott International noted 'we don't see it as a major problem but we would like some verification, or official interpretation from the Russian government'. However, Russia shortly raised Western fears, as it demonstrated its ability to curtail Caspian resource development by simply placing restrictions on oil exports from Kazakhstan. The Azerbaijani 'Contract of the Century' provoked further Russian disruption as the Foreign Ministry made clear that 'we shall not officially recognise this agreement', on the grounds of the threat posed to the Caspian environment. Similarly, the Foreign Ministry called for the resignation of Russian officials who had agreed to the deal. At the same time, Russia re-emphasised proposals for a multinational coordinating committee to manage exploitation of oil and gas in the Caspian Sea, claiming Kazakh and Turkmen support.[153]

Russia further hardened its position, as Yuri Shafrinik, the Russian Energy Minister, stated that Russia was 'obliged to take part in all energy projects undertaken by members of the Commonwealth of Independent States'.[154] Such protests have continued to the present.

However, with some hypocrisy, Russia was actively pursuing the development of its own sector, with the preliminary announcement in mid-1994 of the JKX deal for the InchkeMore field discussed earlier, JKX having completed a detailed technical and economic feasibility study.[155]

However, it is interesting to note that whilst these protests have continued from time to time, the focus of Russian management of Caspian resources shifted after 1994. LUKoil and the Russian Fuel and Energy Ministry determined that they could not afford to be left behind in the scramble for oil, despite the position of the Foreign Ministry. Thus Russia increased its involvement in the other sectors of the Caspian in both production and pipeline projects. This was an attempt to maintain a degree of influence over its 'Near Abroad', and a hand in the potential revenues from any developments.

For example, LUKoil became increasingly involved in the Kazakh sector. More importantly from the strategic point of view, the Russian government approved plans to offer part of its oil pipeline system in exchange for a share in the Kazakh CPC. Within only a month Russia and Kazakhstan had agreed to build the first stage of a pipeline linking Central Asia to Western markets. Moreover, to ensure the deal succeeded, Russia offered to supply Kazakhstan with cheap crude – the agreement was seen as confirmation of 'the Russian government's determination to influence developments in the oil sector of the entire former Soviet Union'.[156]

Similarly, LUKoil's involvement in the Azerbaijani sector increased, as it agreed to a joint venture to develop the Kyapaz and Karabakh fields. Russia also influenced Azerbaijani oil export routes, as it offered financial and political sweeteners in an attempt to persuade the consortium to choose the Russian as opposed to the Georgian route.[157]

Largely as a result of this political and strategic pressure, Russia enjoyed success as Azerbaijan courted its support. Firstly, LUKoil's role in the Karabakh project was greatly increased to give it effective control through a 32.5 per cent share – described as 'a diplomatic move to encourage Moscow to give its blessing to the consortium's project'. Secondly, in 1996, Azerbaijan agreed that Russia would be one of the two routes by which Azerbaijani oil would reach Western markets. Russia was guaranteed the transit of 5 million tonnes of oil per year. In a touching finale in London, President Aliev of Azerbaijan and Mr Alekperov, President of LUKoil, 'vowed to work together to unlock the oil reserves of the Caspian Sea'.[158]

Russia took great steps to develop the regime of its sector. At the end of 1994, LUKoil announced plans to raise between $3 and $7 billion of foreign investment through a flotation of its shares in 1996. By 1995, LUKoil was recognised as a serious player in large energy projects, with excellent political contacts. As a result of this success, LUKoil began negotiations with the American oil company Arco in 1996, to forge a broad strategic alliance to undertake international development projects.[159] The expertise that these developments bring to the Russian sector is evident.

Similarly, Russia lifted its oil tariffs to ensure loans from the International Monetary Fund. Whilst the effect of this decision on freeing oil movement was probably negligible, it nonetheless shows a change in Russian attitude. In 1995, Russia took the first steps in reforming the legislative structure for energy resource development. The Parliament passed a bill allowing PSAs between Western oil companies and Russian firms, further shielding such agreements from government meddling. Western firms said it was the 'vital reform they had needed before proceeding with contracts'.[160] Whilst this legislation was not entirely successful, its subsequent reform has been. In addition, in 1995, Russia granted its first Caspian Sea oil and gas licence, finally confirming the JKX InchkeMore deal discussed earlier.

From this historical overview of resource development, some specific details of the regime may be elucidated. Brief details of the legal and fiscal regime managing oil and gas contribute to the wider picture of an uncertain, unstable and complex regime. These characteristics are further emphasised, when compared to the Azerbaijani system of separately negotiating the legal framework of each development project.

Two sets of legislation originally governed both foreign oil companies and domestic players such as LUKoil. Firstly, legislation on the production of oil, and secondly on the selling and export of it. In the first category, it was 'fair to say that Russia lacked comprehensive legislation'.[161] For example, the fundamental legislative act was the 'Law on Subsurface Resources' of 21 February 1992. This provided the framework for the licensing of exploration and development, through a system of tender or competitive bid auctions. It also dealt with licence terms, environmental protection and application procedure.

However, this was not equipped to deal with a modern Western energy project. There were, for instance, worrying unresolved questions concerning jurisdiction between federal and regional governments, although the Russian constitution did prevent any 'war of laws'. Despite this, Hober notes that the regions did control day-to-day activities within their boundaries. As such, good relations with them were crucial to the success of any natural resource project.[162]

Recognising these shortcomings, on 23 May 1994 President Yeltsin signed a number of decrees designed to speed up the pace of economic reform. This was done largely to appease the foreign oil companies, which were slowing their developments in anticipation of effective legislation and tax reliefs, even thinking of withdrawing from the sector altogether. Similarly, the Law on Amending the Russian Federation Law on Subsurface Resources of 14 July 1994 improved the regime as, for example, it introduced flexibility in the transfer of development rights.[163]

The extent to which these changes helped the Western oil companies was debatable but it provided 'clear proof of the government's recognition of the importance of the oil industry to the Russian economy and of the important role played by foreign investors in this sector'.[164]

A further area of difficulty concerns PSAs, the traditional method of structuring natural resource projects. Originally, in the absence of

Russian legislation, foreign investors were forced to seek approval from Parliament for each PSA transaction. Recognising this deficiency, Presidential Decree 2285 of 24 December 1994 created new regulations to cover this area and updated PSA legislation emerged in 1996.

The Western oil companies, however, 'have been less than enthusiastic about this recently passed production sharing legislation'. Domestic Russian oil companies on the other hand exploited this legislation as a solution to Russia's harsh tax regime and submitted nearly every field for inclusion. This imbalanced reaction to the change to this regime has led to conflict. Western oil companies do not view the new legislation as watertight, and demand that the government pass a number of amendments and normative documents before investment can begin.[165] Meanwhile, Russian companies insist that these imperfections are not serious enough to prevent initial Western finance, on PSAs agreed before the new legislation. Until this is resolved, development is unlikely to progress.

From this discussion it is clear that a number of different laws are developing, making up a 'package' of legislation to govern the regime of this sector. One crucial issue that is yet to be resolved is the coordination and harmonisation of these different legislative acts, so as to avoid contradiction and confusion.

This problem of contradiction was seen clearly with the passing of Part Two of Russia's Civil Code on 1 March 1996. Many of its provisions contradicted existing laws and there is still a great deal of confusion as the law-makers begin to reconcile these inconsistencies, especially in oil pipeline access, licensing tenders and the Law on Production Sharing. As *Russian Petroleum Investor* notes, 'while the end result should be a more investor friendly legislative climate, Western oil companies should be prepared for more legal chaos over the short term'.[166]

The second category of law, governing oil sale and export, indicates similar problems in the regime and some further difficulties. For example, Decree 1007 of 23 May 1994 abolished licences and quotas for exports, in order to liberalise oil exports. However, the nature of the Russian oil industry meant that joint ventures with foreign oil companies would have found it almost impossible to get access to limited pipeline allocation. Recognition of this impact led to Decree 1385 on 1 July of the same year, which returned to the previous system. However, with confusion growing, on 1 January 1995 Decree 1466 again eliminated export quotas on oil, without imposing domestic quotas. This was in response to demands from the International Monetary Fund and the World Bank. It is interesting to note that the loose wording of this document means that it is still unclear whether there will be effective liberalisation of oil exports from Russia.[167]

The nature of the regime is summed up most clearly by Starr who notes that there is a general perception that the Russian Federation has been particularly slow to address the concerns of foreign investors, whereas Kazakhstan and some other states in the FSU are perceived to be more open to creating an hospitable legal and tax environment for oil and gas projects. Not surprisingly, major foreign investment on some projects is being deferred until key uncertainties are adequately resolved.[168] However, this situation is recognised by Deputy Minister Konoplyanik of the Russian Federation Ministry of Fuel and Energy, who appreciates that an improvement to this regime does not simply require greater levels of Western investment and input, but rather a focus on creating a better environment for the existing interaction between Russian oil producers and foreign companies.[169]

The Turkmen sector

Turkmenistan's sector of the Caspian Sea shows stratigraphic features that are similar to that of Azerbaijan – indeed the Aspheron Sill, one of the richer known oil seams in the Sea, runs from Azerbaijan, across the Caspian, to Turkmenistan. As a result, Turkmenistan has been offering joint development contract PSAs for its five Aspheron Sill blocks, including seven fields in various states of operability, and for the entire Turkmen aquatory north of the Sill. Indeed, in 1994, Turkmenistan enjoyed the assistance of the World Bank, as it offered a series of such concessions to Western oil companies at a forum in Paris. However, unlike its Caspian neighbours, Turkmenistan has had a hard time attracting explorers or developers and has been described as 'the slowest of the ex-Soviet Caspian Sea states to develop its energy riches'.[170] It is possible, though, that recent changes to this regime will ensure increased development in this sector.

In overview, it was not until 1993 that oil development in the Turkmen sector moved towards the style of Western projects seen in Azerbaijan or Kazakhstan. Only 'Block II' attracted any attention and even this was not consistent. The two fields in this block, Lam and Zhdanov, were originally operated by the Turkmen state oil and gas company Chelekenneft. Then, in August 1993 operatorship passed to Larmag Energy Assets (LEA) as Larmag signed the 25-year Lannag–Cheleken joint venture with Chelekenneft, where profits were to be shared equally with the Turkmen government.[171]

However, in July 1995, as production had dropped from 80 000 barrels per day to 10 000 barrels per day, and with unrecovered costs of $60 million, LEA sold 60 per cent of its interest to International Petroleum Corp (IPC). It is interesting to note though that IPC withdrew after a few months, because it got 'no cooperation from N6DU Chelekneft or the Turkmen government'. Despite these problems in the Turkmen regime, the Irish company Dragon Oil purchased this 30 per cent stake in October 1995.[172] There have also been recent developments, as PetroAlliance is due to commence a 7000 km survey of the sector in the very near future, which may help motivate further projects.

The development of pipeline projects over this period demonstrated similar levels of activity. Much of this development was fuelled by Russia cutting off the only gas transport pipeline, as it decided to sell its own gas, rather than that of Turkmenistan. As a result, in 1994, Iran and Turkmenistan agreed on a $7 billion gas pipeline linking the Caspian with the Black Sea via Iran and Turkey. This was described as intended to 'break the post colonial stranglehold of the Kremlin on the export trade of landlocked former Soviet Central Asia'. As yet nothing has materialised. Similarly, Turkmenistan expressed plans for a 'pan Asian' pipeline to Afghanistan, Pakistan, India and the Far East and further such proposals in 1996 brought Western companies to the capital Ashgabat, but nothing was finalised.[173]

Indeed, within this underdeveloped sector, the greatest activity has been in the field of statements on cooperation and the need for a common approach to the development of Caspian resources. For example, in 1994 Turkmenistan and Iran agreed to coordinate their efforts in creating a regional cooperation organisation among the littoral states of the Caspian Sea. Turkmenistan and Russia reached a similar agreement in 1995, as President Yeltsin noted, to 'elaborate a common programme for the use of Caspian Resources'. In 1996 President Niyazov reemphasised Turkmen commitment to its partnership with Russia, stating that interaction over the Caspian Sea would remain a priority of bilateral relations.[174]

Within this definite emphasis towards regional cooperation, it is worth noting Tass reports, in 1995, of plans for an offshore joint development project between Iran, Russia and Turkmenistan. In a move away from the West this used the Argentinian oil company Bridas to prepare a large-scale project of seismic prospecting and deep drilling for the Turkmen sector of the Caspian.[175]

There are a number of reasons for the underdevelopment of this sector, but a central problem has been the nature of a very definite legal regime managing the exploitation of oil and gas. Unlike some of the sectors discussed, this regime is definitely not suffering from a lack of a clear legislative framework, but rather from too much of the wrong system.

The low levels of development and performance of foreign oil companies in the Turkmen sector frustrated the government of Turkmenistan into the recent introduction of new regulations to control oil and gas investment. These new rules for production-sharing projects and joint ventures placed foreign investors 'firmly under the thumb of Turkmen officials in a system that makes earning a profit in the former Soviet republic virtually impossible'.[176] Whilst this legislation completed the framework for energy projects in the Turkmen sector, it was felt to be more likely to prove a deterrent to foreign investment. Ironically, much of the work on this legislation was carried out by the Italian National Monopoly Electric Company. The legislation arose because the Turkmen government was unhappy that Western oil companies were making inadequate production gains, and could not be forced to comply with contractual financial obligations. However, this sector's underdevelopment might be better explained by the approach of the Deputy Minister of Oil and Gas Nazdzhanov to legislation: 'we evaluate the draft documents according to one criterion only: their ability to protect Turkmenistan's interests'.

It is not surprising to note that Mobil and Agip are reluctant to invest under this new legislation. Having signed protocols of intent for field development in the summer of 1995, neither has taken any further steps. In the words of an Ashghabat lawyer 'both model agreements treat the foreign investor harshly', but fear of provoking reactions on both sides has lead to a 'silence is golden' philosophy.[177] Only one firm, Petronas of Malaysia, seems to be pursuing plans to develop resources in the sector.

This legislation is harsh for many reasons, a selection of which provides ample elucidation. For example, the Western oil companies are controlled in all aspects of the development, with absolutely no room for manoeuvre. They must present a detailed annual work schedule and budget to Turkmen officials by 1 October in the year of production. Once this is approved, it may not be changed and any unused budget must be paid to the government in hard currency! Moreover, the government may inspect the companies' accounts at any time and any breach of agreement can lead to the termination of the contract, regardless of the loss to the investor. Similarly, officials 'will scrutinise companies closely for rule violations'.[178]

In addition, this legislation only allows exploration and production in new areas and not at all in previously explored territories. The risk of making the commitments demanded by this legislation in untested areas is obvious. The government reserves the right, under undefined 'extraordinary circumstances', to confiscate the oil that foreign investors produce.[179]

In response, LEA's Chairman noted that 'production-sharing agreements must be made more attractive . . . or investors will go elsewhere' and *RPI*'s assessment was that 'most investors will continue to watch from a distance'.[180] However, it is possible that there are shortly to be a series of major changes to this regime. Turkmenistan's First International Oil and Gas Projects Conference in March 1996 attracted 170 delegates from Western oil companies. The results of this were excellent and 'Ashghabat is bound to see increased foreign interest in its oil and gas projects'.[181]

This optimism is founded on three factors, according to *RPI*. Firstly, the Turkmen government has recognised its past mistakes in dealings with LEA and Bridas unilaterally revising their contracts, for example – and has vowed not to repeat them. Secondly, the transport issue is moving forward from the conceptual to the discussion phase. Finally, Western oil companies seem happier with President Niyazov and the long-term stability of Turkmenistan. Further, Minister of Oil Esenov supports his own optimism on the grounds that Turkmenistan is stable and secure, based on its cooperative approach to its Caspian neighbours, namely Russia. It is also predictable and enjoying a recent $500 million contract with foreign investors to modernise the Turkmenbashi oil refinery. This, he believes, is 'a harbinger of other projects' and that foreign investors are starting to recognise the 'vast opportunities in Turkmenistan'; he has begun negotiations with a number of oil majors for eight hydrocarbon blocks, including two offshore in the Caspian.

Perhaps most encouraging is the implicit recognition of the problems seen earlier in the new legislation. Esenov accepts that 'if some of our draft documents elicit concern, we are prepared to consider altering our approach for specific projects'.[182] However, he is determined to ensure that foreign companies do invest all the money they contract to, as he is emphatic that development will not be slowed by companies hanging back. Esenov offers further grounds for optimism, as he intends to follow the highly successful Azerbaijani model of negotiating each block, to ensure that each deal is finalised. Similarly, Turkmenistan intends to build on the security of its regime through involving as many players as possible. This will include Russia, given that much of the Turkmen sector's energy industry is linked to Russia. In Esenov's words, 'the more companies that participate in our projects, the better. Just look at the international consortium formed by Azerbaijan'.[183]

Finally, it appears that the transport problem is moving closer to a solution, with a number of pipeline routes and destinations under serious consideration including Turkey, Iran, China, Pakistan and India: 'the goal is to lay several pipelines to several markets'.[184]

In conclusion, Esenov notes that 'it was impossible for anyone participating in the conference to come away without feeling that Turkmenistan is on the verge of a major investment boom'. Given the changes proposed, he may well be correct. If so, it is possible that market forces will effectively ensure the development of a more effective regime for the management of the oil and gas of the Turkmen sector of the Caspian.

Conclusion

It has been argued that the oil and gas resources of the Caspian Sea are of great importance. Geopolitical stability, economic development and energy provision all make it vital that this resource is managed effectively. Similarly, it has been shown that this transboundary resource is, and almost certainly will remain, managed through its division into five sovereign and independent sectors. All this represents an interesting case study in transboundary resource management. However, a number of more valuable conclusions may be drawn from this that do contribute something useful to this field. In this case there is no specific 'regime for transboundary resource management'. There is no 'joint development zone agreement' such as that seen over a sector of the Bay of Biscay between France and Spain, or between Korea and Japan in the East China Sea.[185] There is no treaty carefully managing the minutiae of resource development to ensure equity for all five littoral states. There is no recognised regional body governing oil production, nor are there regulations harmonising development practice. With the exception of a few conferences and conventions proposing, for example, a Treaty on Regional Cooperation in the Caspian Sea or the joint Declaration on Cooperation in the field of Environmental Protection in the Region of the Caspian Sea,[186] there is no practice of 'joint development' of the resource as a whole, as understood by the agreements mentioned earlier. However, it should be noted that the absence of such a regime for the Sea as a whole is in part the result of the relative youth of the development of this resource. As will be shown, it is possible that such a regime, in some form, may emerge at some stage in the future.

Given this state of affairs, the contribution of this study to this area of research must be questioned. It might be argued that the Caspian offers an excellent example of the implications of a lack, or even mismanagement, of a transboundary resource. There is little cooperation in practice and in a free-for-all oil rush there is no coordination of development in this highly sensitive region. The result is the uneven, skewed and inefficient development of this 'whole' resource, under five very different regimes.

In this void of regulation or control, management of the resource can only lead to a serious crisis for the international system. Desert Storm arose from a tiny resource between only two states – the Caspian resource is the size of the Persian Gulf, with five states. The implications are obvious and become clearer still through a hypothetical parallel of a similar free-for-all in the Persian Gulf between Iran, Iraq, Kuwait, Bahrain, Qatar, the United Arab Emirates and Oman. Surely, it might be claimed, the Caspian Sea is crying out for a regime to manage its transboundary energy resources, even if only the codified delimitation of boundaries, or regulations to ensure equitable hydrocarbon development. Never has the value of definitive 'regimes' for transboundary resource management been more clearly demonstrated.

It is proposed here, however, that this is not the case. The last five years of development suggest that the system of management that has evolved for Caspian oil and gas is the most effective, efficient and peaceful approach for this particular transboundary resource. As such, this system of management contributes greatly to regimes working for the peaceful and efficient management of transboundary resources.

That is not to say that this development has been smooth and trouble-free. However, the long-term peaceful management of this resource may have been guaranteed by those early obstacles. This diverse management of the resource under five different regimes is starting to prove invaluable as the five sectors gravitate naturally, and at their own pace, towards the same most 'user-friendly' regime, in order to achieve economic development and its associated benefits. Nowhere is this organic growth seen more clearly than in the recent changes to the regime for resource management in Turkmenistan, drawing on the experiences of the Azerbaijani sector.

This incremental evolution towards a harmonised regime is far more effective than any imposed homogenising regime, where underlying tensions and *realpolitik* are not accorded due influence. Such an imposed regime would inevitably end up imposing a 'lowest common denominator' of regulation in reconciling all the disparate interests of all the parties.

It is also worth noting that the present regime has encouraged a good deal of inward investment and development by the Western oil companies. This is likely to continue, and, as Rase notes, 'those countries that offer the best terms for commercial development will reap the greatest rewards – non-market considerations and excessively onerous contract terms will slow development and prompt competitors to act'.[187] This free market attitude is not surprising, and is ensuring the development of the regime as discussed, through high levels of investment. It is this investment and economic development that will bring peace, stability and growth to the region – the best evidence of truly effective transboundary resource management.

Moreover, this approach has allowed the involvement of all the littoral states in the development of other sectors of the Sea, ensuring that all states have a financial interest in the success of resource development. Iran, for example, is less likely to disrupt development since its involvement in the Shakh Deniz project.

Those idealists who argue that a definitive regime addressing all interests in the Caspian would provide more effective management need go no further than the investors responsible for recent development. Executives at British Petroleum shudder at the thought of dealing with a regional organisation: 'nothing would ever happen', 'a bureaucratic nightmare', 'too many interests to reconcile'. Dealing with one government's interests has not always been easy – dealing with a regional organisation and the interests of five governments does not inspire investor enthusiasm.[188]

The EBRD has no agenda for encouraging any form of regional regime, accepting unilateral and free market development as the most constructive and efficient route to a peaceful regime. It is interesting to note Bundy's masterly understatement, as a practising lawyer, that 'sorting out some kind of joint sharing arrangement including all five states collectively in all the mineral resources of the Caspian will not be easy'.[189]

What is perhaps most interesting is that the management of this transboundary resource may be naturally evolving to a regime resembling some form of 'cooperation', 'condominium' or 'coordination', as states standardise their regimes and become increasingly involved in resource development throughout the Caspian. All this is not to say that the present regime managing the oil and gas resources of the Caspian Sea is beyond improvement. Much can be done within the existing system that will further assist the peaceful and efficient development of this resource.

On this basis, there is a need for active collaboration between the five littoral states. It would seem prudent for them to end uncertainty and codify the present status of the Caspian as state conduct dictates – through the delimitation of the Sea into five sectors, by an independent boundary commission. In Robert Frost's words, 'good fences make good neighbours'. Nonetheless there is scope for fostering bilateral cooperation through smaller-scale initiation schemes or joint development programmes of specific fields that straddle these potential boundaries. Indeed, it will be illuminating to see how LUKoil deals with its development of the Kyapaz field, since this straddles the potential boundary between the Azerbaijani and Turkmen sectors of the Sea.[190]

Likewise, there is scope for regional cooperation in other areas, such as managing fish resources, sea level rise, the environment and navigation. In short, 'certain issues may be better handled by a division of the Caspian according to normal delimitation practice, while others may be more conducive to arrangements involving all of the States'.[191]

Thus, in conclusion, the management of the oil and gas of the Caspian Sea has a great deal to contribute to the development of effective approaches to the management of transboundary resources. Certainly, there have been problems – not entirely unexpected, given the size, value, location and implications of this resource. What is remarkable and indeed testifies to the effectiveness of this naturally evolving regime is the relatively small scale of the problems involved. In a regime where states are still 'finding their feet', resource development has proceeded and there has been no repeat of the 1991 conflict in the Gulf.

Maybe what this shows is the possibility that this transboundary resource may prove instrumental in ensuring the peaceful management of this unstable region.

Notes

1 C. Schofield and M. Pratt, 'Claims to the Caspian Sea', *Jane's Intelligence Review*, February 1996, p. 75.
2 R. V. Barylski, 'Russia, the West, and the Caspian Energy Hub', *Middle East Journal*, Spring 1995, No. 2.
3 D. George, 'Caspian Equal to Mideast Gulf', *Offshore*, March 1996, p. 34.
4 C. Parry, *Consolidated Treaty Series*, Vol. 62, *1812–1813*, Oceana, 1968, p. 440.
5 Schofield and Pratt, 'Claims to the Caspian Sea', p. 76.
6 Ibid.
7 F. Halliday, 'Iran and the Caspian', *MENAS, Conference Proceedings, 'Oil and Caviar in the Caspian'*, London, 1995, p. 3.
8 Ibid., p. 220.
9 E. Holoboff, 'Russia and Oil Politics in the Caspian', *Jane's Intelligence Review*, February 1996, p. 84.

10 G. Roberts, 'Possible Routes and Probable Obstacles Concerning the Export of Caspian Sea Oil and Gas to Western Markets', 1994, Durham, International Boundaries Research Unit, Caspian File.
11 G. Rase, 'A Washington Perspective on Caspian Oil and the Pipeline Options', *MENAS*, 1995, p. 8.
12 C. Parry, *Consolidated Treaty Series*, Vol. 62, *1812–1813*, Oceana, 1968, p. 440.
13 C. Parry, *Consolidated Treaty Series*, Vol. 78, *1827–1828*, Oceana, 1968, p. 109.
14 R. R. Bundy, 'The Caspian – Sea or Lake: Consequences in International Law', in *MENAS*, p. 4.
15 C. Parry, *Consolidated Treaty Series*, Vol. 78, *1827–1828*, Oceana, 1968, p. 108.
16 L. Shapiro, *Soviet Treaty Series*, Vol. 1, Georgetown University Press, 1950, pp. 92–4.
17 Ibid., p. 93.
18 Ibid., p. 94.
19 Ibid., p. 93.
20 Ibid., p. 94.
21 Ibid., pp. 348–51.
22 M. Pournouri, 'Iran and the Law of the Sea', unpublished PhD thesis, University of Dundee, 1994, p. 359.
23 L. Shapiro, *Soviet Treaty Series*, Vol. 2, Georgetown University Press, 1955, pp. 37–41.
24 Ibid., pp. 140–6.
25 Ibid., p. 143.
26 Ibid., p. 144.
27 Ibid., p. 145.
28 *British Foreign and State Papers*, Vol. 144, *1940–42*, London: HMSO, 1952, pp. 428–31.
29 Ibid., p. 431.
30 P. Orlov, *The Current Digest of the Soviet Press*, Vol. XVI, No. III, 1954, p. 26.
31 M. R. Dabiri, 'A New Approach to the Legal Regime of the Caspian Sea as a Basis for Peace and development', *The Iranian Journal of International Affairs*, Vol. XI, No. I, 1994, p. 32.
32 Ibid.
33 K. Akhmedzyanov, *The Current Digest of the Soviet Press*, Vol. XXVI, No. IV, 23 April 1974.
34 Pournouri, 'Iran and the Law of the Sea', p. 368.
35 Ibid., p. 372.
36 Bundy, 'The Caspian – Sea or Lake', p. 4.
37 K. Yusifade, 'The Status of the Caspian', *Azerbaijan International*, Autumn 1994, p. 30.
38 Ibid.
39 Ibid.
40 N. Sagdeb and M. Javadi, 'Azerbaijan's Contract of the Century', *Azerbaijan International*, Autumn 1994, p. 28.
41 S. Vinogradov and P. Wouters, 'The Caspian Sea, Current Legal Problems', *Heidelberg Journal of International Law*, Band 55, No. 2, 1995, p. 621.
42 Ibid.
43 A. Granmayeh, 'The Caspian Sea in Iranian History and Politics', *Central Asia Quarterly*, Summer 1995, p. 38.

44 Gizzatov in *MENAS*, 1995, p. 6.
45 Ibid.
46 Ibid.
47 Ibid.
48 Ibid.
49 Ibid.
50 Vinogradov and Wouters, 'The Caspian Sea', p. 622.
51 Granmayeh, 'The Caspian Sea', p. 38.
52 N. A. Nazarbayev and B. N. Yeltsin, 'Joint Statement on Cooperation in the Exploitation of the Caspian Sea', 27 April 1996, London, British Petroleum.
53 Ibid., Article 5.
54 Vinogradov and Wouters, 'The Caspian Sea', p. 620.
55 Ibid., p. 622.
56 Granmayeh, 'The Caspian Sea', p. 38.
57 C. Schofield and M. Pratt, 'Claims to the Caspian Sea', *Jane's Intelligence Review*, February 1996, p. 79.
58 *Lloyds List*, 'Dragon chases more funding', 7 March 1996.
59 Granmayeh, 'The Caspian Sea', p. 38.
60 Khodakov in *MENAS*, 1995, p. 5.
61 Ibid.
62 Vinogradov and Wouters, 'The Caspian Sea', p. 620.
63 Khodakov in *MENAS*, 1995, p. 5.
64 Vinogradov and Wouters, 'The Caspian Sea', p. 620.
65 Ibid.
66 Ibid.
67 Ibid.
68 Interfax News Agency, 7/ 11/ 95 (SWB SU/2456).
69 Nazarbayev and Yeltsin, 'Joint Statement on Cooperation in the Exploitation of the Caspian Sea'.
70 Granmayeh, 'The Caspian Sea', p. 39.
71 Gizzatov in *MENAS*, 1995, p. 6.
72 Bundy in *MENAS*, 1995, p. 4.
73 Ibid.
74 S. Leskov and S. Mamedov, *Izvestiya*, 'Russia Strengthens its Position on the Caspian Oil Shelf', *The Current Digest of Post Soviet Press*, Vol. XLVII, 11 November 1995, p. 21.
75 J. Thornhill, 'LUKoil Hopeful on Kazakh Oil', *Financial Times*, 12 April 1996.
76 Vinogradov and Wouters, 'The Caspian Sea', p. 620.
77 C. Hopson, 'Caspian Sea Licence to JKX Subsidiary', *Lloyds List*, May 1995.
78 Granmayeh, 'The Caspian Sea', p. 38.
79 Ibid.
80 Ibid.
81 Ibid.
82 Ibid.
83 Granmayeh, 'The Caspian Sea', p. 38.
84 UNCLOS, 'The Law of the Sea: United Nations Convention on the Law of the Sea', New York: United Nations, 1983.
85 Vinogradov and Wouters, 'The Caspian Sea', p. 614.
86 Bundy in *MENAS*, 1995, p. 4.

87 Bundy in *MENAS*, 1995, p. 4.
88 Vinogradov and Wouters, 'The Caspian Sea', p. 613.
89 Dabiri, 'A New Approach', p. 32.
90 Bundy in *MENAS*, 1995, p. 4.
91 Ibid.
92 Ibid.
93 Ibid.
94 *International Law Reports*, 'Case Concerning the Land, Island and Maritime Frontier Dispute', 1992, Vol. 97, at pp. 112, 266, E. Lauterpacht and C. J. Greenwood, Cambridge, 1994.
95 Ibid.
96 Bundy in *MENAS*, 1995, p. 4.
97 Schofield and Pratt, 'Claims to the Caspian Sea', p. 78.
98 Vinogradov and Wouters, 'The Caspian Sea', p. 617.
99 Bundy in *MENAS*, 1995, p. 4.
100 M. Barrow, 'Ramco Ripe for Soviet Venture', *The Times*, 16 December 1991.
101 L. Smith, 'Amoco Alliance set for Azeri Work', *Lloyds List*, 25 June 1991.
102 D. Hargreaves, 'Western Oil Companies in Caspian Sea Project', *Financial Times*, 4 October 1991.
103 'UK Law Firm Advises Former Soviet Republic', *Yorkshire Post*, 16 October 1992.
104 *Lloyds List*, 'Ramco Oil Deal', 16 June 1993.
105 S. Levine, 'Azerbaijan Cancels Big Oil Contract', *Financial Times*, 28 June 1993.
106 'Azeri Oil and Gas Deal Agreed', *Middle East Economic Digest*, 3 September 1993.
107 M. Mortishead, 'Azerbaijan Wins New Oil Deal', *The Times*, 2 November 1993.
108 *Lloyds List*, 'Caspian Partners Extend Oil Probe', 15 March 1994.
109 C. Hopson, 'Western Consortium Clinches $8 billion Azerbaijan Energy Deal', *Lloyds List*, 21 September 1994.
110 P. Donovan, 'Boost for Exports as BP Wins Share of Oil Bonanza', *The Guardian*, 21 September 1994.
111 *Lloyds List*, 'Russia Refuses to Recognize Agreement', 21 September 1994.
112 C. Freeland, 'Iran Takes Azeri Oil Stake', *Financial Times*, 14 November 1994.
113 C. Freeland, 'Iranian Threat to Oil Venture', *Financial Times*, 11 April 1995.
114 *Lloyds List*, 'Exxon Increases Azeri Interests', 6 April 1995.
115 J. Thornhill, 'Hopes for Russian Oil Deal', *Financial Times*, 11 November 1995.
116 *Lloyds List*, 'McDermott Stake Sale', 13 March 1996.
117 N. Aliev, 'The Contract', *Azerbaijani International*, Autumn 1994, p. 25.
118 'State of the Art Technology Transfer: Chevron and SOCAR', *Azerbaijani International*, Autumn 1994, p. 31.
119 M. Pratt and C. Schofield, 'Caspian Pipedreams – the Prospects for Caspian Sea Energy Exports', 1995, Durham, International Boundaries Research Unit, Caspian File.
120 T. Adams, 'AIOC. Challenges of the Present; Promises of the Future. The First Year', *Azerbaijan International*, Winter 1994, p. 28.
121 P. Springett, 'Groups Row Over Drilling', *The Guardian*, 11 October 1995.
122 Adams, 'AIOC. Challenges of the Present', p. 35.

123 'World Bank Loan to SOCAR', *Azerbaijan International*, Summer 1994, p. 22.
124 'Will Azerbaijan Really Benefit from the Consortium Contract', *Azerbaijan International*, Summer 1995, p. 40.
125 *The Economist*, 'US Foreign Policy and Iranian Oil', 18 March 1995.
126 *Middle East Economic Digest*, 17 July 1992.
127 O. Kuzmin, 'Prospects for Co-Development of Caspian Oilfields Discussed', *Tass*, 26 November 1995.
128 A. Aspandiyaruv, 'Kazakh President Meets Iranian Minister of Oil', *Tass*, 11 August 1992.
129 O. Kuzmin, 'Iran and Russia Oppose Unilateral Actions in the Caspian Sea', *Tass*, 31 October 1995.
130 Ibid.
131 'Iran Seeks to be Outlet for Caspian Sea Oil', *Oil and Gas Journal*, 1 January 1996, p. 30.
132 P. Shammas, 'Energy Cooperation in Central Asia and the Global Perspective', *Iranian Journal of International Affairs*, Vol. V, 1 September 1993, p. 29.
133 N. Ghorban, 'Iran's Role in the Export of Oil and Gas from the Caspian Basin', *MENAS*, 1995, p. 10.
134 D. George, 'Caspian Equal to Mideast Gulf', *Offshore*, March 1996, p. 34.
135 Ibid.
136 *The Economist*, 'Tomorrow's Gusher: Kazakhstan's Oil Industry', 25 July 1992.
137 *Newsweek International*, 'The Rush to Alma Ata. Oil: Western Oilmen and Bankers are excited by the prospect of the Caspian Sea Becoming the New Persian Gulf', 7 February 1994.
138 *Euromoney*, 'No Money and no Pipeline', 1 May 1995.
139 S. Thoenes, 'Kazakhstan Deal to Ease Oil Blockage', *Financial Times*, 27 April 1996.
140 E. Kirillova, 'Rights of Transit and Intervention in the Oil and Gas Industry of the Former Soviet Union', *Journal of Energy and Natural Resources Law*, Vol. XI, No. 4, 1993, p. 269.
141 Ibid.
142 E. M. Kirillova and A. Sarsenbayev, 'What Does 1996 Hold for Investors in Kazakhstan?', *Financial Times East European Business Law*, 95–XI, November 1995, p. 5.
143 B. C. Duval, 'Major Issues in Natural Resources Agreements under Diverse Legal Systems in South America, Africa, the Middle East, the Former Soviet Union and South East Asia', *Oil and Gas Law and Taxation Review*, 6, 1995, p. 235.
144 Ibid.
145 S. Thoenes, 'Kazakhs to Tighten up on Tax Under IMF Deal', *Financial Times*, 28 May 1996.
146 European Bank for Reconstruction and Development, *Financing With the EBRD – A guide for companies and entrepreneurs considering financing projects or investing in the countries of central and eastern Europe and the CIS*, London, 8 March 1996.
147 'With John Deuss Gone, the CPC Appears on the Verge of Major Restructuring', *Russian Petroleum Investor*, March 1996, p. 54.
148 'Outraged with Average Monthly Salaries of $200, Tengizchevroil Employees Contemplate a Strike', *Russian Petroleum Investor*, April 1996, p. 45.

149 Ibid.
150 *Lloyds List*, 'Premier Plans Caspian Sea Exploration', 3 February 1992.
151 A. Robinson, 'Survey of Oil and Gas Industry', *Financial Times*, 3 November 1992.
152 S. Levine and R. Corzine, 'Russians Muscle in on Oil Deals', *Financial Times*, 21 January 1994.
153 *Lloyds List*, 'Barriers Hold Back Kazakhstan', 23 March 1994.
154 *Lloyds List*, 'Russia Oil Ban Sparks Fears', 23 June 1994.
155 *Lloyds List*, 'Caspian Joint Venture for JPX', 23 July 1994.
156 R. Corzine and C. Freeland, 'Russia Raises Stakes on Azeri Oil', *Financial Times*, 5 September 1995.
157 Ibid.
158 J. Thornhill and R. Corzine, 'Leaders for a New Millennium', *Financial Times*, 21 December 1995.
159 J. Thornhill and R. Corzine, 'LUKoil and Arco in Talks on Alliance', *Financial Times*, 21 March 1996.
160 *The Economist*, 'Russian Oil', 14 October 1995.
161 K. Hober, 'A Game Called Russian Oil', *Journal of Energy and Natural Resources Law*, 1995, Vol. XIII, No. 2, p. 99.
162 Ibid., p. 100.
163 Ibid., p. 99.
164 Ibid., p. 96.
165 'Russian Officials' Frustration Grows as Signed PSA Projects Remain Idle', *Russian Petroleum Investor*, April 1996, p. 22.
166 'Adoption of Civil Code Likely to set Off Another Legislative Overhaul', *Russian Petroleum Investor*, March 1996, p. 23.
167 K. Hober, 'A Game Called Russian Oil', *Journal of Energy and Natural Resources Law*, Vol. XIII, No. 2, 1995, p. 102.
168 Ibid.
169 A. Kronoplyanik, 'Russian Oil Industry and Foreign Investment: Legal Aspects and the Problem of Business Risk', *Journal of Energy and Natural Resources Law*, Vol. XI, No. 4, 1993, p. 261.
170 S. Levine, 'Turkmenistan', *Financial Times*, 3 January 1995.
171 I. Esau, 'Turkmenistan Turning Point', *Offshore Engineer*, September 1995, p. 38.
172 *Financial Times*, 'Dragon Buys Interest', 4 October 1995.
173 S. Thoenes, 'Oil Groups Vie to Pipe Turkmen Gas Wealth', *Financial Times*, 20 March 1996.
174 *Tass*, 'Niyazov Voices Commitment to Partnership With Russia', 19 February 1996.
175 A. Kurbanova, 'Argentinean Company to Help Turkmen Oil Complex Development', *Tass*, 6 February 1995.
176 'Wrong Way – Ashgabat's "Framework" Energy Legislation Signals Even Tougher Times for Foreign Investors', *Russian Petroleum Investor*, March 1996, p. 63.
177 Ibid., p. 64.
178 Ibid., p. 65.
179 Ibid., p. 66.
180 Ibid., p. 67.

181 'A Fresh Start – Turkmenistan's Oil Minister on the Republic's New Policy for Attracting Foreign Investment', *Russian Petroleum Investor*, April 1996, p. 55.
182 Ibid., p. 57.
183 Ibid., p. 60.
184 Ibid.
185 Bundy in *IBRU*, 1995, p. 33.
186 Vinogradov and Wouters, 'The Caspian Sea', p. 610.
187 Rase, 'A Washington Perspective', p. 8.
188 Unattributable sources at British Petroleum.
189 Bundy, in *MENAS*, p. 4.
190 J. Delay, *Pipeline News*, No. 18, 4 July 1996, www:http://www.intr.net/cpss/oil/journal.html.
191 Bundy, in *MENAS*, p. 4.

4

Azerbaijan's Energy Policy and its Implications for Russian Security

Avedis Bedros Hadjian

With the collapse of the Soviet Union, a self-contained integrated economic unit fragmented into fifteen.[1] The high level of interdependence among the republics was not perceived as a factor that would enhance mutual trust and foster cooperation. Rather, economic interdependence was and still is considered by the new states as a constraint on their newly acquired sovereignty. Ethnic conflicts and an urgency to break free from Moscow's yoke impelled some of the new republics to pursue the goal of complete independence,[2] if that is possible at all. Azerbaijan was among them.

Baku appeared well positioned to seek the attainment of this objective. Azerbaijan's self-sufficiency in energy protected it against Russia's most formidable lever to retain its influence in the former Soviet republics: cheap energy supplies. Thus Moscow discouraged the new republics' economies from becoming energy-efficient and increased their dependence on Russia. Not being a transit route for Russian oil exports, Azerbaijan was also free from blackmail tactics the Kremlin had indiscriminately employed on Ukraine, energy-poor and traversed by Russia's Druzhba pipeline system.

Azerbaijan indeed was more than self-sufficient in energy. Although in the last few years a general crisis in its industry has made Baku dependent on Iran, Turkmenistan and Russia for gas supplies, it is reckoned that 60 per cent of Azerbaijan's territory is oil-bearing, including its Caspian shelf where 80 per cent of its overall reserves lie. The need for Baku to attract Western investors is paramount, as it lacks the financial means and the technology to develop its offshore oilfields.

Independence was timely. The 1991 Gulf War sparked among Western countries, especially the United States, a new sense of urgency about the need to diversify oil supplies and thus diminish the dependency on unreliable OPEC countries. The opening up of the former Soviet Union's vast reserves to foreign investments appeared as the best opportunity to create a more equilibrated oil market.

Nothing could serve Azerbaijan's interests better. Oil would not only attract Western capital to the country, but this would help, in turn, to protect Baku from Moscow's growing assertiveness towards its 'near abroad'. With its energy interests at stake, the United States would be as interested as the Azeris in their country's independence, especially at a time when Russia, after overcoming its foreign policy's indefinition that followed the break-up of the Soviet Union, was subjecting Azerbaijan to increasing pressure for concessions on military bases and the lease of an early-warning radar. Furthermore, strong Western participation in the oil industry should help to generate a more favourable attitude towards Baku in the West on the Nagorno-Karabakh war, an Armenian-populated enclave within Azerbaijan that was unified *de facto* with Armenia in 1993.

Oil, therefore, is the cornerstone of Azerbaijan's newly acquired statehood and the key to its viability. No other resource can be a better guarantee for Baku's independence, as Caspian oil is considered the most important alternative source to the Persian Gulf for supplies in the next century,[3] when the margin between world production capacity and world demand is projected to narrow.[4] The continuous presence of foreign investors in the country, despite political and military turmoil since 1991, speaks for itself.

Azerbaijan's oil policy, however, has provoked Russia into an assertive policy. It defies Russia's bid for regional leadership, by inviting foreign players, of whom one – the United States – has the political and economic clout to challenge Moscow's hegemony. Free from energy dependence on Russia, Baku has successfully managed to resist the Kremlin's demands for military bases and joint patrolling of Azerbaijan's external borders with Iran and Turkey. However, several constraints limit Baku's room for manoeuvre, offering Russia a leverage over the Caspian republic.

Consistent Russian support for the Armenian separatists contributed to the loss by Azerbaijan of the enclave of Nagorno-Karabakh. Although the ceasefire in the disputed enclave has held for three years now, a definitive settlement has not been reached yet. Geography does not help. Nagorno-Karabakh is an Armenian-populated enclave encircled by Azeri territory which in 1923 became an autonomous region of Azerbaijan. In 1988, war broke out after demands by the Nagorno-Karabakh Parliament for reunification with Armenia. Armenia officially maintains its neutrality in the war between the self-proclaimed 'Republic of Nagorno-Karabakh' and Azerbaijan, but it has been giving material support to the enclave. Apart from the enclave, 20 per cent of Azeri territory is currently occupied by Armenian forces. Baku is not ready to negotiate its territorial integrity, although it has hinted at enhanced autonomy for the enclave once it returns to Azeri rule.[5] Armenian forces control territories close – in some places as close as 30 kilometres – to the existing oil and gas pipeline heading up from Azerbaijan to Georgia.[6]

Azerbaijan is not, as yet, a state based upon the rule of law. None of the presidents who preceded Aliev was able to complete his term, and only the June 1992 elections, in which Elchibey triumphed, were 'free and fair' according to international observers. As an authoritarian state, the government is highly centralised on the president, and the opposition is limited not only by law, but also by membership size.[7] This points to the failure of successive Azeri governments in setting up the mechanisms that govern a working political system after the demise of Soviet rule. Intrigue has played a key role in determining the course of Azeri politics, as successive and thrice successful coups show. More worrying is that there will be little alternative to conspiratorial tactics, as long as restrictions are imposed on political opposition and vote-rigging continues to distort election results. Aliev himself admitted to 'some irregularities' at a press conference in London in 1994 – conveniently away from home – although that seems an understatement of the very Soviet 93 per cent margin that led him to victory.

The fact that its main development projects are on offshore Caspian fields has exposed Azerbaijan to what perhaps amounts to Russia's most powerful diplomatic lever. Moscow denies the Caspian littoral states' right to divide the sea into territorial waters and thus exploit their individual zones, since the only existing demarcation has been established between the Soviet Union and Iran under treaties signed in 1921 and 1940. Moreover, as it is not connected to any open body of water, the Caspian is a 'lake and not a sea' in Moscow's interpretation of the 1982 Law of the Sea. Hence, according to the Russian Foreign Ministry, its resources are subject to joint exploitation by the littoral countries, at least until a new delimitation is agreed among the former Soviet republics on the Caspian's shores.

Geography is the biggest constraint on Baku's potential as a major oil exporter. The value of Azeri oil is contingent upon getting the oil out of the country. Landlocked as it is, Azerbaijan has to rely on hostile or unreliable neighbours. The two pipeline routes agreed on by a Western consortium for the export of the early volumes of oil – one through Russia and the other through its military ally, Georgia – highlight the dilemma for a country determined to attain greater independence from Moscow. But Iran had to be ruled out due to American objections, and, as long as the Karabakh conflict is not settled, Armenia will not be a feasible option. Conflicting goals make the West and Russia vie for the control of Caspian pipelines that will guarantee a crucial position over vital supplies of oil in the next century. The rivalry will be resolved when a decision is reached on the construction of the 'late oil' pipeline which will carry the major volumes of Azeri oil. Control of the flows from this non-OPEC region will guarantee the West its independence from unreliable Gulf producers. As for Russia, an active involvement in the exploitation of the Caspian oil will be the key to recovering its clout as a regional and as a world power.

In the end, Azerbaijan's independence from Moscow, and the impact it could have on Russia's security considerations, will depend on whether there are technically and politically viable ways to circumvent Russia in the development and export of Azeri oil. Much to the dislike of Moscow, Washington's involvement in the development of the Azeri oilfields has turned it into the arbiter between Azerbaijan and Russia. If it is to be effective, any attempt by Azerbaijan to escape Russian influence will require Washington's support. That, however, will depend on the US's readiness to antagonise Russia in its own backyard for the sake of Azeri oil. Is Azerbaijan's oil worth the risk of upsetting the *entente cordiale* that Washington and Moscow seem to have reached on more pressing issues, such as NATO enlargement?

Oil and independence

The productivity of Azerbaijan's oil industry had fallen to record lows when, in 1991, the country gained its independence from Moscow. From having met half of world demand in 1911,[8] its relative importance, even within the Soviet Union, had declined to a point where its production had dropped to around 14.7 million tons in 1980 and to 11.7 million tons in 1991,[9] or around 2–3 per cent of the total pumped in the USSR.[10] This downward tendency continued well into the first half of 1995, when SOCAR's crude oil production was down 1.6 per cent compared with the same period in 1994.[11]

Unsurprisingly, the decline of Azerbaijan's main industry certainly affected the economic performance of the country, especially after becoming independent. No figures are available, but oil is almost the sole source of the state's hard-currency revenue.[12] A gradual rearrangement of the Soviet distribution of labour deprived Azerbaijan of its position as a major oil producer, but did not render it powerless. When martial law followed ethnic riots in January 1990, a virtually acephalous Azerbaijan was still capable of wreaking chaos in the Siberian oil industry. Strikes in Baku and the disruption of transport deprived the Russian oilfields of tools and spare parts of which Azerbaijan was often the sole producer.[13] Oil was the main earner of the Soviet Union and also the principal source of energy, and the upheavals in the Transcaucasian republic hit Soviet economy hard. From 12.5 million barrels per day (mbd) in 1987 and 1988, oil output in the USSR had fallen to 10.3 mbd in 1991, at a time when oil prices were low.[14]

Several intertwined causes explain the slump in the production of Azerbaijan's oilfields:

1 Poor pumping methods generated vast amounts of wastage, while at the same time they depleted the oilfields. Soviet engineers injected water into the wells to bring oil to the surface.[15] This technique, known as waterflooding, also downgraded the quality of the extracted oil and corroded the pipeline system. What emerged to the surface was a mixture of oil, water and gas that had to be separated by additional equipment. As the oilfield aged, the proportion of water in the blend increased and in some Soviet fields it reached as high as 90 per cent.[16]
2 After the Second World War, there was a shift in Soviet drilling away from Azerbaijan towards virgin oilfields in Siberia. As the Azeri fields began to drain, the Soviet government concentrated on the development of newly discovered reserves in Siberian areas, mainly in the province of Tyumen, which turned the USSR into the world's leading oil producer.[17]
3 Azerbaijan became the main centre for the production of drilling equipment and other machinery related to the oil industry in the Soviet Union. This was to the detriment of oilfield development. At the time of its independence in 1991, Azerbaijan supplied around 60 per cent of the matériel employed in the Soviet energy sector.[18]
4 Azerbaijan's markets in the former Soviet republics shrank or disappeared altogether. After becoming independent in 1991, disruptions in transport and a general economic crisis in the former USSR threw intra-republican trade into disarray. Worse still, Azerbaijan's situation was aggravated by the war in Nagorno-Karabakh.[19]

Ayaz Mutalibov's government was too short-lived to have any relevant impact on the development of an independent Azeri economy, but during his tenure negotiations with Western companies began, although sometimes in an unconventional fashion, such as direct deals with company directors without any governmental intervention. Within a week of the fall of Mutalibov's government, Valeh Alasgarov, deputy chairman of Azeroil (currently director of SOCAR's foreign investment division) boasted about joint ventures with Western companies such as BP and Amoco. Although executives from these companies spoke as enthusiastically as Alasgarov did on the joint exploitation of Caspian fields, they were concerned about the lack of legislation to protect foreign investment. Investors were also uncertain about the support they would get from the government. But Alasgarov dismissed such anxieties by pointing out that 'the government here did not interfere with us and will not interfere with us. They know that they cannot develop any policy which runs against the interests of oil production here. Everyone here understands that they must act in this way if we want to co-operate with other countries and with foreign companies.'[20]

Azerbaijan's first moves towards forging links with Western firms coincided with the waning of Moscow's power over the republics.[21] At the time, the rights to develop all three fields had been acquired by different parties at different times.[22] In January 1991, with the war in Karabakh still raging on, the US oil major, Amoco, won Azerbaijan's first tender to explore the feasibility of development of the 1.75–2 billion barrel Azeri field in the Caspian Sea; in October of the same year Ramco and Pennzoil were awarded the rights to exploit the undeveloped portion of the Guneshli oilfield; and in September 1992 BP and Statoil obtained the sole rights to negotiate the development of the Chirag oilfield.[23]

However, the Azeri state oil company SOCAR subsequently decided that the development of all three oilfields should be done on a unified basis and consequently the Azerbaijan International Oil Consortium was formed. Unity would certainly benefit foreign investors, as far as it protected them from Azerbaijan's chronic instability. Needless to say, the government would benefit from their safety too.[24] Foreign investments are the key to the attainment of the three main goals of Azerbaijan's oil policy, which have remained unchanged from government to government in the five years of independent life: reactivation of oil production, modernisation of equipment technology, and an increase in hard-currency revenues.

The potential for the reactivation of oil production appeared high, by the time Azerbaijan became independent. According to estimates of the

Baku Institute of Geology, 60 per cent of the country's territory, including the Caspian sea-bed, was oil-bearing.[25] A Western analyst has pointed out that the current explorations of oil and gas are based on Soviet seismic studies of the 1970s and has cautioned against excessive enthusiasm, wondering why the Soviet Union had not exploited them if they were so profitable.[26] The most likely answer is that the Soviet technology of the 1970s could not do what the Western technology of the 1990s can. As the cases of Brazil's offshore developments and the pumping in Mexico's Fonseca Gulf demonstrate, it is now possible – albeit quite expensively – to extract oil from deep-water fields, though promising prospects below 3000 metres in Azerbaijan, assessed by new seismic surveys, had to be ignored for lack of funding.[27] Only Western companies have the technical means for a profitable development of Azerbaijan's Caspian offshore fields, thought to contain 80 per cent of the country's overall reserves. The deep-water section (more than 200 metres under water) of the Guneshli field, with proven reserves of 155 million tons but with probable reserves of another 100 million tons, accounts for 63 per cent of Azerbaijan's total crude oil output and 78 per cent of its offshore production.[28]

However promising the future seems to be, the current state of Azerbaijan's oil industry is less than rosy. According to the latest data available (1994–5), the food industry has the largest share of industrial output at 31 per cent, with light industry at 19 per cent, and the fuel industry at only 12 per cent.[29] Production has been declining since 1985, and only in the first months of 1996 was there a slight recovery.[30] In 1994, SOCAR, Azerbaijan's major oil producer, extracted 9 562 700 tons of crude oil, a decline of 7.1 per cent from 1993.[31] Worse, the downturn in petrochemicals output in 1995 saw domestic consumption threatening to outstrip supply for the first time.[32] SOCAR has blamed poor equipment and technology for the dramatic fall in production in recent years.[33]

Although emphasis is put on correcting the heavy Soviet bias towards equipment production, investments are encouraged for the modernisation not only of equipment production, but also of the machinery actually employed in the working wells. International investor interest, however, has been limited due to the difficulties of converting production to internationally recognised American Petroleum Institute (API) standards. The Turkish drilling equipment company Pet was the first foreign firm to supply Azerbaijan with equipment production in exchange for petroleum products. In 1995, one joint venture was formed with Austria's Schoeller Blackmann Oil Field Equipment to produce API-certified sucker rods, with production expected to begin in late 1996. With less success, Azerbaijan has sought to reactivate its much neglected petroleum processing industry,[34] and in recent years there has been a shift from petrochemicals production towards finished goods,[35] including mechanical engineering.[36]

If it does not manage to get substantial volumes of its oil to the West, Azerbaijan's exports would be mainly restricted to barter agreements with Iran or to the markets of the CIS republics, unable to pay market rates for its energy.[37] Two-thirds of the country's borders to the west are with unreliable Georgia and hostile Armenia. Azerbaijan usually exported oil by rail to Novorrossisk in Russia and to Odessa in Ukraine, and by tanker across the Caspian Sea to Iran.[38] The only way to improve its economy lies in attracting foreign investors to the country, who after making initial disbursements, will seek to get the oil out to lucrative external markets.

Success in its oil policy will eventually enable Azerbaijan to secure political and economic independence from Russia. Naturally, this objective has remained paramount throughout the last five years. Moscow is still perceived as the main threat to Azerbaijan's independence, and successive Azeri governments have assumed that Western interests in the Caspian reserves will shield the country from renewed Russian hegemonic designs. There have been shifts, however, in Baku's attitude towards Russia, from former President Abulfaz Elchibey's proclaimed goal of 'absolute' sovereignty to Aliev's more balanced relationship with Moscow under the current head of the state Heydar Aliev, who has led the country into the CIS but has consistently refused to allow Russian troops on to its soil.[39]

Western interest in Azerbaijan's oil should also help to put pressure on the Armenian separatists to agree to Baku's sovereignty over the enclave of Nagorno-Karabakh. The war in the enclave is the central issue of Azeri politics. Results at the front have determined the fate of Azerbaijan's leaders.[40] American interest in Azeri oil, coupled with Armenian dependence on political and economic support from Washington (Armenia is the main recipient, in per capita terms, of US aid to the CIS), can become a lever on the separatist enclave.[41]

The economy has suffered from the energy sector's dismal performance in the last five years. Reluctant to impose further burdens on the shoulders of an impoverished population by implementing radical reforms, the Azeri government has assumed that the petroleum industry will cushion the country from the crisis affecting the rest of the former Soviet Union.[42] To some extent this has been borne out. A 1993 IMF report observed that despite the war Azerbaijan's economic performance in 1992 did not compare badly to the rest of the former USSR. The fall in GDP in 1992 was, however, 26 per cent, the best performance in the Transcaucasus but among the worst of the unreformed former Soviet economies.[43] It was not until 1995, when conditions worsened further, that Aliev decided to implement IMF recommended measures, including privatisation and a gradual liberalisation of energy prices.[44] Any hope for a dramatic turnaround in the country's economy, and hence the government's stability, lies in getting Azerbaijan's substantial oil wealth to Western markets under the $7.4 billion production-sharing agreement signed by a consortium of international oil companies in September 1994.[45] Around $78 billion are expected in revenues for the Azeri state and $22 billion for AIOC over the 30–year lifespan of the development.[46]

Elchibey's government

Straightforward as he was in terms of ideological consistency, Abulfaz Elchibey did not manage to carry out a coherent government programme. As the leader of the Azerbaijan Popular Front, he ran for president on a nationalist ticket. When a number of military successes allowed him to shift his attention away from the Karabakh war, he adopted a fairly pragmatic approach to economic issues and gave a boost to negotiations over what were still embryonic deals with Western companies for the development of Caspian oil reserves.[47] Stripped of rhetorical excesses, Elchibey's aims appeared clear: military victory in Karabakh; a firm alliance with Turkey accompanied by a quick disengagement from Russia; thwarting Iranian attempts to extending its political and religious influence to Azerbaijan; and turning around the oil industry with the aid of foreign investment.[48]

With the benefit of hindsight, it is easy to note that such a policy course was impracticable. At the time, however, it made sense, if only in theory. Russia had relapsed into its own borders, and separatism in Chechnya, Tatarstan and Yakutia suggested that it was doomed to shrink even further.[49] Energy-poor Armenia, crippled by the blockade, seemed near breaking point,[50] while in Karabakh bold offensives by the Azeri forces were leading to the recapture of occupied towns and territory. The dispute between Iran and Turkey for regional ascendancy was expected to be solved favourably for the latter, as Teheran's model of Islamic statehood appealed less than the prosperous and secular Turkish democracy. A common cultural and linguistic background would strengthen the bonds between Baku and Ankara.[51] Foreign investors already in

Baku, undeterred by war and political instability, would help finance this somewhat grandiose scheme once oil began to flow from the Caspian's under-exploited fields.[52]

Elchibey began the restructuring of the oil industry with the merger of two production associations, Azneft and Kaspmorneftegaz, responsible for onshore and offshore production respectively, into a single entity called Azerineft. Although the purpose of the merger was to reduce duplication in areas of management and provide a single entity with whom foreign investors could negotiate, in reality the production associations continued to operate separately. Thus Azerineft became a holding company with few resources of its own. The next step, however, was more successful. In September 1992 SOCAR was formed by presidential decree 200, with the aim – more or less accomplished during Elchibey's tenure – of turning it into a vertically integrated firm.[53]

Three main contracts were signed under Elchibey. At a time when foreign investors operated separately, Amoco, a US firm, won Azerbaijan's first international tender to explore the development of the 1.75–2 billion barrel Azeri field in the Caspian Sea. British Petroleum, in alliance with Statoil, won the feasibility study to develop the Dostlug and the Shakh Deniz fields. The Guneshli field, which has estimated reserves of 1.2–1.4 billion barrels, was to be exploited by Ramco Energy and Pennzoil.[54]

Nevertheless, the war effort distracted much of the government's attention. It indeed caused its collapse, when in May 1993 the tide on the battlefield turned against Azerbaijan.[55] The eleven months Elchibey was in power were evidently not enough to execute his policies. Handicapped by political inexperience, he and his entourage of former dissidents were faced by resistance – some authors speak of sabotage[56] – from a powerful bureaucracy, including high-ranking officials in the ministries and state enterprise managers.[57] In other words, the deterioration of Azerbaijan's economic situation in 1992–3 cannot be blamed entirely on the AzPF government. In view of Western companies' determination to invest in Azerbaijan's energy sector, despite a not very propitious atmosphere, a rapid reactivation of the oil industry should have been easily achievable. But several factors conspired against it, some of which, admittedly, were beyond the reach of the government.

Internal rivalries within Azerbaijan's leadership and bureaucracy, and competition among various individuals and cliques to be the one to negotiate the oil deal affected the process of selecting the companies to do the exploration, and sometimes led to sabotage by rival factions of understandings and agreements that had already been reached.[58]

By the time it came to power in June 1992, the Azeri Popular Front had split between 'moderates' and 'radicals'. One had already separated from the increasingly extremist mainstream in early 1990 and formed the Social Democratic Group. With their departure, the power of the 'national democrats' (radicals) within the AzPF grew. Elchibey came from the ranks of this faction, which gained further ascendancy. Despite their calls for the unification of 'northern' and 'southern' (Iranian) Azerbaijan, the radicalism of the 'national democrats' was limited mainly to rhetoric. However, they proved unable or unwilling to contain a number of religious and ultra-leftist and ultra-rightist groups which operated under the wing of the AzPF. Back in Soviet times, these extreme elements were, to the alarm of Moscow, responsible for the tearing down of fences on the Azeri–Iranian border in the enclave of Nakhichevan. They were held officially responsible for the anti-Armenian pogroms in Baku in January 1990 that led to the brutal intervention of Soviet troops.[59]

These rifts continued in Elchibey's government and worsened the already uninviting conditions for foreign investment. Ill-defined ministerial powers paved the way for clashes between the assertive interior minister, Iskender Hamidov (who sympathised with, and later joined the pan-Turkic organisation 'Grey Wolves'), and more moderate ministers and aggravated the cleavage between radicals and liberals, resulting in the harassment of Western investors. For example, the day after BP–Statoil's deal was signed with the liberal-minded Parliament speaker, Isa Gambarov, the managers of Azphonesat, the only private satellite phone operator in Baku which BP had been using for its communications, found their office locked and guarded by police. They were told the local communications ministry had decided it needed to 'supervise' communications.[60] At the time, the post of communications minister was vacant and the police were controlled by Hamidov.[61]

Another obstacle that investors had to overcome was the middle-ranking bureaucracy. Oilfield directors and managers, who had often held their posts since pre-Gorbachevian times, had been more co-operative during the dying days of the Soviet Union and the period of political chaos that ensued in Azerbaijan. Mutalibov and especially Yakub Mamedov's and Isa Gambarov's caretaker governments that briefly succeeded him from March to June 1992, distracted by the war in Karabakh and growing domestic opposition,[62] could not control managers who struck *sui generis* deals with Western firms.[63]

During Elchibey's tenure, however, discussions with foreign firms were centralised in the government again. Thus deprived of their negotiating powers, high-ranking bureaucrats felt displaced by Western executives, much better equipped technologically, and by the Azeri government itself. When BP awarded a tender for the construction of four platform piles to an Azeri company, ShelfProyektStroi (SPS), it organised retraining courses for workers and managers in order to enable them to meet the required standards. BP had to face up to obstructionism provoked by resentful top officials, especially in Azerineft instead.[64]

The linking of oil concessions to the position taken by Western governments on the Nagorno-Karabakh dispute also compounded the conditions for investment. Azeri officials tried to use their oil resources as a lever to redress what they perceived to be undue influence of the Armenian communities in the West.[65] This perception was exacerbated by Act 907 ('Freedom for Russia and Emerging Eurasian Democracies and Open Markets Support Act') passed by the US Congress in 1992 and still in force, which forbade American government organisations from supplying humanitarian aid to Azerbaijan, portrayed as an aggressor by the resolution.[66] The fact that Armenia became the largest recipient of American aid in the CIS served only to confirm this impression to the Azeris.

Eventually this Azeri strategy to extract concessions on the Karabakh issue did not work, and it only delayed the conclusion of agreements between the oil companies and the Azeri government. Azerbaijan's interior minister, Iskander Hamidov, responded to the restrictions imposed by the US Congress by threatening to interrupt negotiations with American oil companies. A deal with Amoco for the development of the offshore Azeri field was almost cancelled. US firms were not alone in bearing the brunt of the Azeri government's anger at the passing of Act 907. A proposal by Ramco to explore the Guneshli field also came under threat. BP, however, was exempted from this penalising treatment for what was seen as a blatant example of Western support to Armenia.[67] The explanation probably lies in the good connections the company had in the Azeri government, and the instrumental role it played in fostering Azeri–British relations, highlighted by the visit that Margaret Thatcher, the former British prime minister, paid to Elchibey on the day an agreement was signed by BP-Statoil for the exploitation of the Dostlug field in the Caspian Sea.[68]

Regional conflicts and rivalries over the projected pipeline routes were an added complication. The war in Karabakh was raging on, Georgia was torn by three wars – between ex-President Gamsakhurdia's followers and Shevardnadze's government forces, against Abkhazian and South

Ossetian separatists[69] – and strained relations with Teheran did not make Iran a feasible option for Azeri oil transit.[70] Russian policy towards the former Soviet republics was still ill-defined and Moscow did not put pressure on foreign investors in Azerbaijan.[71]

Elchibey's confrontational style in foreign policy was another reason for the failure of his government to turn around the oil industry. His pro-Turkish policy bordered on pan-Turkism. This extreme position was matched by an equally unbalanced antagonism towards Teheran, aggravated by his calls for the unification of northern (the Republic) and southern (an Iranian province) Azerbaijan, which implied a non-recognition of Iran's territorial integrity.[72] With a minority of around 20 million Azeris in its northern provinces, Iran had conducted an ambiguous policy towards Azerbaijan, fearing that the war in Karabakh and the subsequent influx of refugees could arouse separatist tendencies among its own Azeri population. Predictably, Iran retaliated by establishing a closer relationship with Armenia, becoming, in fact, its only outlet for supplies when the Azeri–Turkish blockade brought the Armenian economy to its knees.[73]

Elchibey's foreign policy began to show cracks when he was forced to mend fences with Moscow. Although anti-Russian in principle, Elchibey sought to mitigate the more immediate crisis in the oil industry by joining the Russian-sponsored Council of States on Oil and Gas, which the Russian press inaccurately dubbed a 'mini-OPEC'. This body was founded in 1992 in the west Siberian city of Surgut with the aim of reactivating the oil industries in Russia and Kazakhstan, by securing investment and equipment from former Soviet republics. Under the arrangement, Azerbaijan would supply the drilling equipment on which Russia was dependent in return for cheap oil and oil products, which the Azeri industry did not produce in enough quantity to satisfy domestic demand.[74]

While the Azeri government's commitment to foreign investments was unhindered by qualms of a nationalist nature, it was amateurish and oil companies, being profit-seeking *par excellence*, exploited this inexperience to the utmost. Two weeks before the fall of Elchibey's government, the consortium of Western companies, led by BP, and America's Amoco and Pennzoil, paid $70 million for the chance to develop 4 billion barrels of reserves in the Azeri, Chirag and Guneshli fields in the Caspian. 'Seventy million dollars is a lot to you and me, but it's not that much to the companies', as one executive explained. The amount was an advance for a signature bonus of $200 million[75] When Aliev raised it to $500 million, the consortium duly accepted.[76] As Elchibey's government's end approached, the terms of deals worsened even further – there was an agreement with the government on a 50–50 share basis for the development of the Chirag field,[77] and some companies were even preparing for the coming to power of Itibar Mamedov, a man oilmen trusted to keep supporting foreign investments.[78] The growing interest of foreign firms in Azerbaijan's oil industry did not result in substantial investments. Though insufficient to reverse the downward trend in the economy, the influx of money was enough to fuel corruption among government officials and an emerging 'entrepreneurial' class, thus widening the gap that separated them from the majority of the population.[79]

In theory, Elchibey's foreign policy seemed tailored to Azerbaijan's demand for complete independence from Moscow. Backed by Western investment, Baku would be in a position to recover Karabakh by diplomatic pressure and by the military aid Turkey would provide. He achieved neither. Foreign companies were looking for the lion's share in the oil deals, and their governments were not keen on alienating Russia in its own backyard. In fact, Turkey's growing assertiveness during Elchibey's government provoked alarm in Moscow and led to Russia's reassertion on its southern periphery. The anti-Iranian leanings of his government, intended as a way of currying favour with the United States, did not draw any substantial support from Washington but they led Teheran to support Armenia in the Karabakh war.[80]

Political unrest, aggravated by a string of defeats in Karabakh, was exploited by a rebel colonel in Ganja, Surat Husseinov. He marched on Baku to depose Elchibey, who ultimately fled. Husseinov was co-opted by the Parliament speaker Heydar Aliev who, as interim president, named him prime minister. AzPF's unbalanced foreign policy had a heavy bearing on Azerbaijan's political stability, as Russia was actively involved in the undermining of Elchibey's government.[81]

Aliev's government

Heydar Aliev's spell in government has been marked by an expansion of presidential power, accompanied by suppression of dissent and purges among the opposition *à la soviétique*. As secretary of the Communist Party of Azerbaijan, a post he held from 1969 to 1982, his ruling style was described as 'a combination of toughness mixed with public criticism, energetic prosecution of wrongdoing tempered with moralism and calls for discipline'.[82] He has hardly changed. By denouncing plots (on three occasions in 1995) to depose him, he has got rid of unreliable members of his government: for instance, his first prime minister, Suràt

Husseinov, the rebel commander who had joined his forces with Aliev to overthrow Elchibey. He regularly unleashes waves of persecution against opposition parties. Other political opponents were used as scapegoats for the reverses in Karabakh and accordingly jailed (for example, Arif Pashayev, a popular military commander, was sentenced to six years in prison). Alikram Gumbatov, a shadowy figure who led an ethnic rebellion and briefly declared a Talysh-Mugan republic, has been sentenced to death, along with other plotters. His efforts to suppress any opposition to his rule have led him to press Moscow for the extradition of rivals living in Russia, prominent among them Ayaz Mutalibov.[83] So far, Aliev has only got back a former defence minister, Rahim Gaziyev, accused of plotting against him.[84]

Before the November 1995 elections and the second round in February 1996, which Aliev won by a 93 per cent margin, his native Nakhichevan clique's power was circumscribed to the presidential office. The polls, described by a joint team of the UN and the OSCE as 'neither free nor fair', enabled the president to extend his influence over Parliament. Members of Heydar Aliev's family who won seats in Parliament include his brother Jalal, his son Ilham (vice-president of SOCAR) and his son-in-law, Mahmud Mamedkuliev, Azerbaijan's ambassador to the United Kingdom. A popular former foreign minister in Elchibey's government, Tofig Gasimov, had declared his intention to stand for Parliament as an opposition party (Musavat) candidate, but was jailed just before the elections. As usual under Aliev, police resorted to heavy-handed repression to break up protests against Gasimov's arrest. The two most popular opposition parties, the Musavat and the Popular Front, expressed surprise at official intimidation on election day as 'illogical', since pre-voting restrictions limiting those able to stand had ensured that the governing party would get at least 60 per cent of the seats in the legislature.[85]

SOCAR's direction has been reorganised along these lines. Although the holding had been already set up by Elchibey's government, ill-defined ministerial powers and overlapping functions between the various departments hindered the holding's progress. The presidential decree passed on 10 January 1994 finally succeeded in turning SOCAR into a truly vertically integrated state oil company, by dissolving production associations, the refineries and the crude oil pipeline. Since it is still not governed by statute, it enjoys *de facto* a complete monopoly over the petroleum industry. Aliev's authoritarian government has created stable conditions for business, but the juridical status of SOCAR could be a problem should political problems arise. The holding is tightly bound to the head of state and his fate. Since SOCAR was formed by presidential decree, it is assumed that any further structural changes will require a legal act of similar standing.[86] SOCAR is divided up into key departments (Production and Drilling, Refinery, etc.) each headed by vice-presidents who report to the president of the company, who in turn reports to the Board he himself heads and which is integrated by the departmental vice-presidents. All are designated by the President of Azerbaijan, who chose a geologist, Natik Aliev (no relation to President Heydar Aliev), a former instructor in the Oil and Chemistry Department of the Central Committee of the Communist Party of Azerbaijan.[87]

Aliev's policy of filling key government posts with close associates and relatives has governed his appointments to the command of SOCAR. The enormous power Natik Aliev wields is matched by that of SOCAR's vice-president of the Foreign Affairs department, Ilham Aliev, the son of Azerbaijan's president. Although the department commanded by Ilham Aliev is small (around 80 people) and he has kept a low profile in the negotiations with the Western consortium, he is entrusted with the overall responsibility for all activities involving hard currency clients and suppliers. This means that the procurement of all foreign supplies, the export of oil and petroleum products must be channelled through his department and approved by it.[88] In other words, he is the key figure – with direct access to the head of state – foreign investors have to deal with. His position has been further enhanced since he won a seat in Parliament in the last general elections.

The first stage for any foreign investment in Azerbaijan's oil industry is for the potential investor to approach SOCAR – the state company carries out all negotiations on behalf of the government – with a preliminary proposal. SOCAR's chief executives, with perhaps the aid of foreign consulting firms, will then negotiate with the foreign investor and together they will draft a preliminary contract. After having been submitted to various government officials and departments, it will pass through three stages before being submitted to Parliament for approval. The three tiers are: the Presidential Office, the Cabinet of Ministers, and the Economics Committee. Ilham Aliev, vice-president of SOCAR, plays a powerful bridging role between the Presidential Office and SOCAR. The final version of the contract will have to be signed by the foreign investor and SOCAR before being submitted to the Parliament. Once Parliament ratifies the contract it will then go to the president for final consent, if the project is perceived to be of vital importance to Azerbaijan.[89]

Aliev keeps SOCAR's leadership under tight control, by subjecting it to threats and accusations. Protests by oil workers for delays in wage payments were used by Aliev to criticise SOCAR's president. On the same occasion, he warned the Azerigas president, Tariyel Huseinov, that the government possessed information about the sale of fuel to Armenia through Georgia.[90]

In marked contrast with Elchibey's foreign policy, Aliev uses the interest created by oil to strike a balance between the external powers competing for ascendancy over Azerbaijan: Russia, the United States, Turkey and Iran.[91] Also he is hoping that with Western oil companies investing in the country, Western governments will be more supportive of Azerbaijan in its struggles with Armenia and Russia.[92]

Aliev is usually portrayed as having pro-Russian leanings. This may be inaccurate. The yardstick employed is Elchibey's virulently anti-Russian diatribes. Furthermore, Aliev's career at the top of the Communist Party reinforces that perception. In a sign of Aliev's control over the reins of power, in 1995 Azerbaijan became a signatory to the CIS treaty establishing a joint body to manage energy, transport and telecommunications affairs. Although the practical effects of this measure are still unknown, this move, which binds Azerbaijan yet closer to the grouping that has succeeded the Soviet Union, met with almost no opposition.[93]

Whether pro-Russian or not, Aliev's sense of expediency sets him apart from his predecessor, and has enabled him to play upon the disagreements between the Russian Foreign Ministry on the one hand and the Fuel and Energy Ministry and the prime minister, Viktor Chernomyrdin, on the other. Chernomyrdin has been cultivating Aliev's friendship. When in 1994 the then Foreign Minister Andrei Kozyrev sent a letter to the Russian president and the prime minister calling for the imposition of sanctions on Baku after the signature of the agreement with the Western consortium for the development of Caspian oilfields, Chernomyrdin promptly informed Aliev about it. At the same time, the Russian prime minister publicly dismissed the Foreign Ministry's objections.[94] Ever since, the Azeri president has been boasting about his strong links with the Russian prime minister in order to reassure nervous investors.[95] In any case, SOCAR expressed its impatience about continuous Russian pressures by bluntly stating that 'Azerbaijan has already tried to pacify Russia by conceding 10% of its own interests to Lukoil.'[96]

American support also helped Aliev to stand up to Moscow's pressures to pump the 'early oil' only through Russian territory. Washington's commitment to fend off Russian blackmail in Azerbaijan's oil deal was underlined by Clinton's endorsement in his talk on the telephone to Aliev 'for commercially viable and multiple pipelines that would benefit the companies investing in oil development as well as the countries of the region'.[97] Nonetheless, Washington's opposition to Iranian participation forced Baku to exclude Teheran from the oil deal. To soothe Iranian anger, Azerbaijan ceded its own part in the exploitation of the Shakh Deniz oilfield, in which no American firm is involved.[98]

Although as president of Nakhichevan Aliev had built a strong relationship with Turkey,[99] on becoming Azeri head of state he distanced himself from Ankara in order to allay Russian fears about excessive Turkish influence on its southern rim.[100] The relationship between both countries was strained by Turkey's initial refusal to recognise pro-Turkish Elchibey's removal from office and Aliev's highly symbolic move of reimposing visa requirements for Turkish nationals.[101] Mutual distrust, however, was soon overcome by their shared economic interests, especially after Turkey raised its stakes in the oil deal.[102] On the whole, however, Aliev's government has been more reserved than Elchibey in its relationship with Ankara.

His policy towards Karabakh is marked by caution. After a string of mostly unsuccessful offensives, Aliev opted for a Russian-mediated ceasefire in Karabakh, which has held firm for the last two years. In April 1996, the Azeri president and his Armenian counterpart signed an extension of the truce in Luxembourg. There was speculation about whether Azerbaijan would rebuild its armed forces and armoury to relaunch an offensive in Karabakh, but Aliev's commitment to the ceasefire seems firm. The Azeri president had come to consider the 'unending war' a 'triple tragedy' of a permanently displaced population, further occupation of territory and the increase of criminality within the country, fuelled by the easy access to weapons and the dire general conditions.[103]

Unable to turn the tide of war with the Karabakh Armenians, humiliated by having lost a sizeable portion of Azeri territory outside the enclave, and realising the very slim chances of achieving a military victory, the Azeri president is trying to compensate for these losses with his balanced foreign policy and his active promotion of foreign investment.

The government's position is that continued peace will improve Azerbaijan's long-term prospects and the conditions for investments.[104] As the oil revenues begin to flow, high stakes in Baku push foreign powers to put pressure on Armenia, also because of technical considerations in connection with a routing for a 'late oil' pipeline. This policy has scored only modest successes so far, but it may begin to bear fruit soon. As early as November 1993, after signing an agreement to develop offshore fields on the Caspian sea-bed, the Russian Fuel and Energy Minister Yuri Shafranik declared that 'the signing of the treaty between Moscow and Baku will have an effect on a settlement of the Karabakh conflict'.[105] Russian negotiators have hinted that there might be a change in Moscow's policy towards the enclave if Azerbaijan makes concessions on security issues.[106] Armenian authorities were alarmed when in May 1996 Yeltsin expressed surprise at the Karabakh separatists' aim of attaining formal independence.[107] The United States has stepped up its involvement in the negotiations. Washington recently sent a special envoy to the region and, although there has not been a breakthrough yet, pressure on Armenia is mounting.

Aliev scored his biggest success with the conclusion, in September 1994, of an $8 billion agreement with a Western consortium led by British Petroleum–Statoil, for the development of the Azeri, Chirag and Guneshli offshore oilfields, which are estimated to contain between 3 and 4 billion barrels of light sweet crude oil. The accord, dubbed the 'Deal of the Century' by Baku press, represents the largest single foreign investment in the former Soviet Union. When Aliev came to power in July 1993, he cancelled the old deal signed by Elchibey, saying that he could get a better deal than Elchibey had got for Azerbaijan. Aliev had been more anxious to score political points than to impose harsher terms on the oil companies. Nonetheless, he lived up to these promises. According to the new agreement, the Azeri share of profits rose from 70 per cent to 80 per cent.[108] The Azeri government's expected revenues rank in the order of $80 billion over the project's 30–year lifespan, which under ideal conditions should ensure the country's future prosperity.[109]

The agreement with the Western consortium, Aliev emphasised during the signing ceremony, would give access to Western capital and technology, and indicated that the political and economic interests of the West and Azerbaijan were drawing closer together.[110] But, as the Azeri president has come to realise, the more active Western involvement in Azerbaijan is, the more assertive Russian policy becomes.

SOCAR's share has been shrinking since the contract was signed. In order to appease Moscow, the giant Russian oil company LUKoil was given 10 per cent of the government's share. But Azerbaijan secured the financing for its remaining stake in the consortium by selling half of its 20 per cent share to Exxon and the Turkish state oil company, TPAO. Each received a 5 per cent stake, making Exxon the eleventh member of the consortium and raising TPAO's existing stake to 6.75 per cent.[111] SOCAR has reportedly been paid more than $150 million in return.[112]

This has enabled Azerbaijan to meet its funding commitments for the project, clearing the way for full-scale appraisal and development work to begin. The government has not hesitated in giving up the largest slice in order to allow the continuation of the deal.

The government designated the oil and gas sectors, including oil equipment manufacture, as strategic industries and formally excluded them from the privatisation programme agreed with the IMF. This, however, has more propaganda value than any practical effect, and this symbolic gesture is aimed at the opposition Popular Front and the Musavat Party, which have been protesting against the 'sell out of national patrimony' to foreign oil companies.[113] In fact, the government announced that it would be willing to privatise 20–30 per cent of SOCAR to help it overcome its financial difficulties.[114]

Although the oil deal is certainly a big step towards gaining economic independence, it still falls short of an economic guarantee. The money the consortium has undertaken to invest will be spread over time, which means that at each stage AIOC might reconsider its commitment.[115] This should not worry the Azeri government. Dangers that loomed on the horizon only a few months ago are dissipating: Moscow is less vocal in its legal objections to exploitation in the Caspian Sea;[116] works on the Georgian pipeline are reported to have begun;[117] Aliev's grip on power has been consolidated; ceasefires in the separatist regions of Abkhazia and Karabakh have held firm over the last two years.[118] In any case, these relative improvements have not come about only by virtue of the Azeri government's efforts. The problem for AIOC, and for Azerbaijan indeed, is the likelihood of further complications, many of which can be engineered by Russia. Nonetheless, what matters at this stage is that Western oil companies have decided to invest in Azerbaijan, in spite of the country's political situation.

A second North Sea, rather than a second Kuwait

The Azeri government has found itself in the rare position of not being compelled to court potential foreign investors. Indeed, investors themselves decided to explore Baku's wells in the early 1990, when the Soviet Union was beginning to crumble.[119] Azerbaijan's vast hydrocarbon reserves have spared it the daunting task of attracting foreign companies faced by every energy-poor former Soviet republic. An unpropitious environment for any sort of investment, let alone multi-billion dollor projects, has not discouraged Western oil companies from signing an agreement with Aliev's government for the exploitation of the offshore Caspian reserves.

Risks seem to outweigh costs for a country that newspapers little inclined to exaggerate, such as the *Financial Times* and *The Economist*, describe as a promising 'second Gulf'. The *Financial Times* cited industry analysts who speculated that Azerbaijan, together with Kazakhstan and Turkmenistan, could form the world's third-largest oil-producing region, after Siberia and the Gulf.[120]

However, current assessments of the size of Caspian reserves are not conclusive. Even if AIOC's final interpretation of its data eventually proves accurate, Azerbaijan's total offshore reserves stand at 4 billion barrels. According to a conservative estimate, the total regional reserve base (including Azerbaijan, Kazakhstan and Turkmenistan, but excluding Iran and Russia) probably has a capacity of 10.8 billion barrels, a figure that may rise by a further 10 or even 20 billion barrels. Proven reserves therefore constitute 1 per cent of total world reserves of around 1000 billion barrels. If presumed reserve additions prove correct, these figures might rise twofold, threefold or even fourfold.[121]

With around 4 billion barrels of proven reserves in its section of the Caspian Sea, Azerbaijan therefore has 0.4 per cent of total world reserves. Sanctions prevent Iraq's oil from reaching world markets, but Iraqi potential of 2.5 mbd dwarfs the 300 000 barrels per day of Azeri crude expected for the year 2004. These figures, however, are not negligible, and the overwhelming reserves in the Gulf are not the most suitable standard by which to gauge Caspian (let alone Azeri) wealth. Six Gulf countries – Saudi Arabia, Iraq, Kuwait, the United Arab Emirates, Iran and Qatar – hold between them almost two-thirds of the world's proven reserves. Furthermore, being mainly deep-water offshore fields, Caspian reserves are far more expensive to exploit than Middle Eastern ones. The size of Caspian reserves is within the range of those in the North Sea, where the share controlled by the United Kingdom and Norway amounts to 13.9 billion barrels of proven reserves.[122] Even the president of the Western consortium that will develop Azerbaijan's offshore fields has spoken of the Caspian as an 'untested North Sea'.[123]

While it will hardly become a second Gulf in terms of oil supply, some Western oil executives involved in projects in the region believe that Azerbaijan's reserves – together with those of Kazakhstan – are large enough to alter world energy trading patterns by the end of the next decade.[124] That can happen only when the oil is piped out of the region into Western markets, which is the biggest obstacle they face, for a range of complex reasons.

After the 1986 prices slump, oil demand picked up pace again. It will keep rising, if only to sustain economic recovery in those countries just recovering from the setbacks caused by the 1973 crisis and its by-products (the 1980s debt crisis probably being the worst among them). Unlike in the mid-1980s however, the market balance today looks more precarious. A decade ago the world oil industry was able to meet growing world demand by operating at 80 per cent of its productive capacity. Currently it is up to 92 per cent, even if Iraq were taken into account. Based on these facts, some authors foresee a further narrowing margin between world oil production capacity and world demand for the next decade.[125] The 1973 crisis showed that a tight market is exposed to shocks in a way an oversupplied market is not.[126]

Projections of a tight oil market in the future, however, may be inaccurate or may have been intentionally exaggerated by interested parties in order to reinforce the case for Caspian oil.[127] Adamant on isolating Iran for its alleged support of international terrorism and on preventing Iraqi oil from reaching oil markets, the United States has an interest in promoting the Caspian as a viable source of oil. Currently less than 30 per cent of world supplies come from the Middle East, and by 2004 – when Azerbaijan is expected to produce 300 000 barrels per day – it could be up to 45 per cent, or 28 mbd (up from 18.3 mbd today).[128] Over-dependence on only one source is disturbing for Washington.[129] Apart from Iran and Iraq, the continuity of the Saudi regime cannot be taken for granted and its replacement may not necessarily be responsive to the US government.

Thus, the opening up of the Azeri economy to foreign investment was timely. It coincided with the quest by the Clinton administration for alternative suppliers of oil, in order to diminish its reliance on the Middle East countries. The boost that Washington's backing has given to investment in Azerbaijan has served oil companies well. Outside OPEC, the United States oil industry has been depressed for the last years and its oil imports will probably continue rising. That leaves out emerging markets which only in recent years have been opened to foreign investors such as Colombia, Argentina and Vietnam, and certainly Kazakhstan and Azerbaijan. With the Russian oil industry having converted from state monopoly into a private oligopoly with little foreign participation, Azerbaijan's and Kazakhstan's oilfields represent attractive opportunities to exploit. Sensitive as they are, the stock markets mirrored exaggerated expectations created by talk of Azerbaijan as a 'second Kuwait'. The AIOC agreeement with the Azeri government drove up the share prices of the companies involved in the deal.

If recent history is anything to go by, there is no reason not to expect turmoil in the Middle East. By the same token, one cannot rule out renewed conflict in Azerbaijan. The key difference is that in Azerbaijan foreign companies have a strong foothold and that, unlike the Gulf states in the 1970s, the magnitude of reserves controlled by Azerbaijan does not allow it to challenge the world markets. Baku could never be in a position to trigger a world crisis of OPEC-like proportions. Bankrupt ever since it became independent, Azerbaijan depends heavily on foreign investment for its viability as an independent state.

The opening up of the Caspian reserves to Western investment may relieve the West of over-dependence on the Gulf countries. It should also deprive an increasingly assertive Russia of the opportunity to blackmail the Caspian countries back into submission. Western governments would not contemplate idly the prospect of Russia – already the biggest single producer of oil in the world – controlling another major source of supplies, while the OPEC countries are still sitting on the overwhelming majority of proven reserves.

But it is premature to speak of the Caspian, as some authors do, as a 'third major energy hub' (after the Gulf and Siberia).[130] The long-term prospects for Caspian oil will depend on future developments in Iraq. As long as Saddam Hussein remains in power, it can be safely assumed that the United States will bar Iraqi oil from international markets. Under the UN scheme known as 'oil for food' (UN Resolution 986, May 1996), Iraq is allowed to export 2 billion dollars of oil every six months, which amounts to around 700 000 barrels per day, depending on the oil price. If the UN sanctions were lifted, however, Iraq could have the capacity of exporting between 2 mbd and 3 mbd. This could also mean that the Iraqi government would be ready to open the oilfields to foreign companies for development and, unlike the Caspian offshore fields, they are easier to exploit and pipe out. Even if that did not happen, a full return of Iraqi oil to the market in an unregulated way could push oil prices further down. Cheap as they are today at 17–18 dollars per barrel on average, they could fall to as low as 10 dollars a barrel.[131]

Therefore, the question is when Iraqi oil will start to flow again. The longer it is held back, the better for Azerbaijan and the other oil-producing Caspian countries. Though unlikely, if Iraq's comeback occurs before the pumping of 'early oil' in mid-1997, the whole Azeri deal might be called into question, because in that case a market saturated with cheap oil would make the Caspian pipelines venture unprofitable. Since the AIOC will invest in stages it may be free to withdraw if the agreement with Baku stops making sense. If, on the other hand, the pipelines are already in place by the time of Iraq's return to the markets, they will still be used for exports. By then, the bulk of AIOC's capital for oilfield development would have been spent already and the lines would be working at operating costs. The pipelines would not generate a return on the invested capital, if oil prices remained low over prolonged periods of time, but they would still produce an income.[132]

The longer-term prospects for Azeri oil may be less promising. Sooner or later Iraq will return to the fore. Even if the 'early oil' pipelines are operating by then, the case for a 'late oil' system would be less compelling, as the potential benefits would not seem worth the enormous expenses to be incurred (as much as 2 billion dollars) and the geopolitcal obstacles to be overcome. Currently, non-OPEC countries supply 60 per cent of the total world production from 25 per cent of the total oil reserves. In contrast, the output of OPEC's six most powerful Arab members is only two-fifths of world production, although they possess two-thirds of the world's proven recoverable reserves of over one trillion barrels. As oil is a depletable resource, non-OPEC output will begin to decline sooner than OPEC's and this imbalance will disappear.[133]

OPEC, however, is not the most immediate threat facing Azerbaijan and the Western governments which back the development of its oil industry. They, and the foreign investors working there, will have to deal with an increasingly assertive Russia. In its bid to restore its authority in the 'near abroad', the Russian government, and Russian high officials with personal stakes in the Azeri deal, are also vying for the control of Caspian reserves and pipeline routes.

Azerbaijan's independence and Russian security

One of Russia's favourite ways to retain authority over the 'near abroad' has been by supplying cheap energy, as a lever of political influence. Although opposed by the IMF and the World Bank, Russia's energy pricing has been determined by this regional policy goal. It is estimated that in 1992 Russian subsidies in the prices of oil and gas supplies to the former Soviet republics reached around $15 billion.[134] The rationale of this policy was not only political. Since Russian energy exports, through the Druzhba pipeline, should traverse the territory of some of these countries, Moscow has held control over them by keeping their energy demands steady, using low bills as a lure. Some of the energy-deficient republics, like Belarus, have come to consider this dependence level as another reason to keep strong links with Moscow. Others, especially Ukraine, resent this situation but cannot afford to pay market rates for other sources.[135]

Self-sufficient in oil and partially dependent in gas (its industrial crisis prompted it to import gas from Turkmenistan and Russia in 1994–5), Azerbaijan is protected against this Russian practice. Moreover, the attraction Azeri oilfields exert on the West would actually allow Azerbaijan to escape Moscow's influence. Compelling security concerns make the Kremlin resist Azerbaijan's moves away from Russia's sphere of interest.

Unlike the British empire, maritime *par excellence* and decentralised, the Soviet Union was a territorial and heavily centralised empire.[136] The USSR was an extension of Russia in geographical contiguity and political system, whose borders broadly coincided with those of the Russian empire, where Russians were an overwhelming majority and Russian was the common language. These factors contributed to the perception by the Russian leadership of the Soviet Union as a single, albeit multi-ethnic, country, rather than a state made up of different countries.[137] A corollary of that premise is that the collapse of the Soviet Union was, in a territorial and historical sense, a shrinkage of Russia.

That has worrying implications for the Russian Federation, because, like the Soviet Union in the past, the Russian Federation is itself a multi-ethnic country. This is especially true in the Caucasus, where unlike most of Siberia, local ethnic groups are in the majority and, in some cases, homogeneously so within the boundaries of the autonomous regions or republics.[138] Although subsequent events have not borne out Moscow's fears about separatism in the Russian part of the Caucasus at the instigation of Turkey or Iran, Chechnya's *de facto* independence from 1991 to 1994 was a challenge to Russia's territorial integrity. In a region where at one time there were five simultaneous wars – Nagorno-Karabakh between Armenians and Azeris; Abkhazia, South Ossetia and a civil war in Georgia; North Ossetia against Ingushetia in the Russian Federation itself – the Chechen example conveyed a high potential for further dismemberment, this time within the Federation itself.

In 1992, when Russia foreign policy was beginning to take shape, the Chairman of the Supreme Soviet's Joint Committee on International Affairs and Foreign Economic Relations, Yevgeny Ambartsumov, formulated foreign policy recommendations first presented in a closed session of the Soviet in June 1992. Dubbed 'Russia's Monroe Doctrine', the document began with the assertion that Russia 'has no integral conception of foreign policy for the nearby or distant foreign countries'. Hence, its essential recommendation was that 'as the internationally recognised successsor to the USSR, the Russian Federation should base its foreign policy on a doctrine declaring the entire geopolitical space of the former Union to be the sphere of its vital interests (like the United States

Monroe Doctrine in Latin America) and should strive to achieve understanding and recognition from the world community of its special interests in this space. Russia should also strive to achieve from the world community recognition of its role as political and military guarantor of stability in the entire space of the USSR.'[139]

These assumptions, embodied in 1993 by the Russian military doctrine imply the following goals:

1 *The priority of the FSU or the 'near abroad' in Russian defence policy.* This notion is based on the belief that the security of the 'Russian state' is inextricably linked with the security of its Asian periphery. A corollary of this concept is that events in Transcaucasia will have an impact on North Caucasus. It has crucial implications for Azerbaijan, as shown below.[140]
2 *The necessity of maintaining Russian predominance in the region.* Security considerations and high economic interdependence with the republics, led Russia to assume the mantle of the Soviet Union as the 'continuer state'.[141]

Russia has been pressing Azerbaijan to allow Russian military bases on its soil, to patrol its borders with Turkey and Iran, and to lease the early-warning radar at Gebele (north-east Azerbaijan). Azerbaijan is important in Russian security considerations because of its proximity with Chechnya and border with Daghestan (another potentially explosive autonomous region), and its borders with two regional rivals: Iran and Turkey. Transcaucasia is inseparably linked with North Caucasus, which is an integral part of the Russian Federation. Hence, Moscow proceeds from the fact that its internal security is indivisible from the security of the three Transcaucasian republics. This has far-reaching implications for a multi-ethnic country like Russia with restive non-Russian ethnic groups in the North Caucasus area.[142]

Events in Transcaucasia naturally affect the Russian Northern Caucasus. Although the upheavals in the region have not escalated to the extent initially feared by Russia, the war in South Ossetia created the conditions – in the form of traffic of weapons and activity of armed gangs – for clashes between North Ossetia and Ingushetia, both autonomous regions within the Russian Federation. War in Abkhazia generated unrest in the ethnically related autonomous republic of Adyghe, also in the Russian Federation. Chechnya's *de facto* independence from 1991 to 1994 was a focus of instability in the area, although arguably the Russian onslaught probably worsened the situation.[143]

Although Moscow may have manipulated national conflicts in the 'near abroad', it has an interest in preventing the propagation of ethnic strife into the territory of the Russian Federation. Its only common border with Azerbaijan is in Daghestan, which separates in two halves of 500 000 a Lezgin community.[144] They live in the southern part of Daghestan, an autonomous republic within the Russian Federation with 35 minorities, including Chechens, where Lezgins represent the biggest single ethnic group in a total population of 1 million. Azerbaijan's Lezgins live in the north-east of the country. Over the last five years, this minority has been calling for the unification of the Russian and Azeri parts inhabited by them, to form an independent state of Lezgistan.[145] As the Chechen war demonstrates, Russia, unlike the Soviet Union, is not capable of curbing violence in the Caucasus.[146] A Lezgin revolt in Daghestan could spark a wider ethnic conflict in a republic where more than 30 minorities are exposed to the tensions that strain their kin in neighbouring countries and autonomous republics, like Chechnya in the east.[147] Relations between the different ethnic groups have been strained since the Chechen terrorist attack in the Daghestani city of Pervomaiskoye in January 1996.[148] It is also true that the Chechen war's example of no-winners can be effective enough to deter other potential separatist groups.

Daghestan does not seem to be on the verge of an ethnic crisis, but this does not diminish its importance in Russia's security scheme. One of the routes chosen by the Western consortium for the export of Azeri oil, the Russian pipeline running from Baku to Novorrossisk, passes through the Daghestani capital of Makhachkala. In this greater sense, Daghestan's strategic importance is higher than Chechnya's because while a loop to avoid Grozny is feasible, transit through Daghestan is unavoidable, as it is the only border of Russia with Azerbaijan. In fact, the two Russian pipelines that carry Azeri oil – Baku–Novorrossisk and Baku–Tikhoretsk – run through Makhachkala, the Daghestani capital.[149] Political stability in Daghestan is intimately connected with the viability of the Russian routes for the export of Azeri oil. In other words, a Chechen scenario in Daghestan would disrupt the Druzhba line from Baku to the Russian terminals.

Assuming the indivisibility of its security from that of Transcaucasia, Russia considers its forward defence to begin at the borders of the former Soviet Union and not the Russian Federation. This premise is codified in the near-abroad military doctrine , which upholds Russian assertiveness in view of the indivisibility of Russia's internal security and the former Soviet republics' external security. Far from theoretical, these objectives were reflected in the creation of a unified security system in the Caucasus and in the revision of the CFE quotas in the North Caucasus Military District.[150]

Ill-defined borders within the Soviet Union contribute to that perception. The problem, common to all the former Soviet republics, is particularly acute in the Caucasus and Central Asia.[151] Russia's new southern boundaries are often not much more than imaginary lines, and not very clear ones at that. Potentially disturbing for the new republics, they are still not fully recognised either by constitutional arrangements or by international treaties upheld by the current Russian government.[152] Only Soviet borders were properly delimited, set up and manned.[153] Erecting new border infrastructure would be expensive; more than patrolling the older Soviet borders in any case. It could also give rise to demarcation disputes, a danger contained by the status quo sought by Russia regarding security on the borders of the former Soviet Union, which its army is better equipped to guarantee.[154] These concerns have been reflected in Russia's successful renegotiation on the level of forces on the flanks allocated by the CFE treaty.[155] As the treaty was signed by the Soviet Union, Russia argued that the limits prescribed for its two flank areas, the Leningrad Military District and the North Caucasus Military District, did not apply any more. While both flanks were considered rear areas in a Soviet Union that included the Baltic (Estonia, Latvia and Lithuania) and the Transcaucasian republics, they are now border districts in the Russian Federation. It was illogical, argued Yeltsin, to expect 15 per cent of forces level in two regions that together make up half of European Russia. Once again, the Kremlin successfully warned of the threats posed by radical Islam to stability in the Caucasus, an argument usually taken at face value by Western governments and prominent figures.[156]

In Azerbaijan, however, that status quo does not exist. Russia does not control the Azeri borders with Turkey and Iran. Baku's resolve to supervise its external borders was reflected last year by the visit of Ramil Usubov, Azerbaijan's interior minister, to Teheran. Usubov told his Iranian counterpart, Ali Mohammad Besharati, that the Azeri government would appreciate Iranian expertise in its campaign 'against terrorism and drugs'.[157] It is an obvious response to the most common charges Russia invokes for the closure of its border with Azerbaijan, which puts pressure on Baku. So far, the head of the Russian Border Guard Service, Andrei Nikolayev, has only managed to initiate an agreement with Aliev on the policing of their common border, and has only obtained a pledge from the Azeri president that measures would be taken to prevent criminals and terrorists from entering Russian territory through Azerbaijan.[158] Russia has in the past accused Azerbaijan of allowing Turkey to trans-ship arms and personnel to Chechnya across Azeri territory. Another agreement between both countries signed in May 1996 also fell short of what Russia had wanted. It was on cooperation in the prevention of terrorism, illegal trafficking in arms and drugs and illegal migration.[159] Azerbaijan remains adamant in its opposition to having Russian troops supervising its border with Iran and Turkey, which leads to Russia's essential defence concern: fears of a security vacuum.

In the first years after the collapse of the Soviet Union, Moscow feared the existence of a security vacuum in Azerbaijan to be filled by external players; more concretely, that a withdrawal of Russia from the former Soviet southern periphery would open the way for a growing influence of regional powers like Turkey and Iran – a disturbing prospect given the state of border security in Russia, as described above. In the case of Azerbaijan, both Western pressures and Elchibey's virulent anti-Iranian views kept Teheran's influence in check. One of Yeltsin's advisers, Andranik Migranyan, warned that Azerbaijan was 'running away' from the CIS and 'unambiguously' gravitating towards Turkey, whose interests in Transcaucasia were supported by the West.[160]

AzPF's foreign policy appeared to lend credence to those claims. By feeding Armenian fears of Turkish intervention, Elchibey prompted the Armenian government to strengthen its security links with Russia and attracted Russia's hostile attention at a time when it was not objecting to Baku's oil deals with Western companies.[161] He highlighted his ignorance of regional geopolitical imperatives when, in April 1993, he even telephoned the Israeli prime minister, Yitzhak Rabin, to request – unsuccessfully – Tel Aviv's support against a successful Armenian offensive, that finally precipitated his downfall.[162]

The AzPF had, in fact, re-established commercial links with Russia and had signed a treaty on friendship and mutual security, but Elchibey was keen to make clear the transient nature of these arrangements.[163] The long-term objectives – or, judging from his rashness, not so distant – of the government of Abulfaz Elchibey were a source of concern for Moscow. AzPF's discourse made matters worse. On coming to power, the AzPF called for a *jihad* against 'Armenian infidels'.[164]

From the moment it assumed power, the Azerbaijan Popular Front made it clear that the oil reserves would be used to secure definitive independence from Russia by forging closer links with Turkey and the West. Turkish cooperation with Elchibey's government went beyond mere words of support. In the early summer of 1992, shortly after

Elchibey's election as president, Western journalists reported that some 150 retired Turkish army officers were serving as military advisers in Azerbaijan. These reports were denied by the Turkish government. In November 1992, shortly after the signing of the bilateral Russian–Azeri treaty on friendship and mutual security, Elchibey paid a state visit to Turkey during which he reportedly signed a military cooperation agreement with Ankara. Elchibey was quoted by Russian newspapers as denying this. However, when in April 1993, following the occupation of Azerbaijan's Kelbajar district, Armenian forces were reported to have found Turkish weapons, Turkish officials admitted that Turkey was supplying arms to Azerbaijan.[165]

Russia's response to this situation has been the establishment of a unified security system with the other Transcaucasian states. Its goal of securing a military foothold in the Transcaucasus has reached its ideal level in Azerbaijan's enemy Armenia. The smallest Transcaucasian republic is the only CIS member to have a combined air defence system with Russia.[166] Surrounded by neighbours that range from unreliable to hostile, Armenia does not need to be pushed to request the Russian troops 'to stay', as Grachev explained in 1992.[167] In June 1994 Armenia and Russia signed an agreement of military cooperation for 25 years, providing for Russian military bases and joint patrolling of the borders with Iran and Turkey.[168]

Georgia was initially reluctant to allow Russian bases on its territory, making it contingent on Moscow's support on the issue of Abkhazia. However, it has signed an agreement with Russia to patrol its borders with Turkey and allow the re-establishment of three Russian military bases.[169]

Azerbaijan is the missing piece. It has persistently rejected the stationing of Russian troops on its soil. Such a move would be an effective check on Azerbaijan's policy of attaining a high degree of independence from Russia. A Russian army would be the ultimate lever over Azerbaijan. If the past record of the Russian military is anything to go by, Baku has reasons to distrust it: it helped overthrow Elchibey by supplying the weapons to Surat Husseinov's army,[170] and it was charged with spiriting him away to safety and with allegedly planning plots against Aliev. More importantly, Russia is widely blamed as the country that helped Armenia to occupy Nagorno-Karabakh.[171] Although it cannot be completely ruled out – as Aliev might agree to it in exchange for Russian help in the secessionist enclave – a decision to allow back Russian troops in Azerbaijan would be extremely unpopular and would put further strain on the government.

The same can be said of Azerbaijan's refusal to lease the early-warning radar station at Gebele to Moscow. As it does not need the installations, Baku is using Russian interest as a bargaining chip to obtain Moscow's support on Karabakh. Azerbaijan's intransigence over the latter issue prompted the former Russian Defence Minister, General Pavel Grachev, to declare impatiently that Russia was 'going to create a single Armenian–Georgian–Russian unified air defence system, even if the Azeris refuse'. However, Moscow's continuous insistence on recovering Gebele signals that the need for this radar which monitors aerial movements from the Persian Gulf to China has not receded.[172] Aliev has shown more flexibility towards Russian interest in getting a lease, but to date he has stopped short of ceding to Moscow. In fact, Moscow could assert property rights on Gebele. After the dissolution of the Soviet Union, Russia signed an agreement with Azerbaijan, by which Moscow assumed Azerbaijan's share of the Soviet external debt in exchange for its renouncing of claims on Soviet assets.[173] The Azeri president's repeated statements that Gebele is Azeri property point to Baku's concern about the Kremlin's attempts to establish a permanent foothold in the country.[174]

Russian predominance in the region

Russia's bid for hegemony in the 'near abroad', legitimised in its 1993 security doctrine, had the following implications for the Transcaucasian republics:

1. Russia must be the main intermediary between the region and the outside world.
2. No other country should be allowed to establish a presence in the region that could rival Russia's.
3. Under no circumstance should this region become a source of threat to Russia or serve to isolate it from the rest of the world.
4. A political leadership responsive to Russia must be favoured in the Transcaucasian republics.[175]

The compelling factors that have driven foreign oil companies to invest in Azerbaijan introduced a new element: direct American involvement in Russia's southern periphery. In the first two years following the collapse of the Soviet Union, Russian authors and policy-makers (Grachev, Ambartsumov, Migranyan) calling for assertiveness in the Caucasus only regarded the United States as a rival in that it promoted an active Turkish foreign policy in the Transcaucasian area. At a time of rising ethnic conflicts and nationalism, the threats to Russian hegemony had an ideological dimension (pan-Turkism, Islamic fundamentalism) and a military one (Turkish warnings about intervening against Armenia, and Turkish military aid to Azerbaijan).

With the signature of the oil agreement between Baku and the oil consortium in 1994, it became clear that the economic factor prevailed. Western interest in Azerbaijan's vast hydrocarbon reserves was the best guarantee for its independence from Russia. Disturbingly for the Russian government, the Azeri oil attracted external powers capable of disputing Russian leadership in the region. Short of capital and technology, Russia was not in the economic position to compete with the external powers that brought with them both the money and the technology necessary to exploit Azerbaijan's deep-water fields.

The 'Great Game' days gone, Britain has preferred to keep a low profile. London's interests are essentially economic in nature, and would not jeopardise them by questioning Moscow's regional policy. Unwilling to provoke Russia, the British government has always sought to accommodate the Kremlin's interests, even at the time when the consortium was openly reluctant to route its pipelines through Russian territory. Nonetheless, since British Petroleum, in partnership with Norway's Statoil, has the largest share in AIOC, United Kingdom's role, albeit discreet, has been inevitable. London has been the capital where the negotiations have been conducted and Heydar Aliev's sojourn to the United Kingdom in 1994 was hailed as a diplomatic success by the Russian press, which contrasted markedly with the opaque visit by the Armenian president a few days earlier.[176] Apparently the Foreign Office has been giving some military help to Baku because, as 'a very senior official' explained to Caroline Cox (House of Lords), Britain has 'oil interests in Azerbaijan'.[177]

Britain, an unlikely candidate to dispute Moscow's ascendancy over the region, is worth mentioning if only for one reason: the Russian reaction to the signature of a cooperation treaty between the United Kingdom and Azerbaijan in March 1994. Shortly after the agreement was concluded, the British embassy in Moscow received a letter from the Russian Foreign Ministry, warning that given the indefinite legal status of the Caspian Sea, Moscow would not recognise the legitimacy of the exploitation of the offshore reserves.[178] The British ambassador in Baku received a similar note. While the issue of the Caspian's legal status is considered separately, it is important to analyse here what the letter by itself reveals about the Russian government's perspective and ways of negotiation.

The démarche upholds, in an orthodox fashion, the principles and goals of the 'near abroad' policy.

- *Russia's warning implies a claim on preemptive rights over Caspian energy ventures*, whether on sound legal grounds or not.
- *Moscow considers foreign economic participation in Azerbaijan a political move*, which accordingly must be settled by diplomatic means between the Russian and the foreign government concerned, Britain in this case. The timing and the tone of the letter indicate that Russia considers this an issue in its relations with the West[179] or, in any case, an assertion of its ascendancy over Azerbaijan.
- *Azerbaijan is ignored as a player altogether.* Baku's views on the issue are not even sought by the Russian Foreign Ministry, despite the fact that it was the Azeri government who signed deals with Western companies and governments, and not the other way round. This is illustrated by the fact that Russia sent a similar letter to the British ambassador in Baku. In other words, Azerbaijan is seen as acting on behalf of an external power against Moscow.

Prior to their interest in Caspian oil, Western countries, especially the United States, acquiesced to Russian assertiveness in Azerbaijan, recognising it as the only power capable of imposing a certain degree of stability in a country torn by war and political turmoil.[180] It was the necessary corollary of a support for Yeltsin's 'reformist' government, based on the assumption that it would have beneficial effects on the former Soviet republics. As Under-Secretary of State Strobe Talbott put it, US policy was 'focusing on those areas of the globe where success in one country or region will have an influence on surrounding areas'.[181]

The realisation of Azerbaijan's oilfield potential introduced a shift in American policy, from its somewhat complacent view on Russia's claims regarding the 'near abroad', towards a firmer attitude. Foremost among American energy policy priorities is the diversification of oil supply sources. Although in the last decade almost all the growth in world oil demand has been met from production outside OPEC, long-term prospects look more worrying. Arco and Chevron are among the American companies who are already feeling the crunch. Over the past ten years both firms have failed to replenish their oil reserves as fast as they have used them up.[182]

The opening up of the Caspian reserves will relieve the United States of over-dependence on the Gulf countries, where an anti-American mood is on the rise even in usually 'friendly' states, as reflected in the recent attacks against US military bases in Saudi Arabia. American concerns were reflected last year in the deputy US energy secretary's tour of seven former Soviet republics. During his visit Bill White stressed his government's support for the rights of the new states to develop their natural resources free from Russian meddling. He openly upheld Azerbaijan's position of routing one of AIOC's early oil pipelines through Georgian territory, despite Russia's pressures to make its Druzhba system the sole export alternative. In what appears to be a confirmation of the hypothesis outlined above, he urged Azerbaijan's government to 'think of itself as a future major oil producing nation, and of Russia and Iran as competitors'. He bluntly stated that 'for political reasons' Iran and Iraq could not be counted on to cope with the growth in world demand. On the other hand, drilling in the Amazon and the Arctic was no longer possible 'for ecological reasons'. The oil, he concluded, should come from 'the western hemisphere, including the US, and central Asia'.[183] Russian fears that the US, increasingly concerned for the security of oil supplies, is using Azerbaijan as a base to increase its control over the Caspian, are not, then, misplaced.[184]

Seen in this context, the US's foremost goal of supporting the 'independence of the countries of the region'[185] assumes a new dimension. Washington will go to greater lengths to shield the oil-rich Caspian states from Moscow's encroachments. Azerbaijan benefited from the American government's involvement in the oil deal, when in October 1995 Bill Clinton, in a now famous telephone conversation, urged Aliev to resist Moscow's pressures to export the oil only by the Russian pipeline.[186] It was after this conversation that the AIOC agreed to a dual system of northern (Russia) and central (Georgia, Turkey) routes for the 'early oil'. The US encourages a diversification of routes to promote commercial competition and thus keep tariffs low and, above all, avoid the risks associated with dependence on a single route.[187]

Nonetheless, Washington's policy in the area is constrained by the global nature of this interest. Hence, it opposes the routing of a pipeline through Iran – while it seems to be the best option – and is also against Iranian participation in deals involving American companies (although it has also pressed other Western firms, with mixed results, not to work with the Iranian state oil company).[188] Teheran's support for terrorism to undermine the Middle East peace process is the avowed justification of this policy.[189] While its consistency is undeniable in a political sense, Washington's inflexibility towards Iran may end up dragging Azerbaijan into the Middle East's complicated diplomatic equation, depriving Baku of an ally that could help balance Russia's pressures and Armenia's dominant position in Karabakh in the process. In fact, as a response to its exclusion, Iran explicitly sided with Moscow in the dispute over the legal status of the Caspian Sea, and further strengthened its links with Yerevan. Despite the fact that it is the largest recipient of American aid in the CIS, neighbouring Armenia has not been castigated for its close links with Teheran, and so is being left free to conduct a more equilibrated regional foreign policy than Baku.

More than any other country, Turkey had grand designs on Azerbaijan after the collapse of the Soviet Union. These policies were epitomised by Turgut Ozal's assertive policy towards Azerbaijan, which reached its peak during Abulfaz Elchibey's markedly pro-Turkish government, as shown earlier. Turkey had the advantage of common ethnic, linguistic, religious and cultural features with Azerbaijan, and strove to present itself to its brethren in Baku as a model of a secular and modern Islamic state, in obvious competition with Iran.[190] Ankara's endeavour was backed by the government of George Bush. In the confused situation that had arisen after the collapse of the Soviet Union, the United States feared the spread of Islamic fundamentalism into the new republics promoted by Teheran.[191]

A retreating Russia provided an excellent opportunity for the Turkish government's pretentious schemes. Although external observers emphasised the ideological aspect of Turkey's bid for leadership in Azerbaijan, qualifying it as pan-Turkism, Azerbaijan's oil played a relevant role in Ankara's aim to strengthen the links with Azerbaijan. Turkey would be able to reactivate its oil terminal at Ceyhan, which, at a daily cost of $4 million in lost revenues, has remained idle since the embargo imposed on Iraq in 1990 interrupted the flow from Baghdad. Thus, Russia's aim of becoming the main intermediary between Azerbaijan and the outside world would be jeopardised. By way of oil exports, Azerbaijan's gateway to the external markets would have been Turkey. Geography, economic factors, and American and Azeri support enhanced its position *vis-à-vis* Russia.

Moreover, Turkey's decision not to allow the passage of a higher number of tankers through the Bosphorus straits, citing the increased risk of accidents, would be a big step towards isolating Russia. As seen from Moscow, such a measure would not only violate the 1936 Montreaux Convention on free navigation in the straits, but it would also be tantamount to closing to Russian oil exports (with 60 per cent of its trade, the country's main earner of hard currency) since it is the only waterway linking the Black Sea to the world's oceans via the Mediterranean. Russia plans to bypass the straits by building a pipeline through

Bulgaria and Greece. But the Turkish objections alerted Russian analysts to the fact that the energy corridor being developed from the Caspian to Turkey was effectively cutting off Russia from its southern periphery. Moscow's subsequent decline would be comparable, in the eyes of a group of Russian historians, to 'the opening of the sea route to India around Africa and the discovery of America, which consigned the Italian city-states to the periphery of European politics'.[192] This signalled the emergence of Turkey as a new regional leader on the Russian Federation's southern borders which, these authors pointed out, was backed by 'international organisations' in its decision to restrict navigation in the straits.[193]

While Turkey has certainly not dropped its objections to tanker passage through the Bosphorus, its position as the foremost foreign influence over Azerbaijan has been weakened. For all its sonorous promises, Ankara's military assistance was, in hindsight, symbolic, and in any case did not make a difference in Baku's efforts to recover Karabakh. Unable to project military power, Turkey has lost ground in Azerbaijan.[194] It has also been unable to honour its initial pledges of economic aid to Azerbaijan and the Central Asian republics which, in the hope that they would be backed up by the US, had reached the unrealistic figure of 1200 billion dollars (80 per cent of its total reserves) for its 'Asian Marshall Plan'.[195] Thus, during his official visit to Azerbaijan in 1995, the Turkish president stressed that his country did not intend 'to compete with other states for influence in the region'.[196] Yet its strategic position as a competitor for the export routes of Caspian oil makes Turkey a power Russia has to reckon with. Turkey remains the most serious contender for Russia in the bid for the 'late oil' from Baku.[197]

Russia's long arm

Its appeal for Western investors has not protected Baku from Russian manipulation in its economy, politics or the war against the Armenian separatists in Karabakh, the issue that, by far, dominates Azeri politics. Heavy losses on the battlefield caused the downfall of two presidents, Ayaz Mutalibov in 1992, and Abulfaz Elchibey in 1993. A ceasefire has held firm for the last two years, thus giving Azerbaijan a respite from a war in which it has been the losing side, and allowing it to concentrate its attention on the oil deals. A resumption of the war would throw the country into disarray again and, naturally, mar the prospects for the development of its Caspian oilfields. At the same time, it should be noted that at the peak of the war in 1992, foreign investors did not withdraw from Azerbaijan.

It is Russia's tilt towards Armenia in the war what explains the separatists' gains. First-hand evidence abounds. There are many accounts by Armenian witnesses of the unexpected Russian military help in the sweeping advance of the Armenian forces of Karabakh in 1992, which resulted in the massacre of Azeri civilians in the town of Khojali, a turning point in the escalation of the conflict into a fully-fledged war. These tales are confirmed by an American commentator who reported Russian support that included the participation of dozens of tanks and armoured personnel carriers of the 366th Army (Russian) stationed in Stepanakert, the capital of Karabakh.[198] An Azeri reporter with the BBC, who was part of a human rights delegation to briefly recovered territory in Karabakh in 1993, found written instructions from Russia's 7th Army based in Yerevan.[199]

In mid-May 1994, Grachev convened a meeting of the defence ministers of Armenia, Azerbaijan and the self-proclaimed Republic of Nagorno-Karabakh, where they agreed to a ceasefire. Although Grachev's terms included the deployment of peacekeeping forces from the CIS, Azerbaijan never agreed to what would be tantamount to a Russian contingent in the enclave. What Grachev had achieved was to push aside the influence of the CSCE in the mediation of Armenia and Azerbaijan. Latent tensions between the different approaches of the West and Russia surfaced during Yeltsin's meeting with Clinton in New York in late 1994. While the Russian president insisted that Moscow wanted the role of 'main peacekeeper', Clinton insisted that all Russian actions in the region must correspond to international norms and be monitored by the UN and the CSCE, which led Yeltsin to accuse Washington of wishing 'to seize the initiative in mediation for itself'.[200]

Eventually the Kremlin's position prevailed when the CSCE Budapest summit in December 1994 resolved to back Moscow's efforts at mediation in the enclave. The delegates agreed to merge the CSCE Minsk Group, in charge of the Karabakh issue, and the Russian negotiation processes within the framework of the OSCE. Although peacekeeping forces were never stationed – both Armenia and Azerbaijan agreed that there was no need since the ceasefire has held for two years without them – the diplomatic initiative lies entirely with Russia.[201]

In January 1996, following a summit of CIS leaders, Boris Yeltsin warned the Armenian separatists in Nagorno-Karabakh not to have expectations that it would receive independent status from Azerbaijan. At that meeting, the Russian president and his Azeri counterpart were reported to have progressed in their negotiations for base rights at the Gebele early-warning radar station. Further confirming that they hold the keys to the settlement, Russian negotiators recently hinted that Azerbaijan would be rewarded with a shift of Russian policy over the disputed enclave towards one more sympathetic to Azerbaijan, if Baku adopted a more responsive attitude towards Moscow's security demands.[202]

Aliev's determination to clear the political arena of actual or potential challengers to his power has offered Moscow another useful tool. Many of his opponents live in Moscow, including his two most powerful rivals, the ex-prime minister Surat Husseinov, and Ayaz Mutalibov, the ex-president widely blamed for Azeri defeats in Karabakh and also accused of conspiratorial schemes (which, indeed, have been quite useful to the Azeri president to clean the political arena of opponents).

Thus, after having lived unmolested in Moscow for three years, Rahim Gaziyev, who acted as defence minister in Elchibey's government, was detained by the Russian police in April 1996 and was promptly sent to Baku two days later, where a trial *in absentia* had sentenced him to death on charges of plotting against Aliev. But Gaziyev has much less political weight than Mutalibov, who is believed to have retained popularity among the population.[203]

A few days before Gaziyev's arrest, Mutalibov was detained in Moscow in April 1996. The sympathy he commands among Moscow's political class became manifest by the uproar his arrest caused in Russia's Duma. All the factions joined in their support of the Azeri ex-president and voted unanimously against the decision to extradite him. Communists and nationalists hailed Mutalibov as 'Russia's friend', while democrats and centrists held that his civil rights were being infringed. Russia released Mutalibov in May 1996, after a statutory month's detention, on grounds of insufficient detail in the charges brought against him for extradition. The Russian Federal Prosecutor General Office did not find any proof that he was involved in criminal activities.[204]

The treaty governing extraditions between Russia and Azerbaijan, in force since 1995, says that the person whose extradition is requested by one of the sides can be held for up to a month until a final decision is made. During that period, the side requesting the extradition must produce evidence that the detainee was involved in specific crimes. But, according to Article 61 of the treaty, an individual can be extradited on the condition that 'the deeds that caused the question of extradition to be raised are criminal actions under the legislation of both countries'.[205]

Despite his wish to have Mutalibov safely locked away in Baku, Aliev did not initiate formal criminal proceedings against him. Mutalibov was arrested on charges brought against him in 1993 by Elchibey's government for 'stealing weapons and creating armed formations', both punishable under Russian law. The Russian prosecution found no evidence to back up these accusations. As for the other counts, no proof was even sought as they were not punishable in Russia, although they include the more serious charges of inviting Russian troops to quell general agitation in Baku, the unopposed surrender of Azeri towns in Karabakh in the spring of 1992, and alleged attempts to overthrow Elchibey at about the same time.

Russian reluctance to extradite Mutalibov contrasted sharply with the readiness to hand back Gaziyev. Legal niceties could hardly be the reason, as the charges for conspiratorial plans that paved the way for Gaziyev's extradition were not even considered in Mutalibov's case, as they were not 'indictable in Russia'. But the prospect of his extradition, made credible by Gaziyev's prompt return to certain death in Baku, gives the Azeri government an incentive to offer Russia concessions on other issues. The timing of the arrests did not escape the attention of observers in Baku. They coincided with ongoing conversations with Primakov on a settlement of the legal – or rather political and economic – dispute in the Caspian Sea and the incorporation of Azerbaijan into a unified CIS security system in Transcaucasia.[206]

Mutalibov's extradition is a bargaining chip the Kremlin can use again. He was arrested once in May 1995 for 'not having a Moscow residence permit', but was released within hours. But he is still not completely shielded against the letter of Russian law.[207]

Timing usually gives the clue to the reasons behind Moscow's moves. Shortly after the signing of the oil deal with the Western consortium in late 1994, Russia closed its border to Azerbaijan's road and rail traffic. Flights between Moscow and Baku were also interrupted, to be resumed a few weeks later. The officially cited reason for the unilateral closure of the crossings between both countries were the rapidly deteriorating conditions in Chechnya.[208] War had erupted once again in the separatist republic in December 1994 and Grozny was being subjected to heavy pounding.[209] Therefore, 'temporarily, pending a special directive', admission to the Russian Federation of persons, means of transport, freight and goods from Azerbaijan and Georgia, was being suspended.[210] The opportune discovery in August 1995 of a Turkish spy ring accused with providing the Chechens with 'communication links' with Ankara only strengthened Russia's rationale for the closed borders policy, as they had gained access to Chechnya through Azerbaijan's border with Daghestan.[211]

Russia's measure amounted to a *de facto* blockade of Azerbaijan, as the country lost access to its main source of spare parts imports and a major market for its exports. The economy was badly hit. Russia at the time accounted for 60 per cent of Azerbaijan's external trade, but within three months it had fallen to just 10 per cent.[212] In the first half of 1995 there was a 27 per cent plunge in industrial production,[213] and the Azeri government estimates that the trade losses neared $30 million in the first month after the borders closure.[214] Russia lifted the road blockade in May 1995, but has maintained the rail stoppage.[215]

The transport stoppage also affected sea traffic, if only for a short time. That was long enough, however, to highlight another Russian lever to which Azerbaijan's oil industry is potentially exposed. As existing Soviet-era technology is obsolete or at best below the standards required for many of the new projects on the Caspian sea-bed, drilling equipment, including large and heavy pieces, imported from Europe by the foreign companies operating in Azerbaijan, must be shipped through Russia's Volga river system to Caspian ports.[216]

However enormous its capacity for inflicting damage on its periphery, Russia has not achieved its security goals in Azerbaijan. No military bases have been stationed yet, nor has the Gebele radar been leased. This indicates that Azerbaijan has moved towards the attainment of even greater independence from Russia, to the point that it is being successful in its resistance to being dragged into the 'near abroad'. Western investment in Caspian oil is not an explicitly anti-Russian move, but it is helping Baku escape from Moscow's 'sphere of influence' by making Azerbaijan's economy viable. The equally independence-minded Georgians ended up succumbing to Russian manipulation of ethnic rivalries and political conflicts. True, Azerbaijan lost Karabakh to Moscow's Armenian allies and a settlement of the enclave's conflict on Azeri terms ultimately depends on Russia. A decision on Gabele's lease and Russian military bases lie with the Azeri government. As soon as the oil starts to flow, Azerbaijan will have time on its side for the exchange of these bargaining chips.

Conclusion

Both Russia and the United States are vying for control of Caspian oil. Washington is committed to muster influence in a region that will enable it to reduce its energy-dependency on unreliable Middle Eastern OPEC members. As seen from Moscow, its regional leadership is at stake. Control of Azerbaijan's pipelines will secure its ascendancy over the 'near abroad', and may help it recover part of its past global prestige. At the same time, it is misleading to speak of Russia as a unitary, rational actor. Different groups within the Russian government have conflicting interests in Azerbaijan. Writing conventions make us speak of 'Russia', which thus becomes a misnomer for individuals in the government. We are therefore led, or misled, to analyse decisions and motivations in a systematic way, while a closer view shows a chaotic process of policy-making in which government and personal interests overlap, as corruption blurs the difference between both. When bribes and stakes rank in the order of millions of dollars, greed becomes a powerful determinant of the position of high officials on certain issues. Their decisions are acts of state, whatever the motivations behind them. Provided information is available, it would be possible to disentangle the web of interests that give rise to certain actions. In that case, however, the general view may be sacrificed to the details. Only a substantial amount of reliable information might enable us to assess accurately the weight of corruption in Moscow's policy towards Azerbaijan. Until or if that becomes possible, the role of corruption should not be overplayed. There are few reasons to doubt that former Soviet and Russian governments were less corrupt than the current one, but to our knowledge no author has been able to demonstrate that 'personal stakes' of high-officials may have been powerful enough to alter Moscow's security interests.[217]

Oil has made Azerbaijan an issue in the bilateral relations between the United States and Russia. It was on the agenda when in September 1994 Clinton and Yeltsin discussed peacekeeping in Karabakh and Moscow's position on the development of the Azeri offshore Caspian fields.[218] Apart from their potential contribution to reducing overdependence on Persian Gulf oil, the fact that Baku's oilfields could become an outlet for Iranian economic presence in the region has made it very important for the Clinton administration to step up its diplomatic activity in the Caspian area. No political divide applies to the assessment of the relevance of the Caspian oilfields for American economic and political interests. Changes are unlikely in the regional policy of the White House even if the Republican candidate Robert Dole emerges victorious in the presidential elections. Despite understandable Azeri fears,[219] Dole, a notorious pro-Armenian, is as keen as Clinton on the greater independence from OPEC that the Caspian oilfields seem to promise.[220]

Two examples illustrate the respect that Washington's word commands in Baku. The first one is that the Azeri government did not hesitate to annoy Teheran by not allowing it to take up its agreed share of 5 per cent in the AIOC deal, due to American objections. The second is that Aliev gave in to Clinton's pressures for a dual pipeline system rather than to Moscow's demands to export the Azeri crude only through the Russian line.[221] Although the double route strategy did not elicit any protest from the Kremlin – perhaps because the other line, after all, will run through responsive Georgia[222] – the sequence of steps that led up to it indicates the emergence of a new geopolitical reality for Russia. For the first time since the collapse of the Soviet Union, the United States challenged – successfully – Moscow's bid for hegemony in the 'near abroad'.

Although by means of officials whose views 'do not necessarily reflect those of the US government', the Clinton administration also disputes Russia's stand on the legal status of the Caspian Sea.[223] As mentioned above, the deputy US energy secretary was frank during his tour of former Soviet republics last year, when he expressed Washington's support of their right to develop their own resources independently and to look at Russia as a 'competitor'.[224]

In historical perspective, the increasing American involvement in Azerbaijan may mark the beginning of a new stage in the shrinkage of Moscow's clout as a world and regional power since 1989. With the collapse of the Berlin Wall, Russian influence reverted to the Soviet borders; the independence of the Soviet republics ensued two years later; NATO's enlargement to include Eastern European countries (Poland, the Czech Republic and Hungary are in the first tier) represents a third stage, insofar as an expansion of the Western military alliance into what was Moscow's *cordon sanitaire* in post-war Europe was perceived, in the words of former foreign minister Andrei Kozyrev, as a continuation of 'a policy aimed at containment of Russia'.[225]

By actively pursuing its own agenda in Azerbaijan, the United States government is now contesting Moscow's influence in the area its 1993 military doctrine proclaimed as Russia's 'near abroad'. For Russia, this means that its sphere of influence is contracting even further, now to affect the buffer of former Soviet republics which, as stated elsewhere, Moscow considers its forward line of defence.[226] In other words, the West is approaching Russia's gates. As for the United States, this supposes a shift away from the Clinton administration's previous stance of implicitly recognising the former Soviet republics as Russia's sphere of influence,[227] towards a more assertive regional diplomacy.

When it still finds it hard to swallow NATO's enlargement into the East, the Russian government is witnessing that one part of its southern periphery, Azerbaijan, is becoming susceptible to American influence, sometimes in contradiction to Moscow's interests, as reflected by the decision on the pipeline routing. In other words, the US commanding role in the development of Azerbaijan's oilfields is checking Russia's hegemonic tendencies in its own backyard.

The Russian foreign ministry sees American participation in the development of Caspian oilfields in the old terms of East–West confrontation. Thus, at a conference in October 1995, Alexander Khodakov, director of the Legal Department of the Russian Foreign Ministry, stated that 'third countries should have no right to dictate to the Caspian states, in what ways and by which methods they should perform their activities in the Caspian Sea'. After considering that any form of 'political or economic pressure exerted on the Caspian states by third states was still less acceptable', Khodakov pointed to the 'complete absence of legal guarantees for investments of the oil consortium, if Azerbaijan launched unilateral actions for changing the legal status of the Caspian Sea'. This, he indicated, should have a 'sobering effect on the Americans, who are inclined to ignore the exclusive right of the Caspian states to dispose of their own natural resources'.[228]

A group of Russian historians also voiced similar concerns. Since the former Soviet oil-bearing republics had 'flung their doors open to the West', the Western countries – argued these academicians – were making inroads into Azerbaijan and Central Asia, where they were creating 'windows to the Mediterranean', i.e. Turkey. In what ominously appears as a suggestion to the Russian government as to how to block this penetration, they stressed that 'only potential social, economic or political instability in the aforementioned regions could slow this process, since Western businessmen are unlikely to invest their money in risky ventures'.[229]

It is undeniable that a greater role by the United States in the exploitation of the Caspian reduces the scope for Russian economic influence in the region. American presence in Azerbaijan is a setback for Russia's regional leadership ambitions, for it is not in a position to compete with the US. The technological and financial power Washington wields, which Moscow lacks, are indispensable for the development of the Caspian deep-water offshore fields.

But there the rivalry ends. After certain initial reluctance, the United States consented to Russia's demand for being the sole peacekeeping force in Nagorno-Karabakh and, although no Russian force is guaranteeing the ceasefire in the enclave, Moscow retains its role of arbiter between Armenia and Azerbaijan.[230] Despite Turkey's strong objections,[231] Washington also appeared to agree to Russian demands of upwards revisions of CFE limits on its flank regions, including the

North Caucasus Military District.[232] Furthermore, in response to frequent concerns voiced by the Azeri government about Russian pressures to station troops in the country, American diplomats have replied that it 'was part of Azerbaijan's internal affairs'.[233]

In other words, Washington's and the West's involvement in Azerbaijan begins and ends with oil. The fact that Moscow's claim on special rights on its 'near abroad' is being eroded by heavy Western investment in Azerbaijan creates resentment in the Kremlin, but it is not tantamount to a confrontation on security policy in the way NATO's eastward enlargement is.[234] With a sizeable part of its anticipated supplies for the next century at stake,[235] there is no reason why the American government should provoke Russia so as to mar the prospects for the Azeri oil deal. True, Clinton advocated a dual pipeline system despite Moscow's wishes. His compromise solution, however, can also be seen as a concession to Russia. Only a political interest to appease Russia made the Baku–Novorrossisk line a viable option, otherwise resisted by most of the foreign companies developing Azerbaijan's oilfields.[236]

For the sake of a balanced relationship with Russia, the United States was ready to bow, at least partially, to Moscow's demand for a line to Novorrossisk. More questionable is whether it served Azerbaijan's interests. Baku is as keen as Washington on not estranging the Kremlin, but perhaps not to the point of leaving its statehood's lifeline – oil exports – hostage to Russia's whims, as the Kazakh example eloquently shows. The Georgian route was one of the main options but it does not represent a really independent alternative, now that Georgia has reverted to its Soviet role as a Russian outpost in Transcaucasia. If Azerbaijan's oil is to guarantee greater independence from Russia, none of the pipeline routings seems to be the choice in the right direction. A route through Iran, politically stable – if not likable – and Azerbaijan's only neighbour free from Russian influence, had to be ruled out, again for American foreign policy considerations.

This has left Azeri oil pipelines at the mercy of Russia and Russia's ally, Georgia, and irked the Iranian government. Ever since, Teheran has been siding with Moscow over the legal status of the Caspian Sea,[237] despite having taken up the offer of a 20 per cent stake from SOCAR's share in the $4 billion development of the offshore Shakh Deniz oilfield, in which no American company participates.[238] Baku cannot afford to anger Iran, always sensitive to the potential for conflict within its own Azeri population of around 20 million, who enjoyed 'independent' statehood in northern Iran under the aegis of the Russian army from 1945–6,[239] and whose nationalist feelings have been aroused by the

Karabakh war.[240] During Elchibey's anti-Iranian reign, Teheran retaliated with a less ambiguous tilt towards blockaded Armenia, and, by continuing to supply energy and goods, is helping Azerbaijan's rival to overcome Baku's blockade.[241]

Yet the constraints imposed on Azerbaijan by American foreign policy interests are made up by one crucial benefit. As shown above, the United States is also the only power capable of restraining Russian hegemonic tendencies. Assuming that Moscow or other factors do not hamper the exports of oil, Washington's strong interest in developing the Azeri oilfields will help the Caspian republic to obtain profits in the range of 80–100 billion dollars over a period of 30 years.[242] By paving the way for Azerbaijan's integration into Western markets, oil should help Baku reduce its dependence on Russia, and would enable it to increase its trade with hard-currency suppliers and buyers: although reorientation towards markets outside the former Soviet Union is still continuing, in 1993 the CIS republics still accounted for 60 per cent of Azerbaijan's exports and 47 per cent per cent of its imports.[243] Its role as a major oil producer should also enhance Azerbaijan's stature as a regional power, which in turn would enable it to deal with Moscow from a stronger position, as its successful resistance to Russia's military demands demonstrates.

It cannot, however, be the sole pillar of Azerbaijan's sovereignty. A startling fact of international politics is that vast oil reserves happen to be in 'problematic' places. In many cases, the converse is true: it is oil exploitation that makes these places problematic. If it is not backed by an effective administration, oil wealth does not necessarily bolster a state's institutional strength or its economy. The cases of Angola, Venezuela, Libya or Iraq, just to mention a few, show that a large energy resources base need not imply a promising future either for the country or its population.[244] Azerbaijan seems set on the latter course, judging from the mismanagement that is resulting in declining levels of oil production[245] and recent reports about the widening gap between an impoverished population, whose average salary stands at about 20 dollars a month, and a suspiciously wealthy political elite.[246]

Unpredictable as history is, other factors could diminish Azerbaijan's relative importance as an oil producer. However unlikely in the near future, an opening up of Saudi Arabia's oilfields to foreign investments or the fully-fledged return of Iraq to international markets would reduce the weight of Caspian reserves in world economy. There have been predictions about the major OPEC producing countries, which control two-thirds of world existing reserves, eventually needing to invite foreign companies to finance their costly capacity expansion programmes.[247] In any case, the power and the wealth associated with oil cannot be taken for granted on a permanent basis by Azerbaijan, as its oilfields will reach maturity in 30–40 years and then begin to decline.[248] Without oil, and therefore with probably much more nuanced American backing, Azerbaijan will be left to its own devices, hostage again to its hostile geography.

There is no need to look that far into the future, however, to note that Azerbaijan's oil potential cannot be the only base for its independence. A glance at Abulfaz Elchibey's government reveals the limits of a policy inspired by the belief that oil can solve every national problem. Elchibey embodied the ideal president for Azerbaijan. A former anti-Communist dissident with a humanistic background, his policy towards foreign investment was pragmatic in its readiness to exploit the country's reserves with Western companies. The strong relationship he had set about to build with Turkey, the country Washington envisaged to spearhead Western policy towards the region, coupled with his actively anti-Iranian policies could have only pleased the United States. Russia, meanwhile, had relapsed into its own borders and seemed unable to articulate a consistent policy towards Transcaucasia.

As shown earlier, Elchibey's policy only exacerbated Moscow's fear of greater Turkish involvement on its southern rim and contributed to precipitate an assertive Russian policy towards Azerbaijan. Acute political and military crisis, partly engineered by the Kremlin, hindered progress in the negotiations with foreign oil companies and led to his government's downfall. The allies on which he had pinned his hopes, Turkey and the United States, were absent.

Since Persia ceded the northern part of its empire (including what now constitutes the Republic of Azerbaijan) in the Turkmenchai Treaty of 1828, Russia has been the dominant power in the Caucasus continuously but for three years between 1917 and 1920. Oil did not shield Azerbaijan from Russian occupation in the past, even though it led Britain to send a military contingent in 1918 to occupy Baku and protect the oilfields in the middle of civil war and chaos. In the end, Russia prevailed. Historical parallels can be unreliable. Facts, however, are harder to contest. Washington's interest in Azerbaijan is as transient in nature as Caspian oil reserves are, whereas Russia's geography and history, and the security demands they create, tend to be of a more stable nature. As such, they will remain a factor Baku will have to deal with throughout its independent life. Oil will not ensure 'complete independence' (if such a thing exists at all) from Moscow. But if it helps Azerbaijan to diversify its economy and thus secure its integration into Western markets initiated by its oil exports, Baku will be on a stronger footing to manage its inescapable interdependence with Russia.

Notes

1 Andrew Apostolou, 'The Problems of Creating Economies in Central Asia', p. 58, in Anoushiravan Ehteshami, ed., *From the Gulf to Central Asia*, Exeter, 1994.
2 Karen Dawisha and Bruce Parrott, *Russia and the New States of Eurasia*, Cambridge, 1995, p. 161.
3 Rosemarie Forsythe, *The Politics of Oil in the Caucasus and Central Asia*, Adelphi Paper 300, 1996, p. 7.
4 Joseph Stanislaw and Daniel Yergin, 'Oil: Reopening the Door', *Foreign Affairs*, September/October 1993, Vol. 72, No. 4.
5 Press conference by Heydar Aliev at NATO's headquarters, Brussels, 24 April 1996.
6 John Roberts, *Caspian Pipelines*, London, 1996, p. 23.
7 The official party New Azerbaijan was reported to be the largest by already outdated figures (see *Nezavisimaya Gazeta*, 27 August 1993). It had 'several thousand members'.
8 Fuad Kuliev, 'Prospects for Foreign Investment in Azerbaijan's Oil Industry', *The Oil and Gas Guide to the Former Soviet Union*, Summer 1995, p. 1.
9 *EIU Country profile 1995–96: Georgia, Armenia, Azerbaijan*, p. 62.
10 Andrew Seck, *Oil and Gas Investments in Azerbaijan (part 2)*, Centre for Petroleum and Mineral Law and Policy Paper, University of Dundee, 1994, p. 1.
11 *EIU Country Profile 1995–96*, p. 62.
12 *Armenia, Azerbaijan and Georgia: Country Studies*, Washington, 1995, p. 125.
13 Quentin Peel, 'Moscow to Draw Up Emergency Oil Strike Measures', *Financial Times*, 31 March 1990, p. 2.
14 'On the Brink', *The Economist*, 16 March 1991.
15 Ibid.
16 Thane Gustafson, *Crisis Amid Plenty: the Politics of Soviet Energy under Brezhnev and Gorbachev*, Princeton, 1989, p. 114.
17 Ibid., p. 64.
18 *EIU Country Profile 1995–96*, p. 63.
19 *Armenia, Azerbaijan and Georgia: Country Studies*, pp. 115–16.
20 John Lloyd, 'Azerbaijan Expects to Climb Oil Reserves League', *Financial Times*, 12 March 1992.
21 Neil Buckley, 'Developing the Last Great Oil Frontier', *Financial Times*, 7 August 1992, p. 22.
22 Seck, *Oil and Gas Investments*, p. 52.
23 *EIU Country Profile 1992–93: Georgia, Armenia, Azerbaijan, Central Asian Republics*, pp. 49–50.
24 'Historical Beginnings: the AIOC–Azerbaijan International Operating Company', *Azerbaijan International* (SOCAR section), Vol. III, 2, Summer 1995, p. 33.
25 Elizabeth Fuller, *Azerbaijan at the Crossroads*, London, 1994, p. 24.
26 Apostolou, 'The Problems of Creating Economies in Central Asia', pp. 67–71.

27 Robert Corzine, 'Explorers Target New and Old Territories', *Financial Times*, 13 December 1993. Andrew Seck, *Oil and Gas Investments*, pp. 11, 16.
28 Seck, *Oil and Gas Investments*, p. 15.
29 *EIU Country Profile 1994–95: Georgia, Armenia, Azerbaijan*, p. 58.
30 *EIU Country Report*, 4 June 1996, 2nd quarter, p. 38.
31 *EIU Country Profile 1995–96*, p. 62.
32 *EIU Country Report*, 12 June 1995, 2nd quarter, p. 34.
33 Ibid., p. 34.
34 Andrew Seck, *Oil and Gas Investments*, p. 27.
35 *EIU Country Report*, 6 November 1995, 4th quarter, p. 39.
36 *EIU Country Report*, 5 March 1996, 1st quarter, p. 36.
37 *Armenia, Azerbaijan and Georgia: Country Studies*, p. 121.
38 *EIU Country Profile 1992–93*, p. 50.
39 See Fuller, *Azerbaijan at the Crossroads*, p. 13.
40 Ibid., p. 19.
41 *Armenia, Azerbaijan and Georgia: Country Studies*, p. 68. See also *Azerbaijan International*, Vol. II, 3, Summer 1996, p. 41, which cites the UN as a source to report that Armenia gets 50.1% ($5 820 406) of US Humanitarian Aid for the Caucasus via the UN, compared to 2.9% ($339 102) for Azerbaijan.
42 *EIU Country Profile 1994–95*, p. 54.
43 *EIU Country Report: Georgia, Armenia, Azerbaijan*, 10 September 1993, 3rd quarter, p. 36.
44 *EIU Country Report*, 12 June 1995, 2nd quarter, p. 32.
45 Nasser Sagheb and Masoud Javadi, 'Azerbaijan's "Contract of the Century" Finally Signed with Western Oil Consortium', *Azerbaijan International*, Vol. II, 4, Autumn 1994, p. 26. See also John Lloyd and Robert Corzine, 'Azerbaijan's Oil Deal is Signed in Face of Russian Protests', *Financial Times*, 21 September 1994. Some sources, for example the EIU, refer inaccurately to an investment of $8 billion (see *EIU Country Profile 1994–95*, p. 54).
46 'Will Azerbaijan Really Benefit from the Consortium Contract?', *Azerbaijan International* (SOCAR section) Vol. III, 2, Summer 1995, p. 40.
47 *EIU Country Profile 1994–95*, p. 51.
48 For a detailed analysis of Elchibey's government see Shireen Hunter, *Post-Soviet Transition in the Transcaucasus*, Centre for European Policy Studies, CEPS Paper 61, 1994, pp. 91–7. See also Tadeusz Swietochowski, *Russia and Azerbaijan: a Borderland in Transition*, New York, 1995, pp. 221–6.
49 Dawisha and Parrott, *Russia and the New States of Eurasia*, pp. 135, 169. For an account of Tatarstan's moves towards independence see Radik Batyrshin, 'Tatarstan: Parliament Will Adopt a New Constitution', *Nezavisimaya Gazeta*, 27 October 1992, p. 3, and Tagir Agliullin, 'Traditional Confrontation is Maintained at the Republic's Supreme Soviet Session', *Nezavisimaya Gazeta*, 29 October 1992, p. 1.
50 *Armenia, Azerbaijan and Georgia: Country Studies*, pp. 48–52.
51 Alexei Vassilev, 'Turkey and Iran in Transcaucasia and Central Asia', pp. 129–33 in *From the Gulf to Central Asia*, ed. Anoushiravan Ehteshami. See also Maksim Yusin, 'Teheran Declares "Great Battle" for Influence in Central Asia. Russia, the US and Turkey Seek to Prevent Iran from Winning that Battle', *Izvestia*, 7 February 1992, p. 7.

52 Hunter, *Post-Soviet Transition*, p. 95.
53 Seck, *Oil and Gas Investments in Azerbaijan*, p. 5.
54 *EIU Country Profile 1992–93*, pp. 49–50.
55 Ibid., pp. 51–2.
56 See for example Elizabeth Fuller, *Russian Strategy in the Transcaucasus since the Demise of the USSR*, Bundesinstitut für Ostwissenschaft paper, Koln, 1994, pp. 19–20. Also Timothy Goltz, *The Hidden Russian Hand*, Foreign Policy, Fall 1993.
57 Hunter, *Post-Soviet Transition*, p. 93.
58 Ibid.
59 Fuller, *Azerbaijan at the Crossroads*, pp. 3–4.
60 Neil Buckley, 'Bringing Oil to Troubled Waters', *Financial Times*, 14 September 1992, p. 12.
61 Leonard Geron and Alex Pravda, *Who's Who in Russia and the New States*, I. B. Tauris, 1993.
62 Swietochowski, *Russia and Azerbaijan*, p. 219.
63 John Lloyd, 'Azerbaijan Expects to Climb Oil Reserves League', *Financial Times*, 12 March 1992.
64 Neil Buckley, 'Bringing Oil to Troubled Waters', *Financial Times*, 14 September 1992, p. 12.
65 Hunter, *Post-Soviet Transition*, p. 93.
66 Ibid., p. 107.
67 *EIU Country Report: Georgia, Armenia, Azerbaijan, Central Asian Republics*, 6 March 1993, No. 1, p. 30.
68 Neil Buckley, 'BP and Statoil in Deal to Develop Caspian Sea Field', *Financial Times*, 8 September 1992, p. 32.
69 For a brief account of Georgia's civil and separatist wars see *Armenia, Azerbaijan and Georgia: Country Studies*, pp. 166–75.
70 John Murray Brown, 'Turkey and Azerbaijan Sign Oil Pipeline Accord', *Financial Times*, 10 March 1993.
71 Maxim Shashenkov, 'Russia in Central Asia: Emerging Security Links', pp. 168–9, in Ehteshami, ed., *From the Gulf to Central Asia*.
72 Dawisha and Parrott, *Russia and the New States of Eurasia*, pp. 224–5. See also Swietochowski, *Russia and Azerbaijan*, p. 223.
73 Fuller, *Azerbaijan at the Crossroads*, p. 16. For Armenian–Iranian relations, see Christopher Walker, *Armenia: the Survival of a Nation*, London 1995 edn.
74 Radik Batyrshin, 'Post-Soviet OPEC Created', *Nezavisimaya Gazeta*, 3 March 1993, p. 3.
75 Steve Le Vine, 'Oilmen Ignore Azerbaijan: Foreign Oil Companies are Taking Political Turmoil in their Stride', *Financial Times*, 23 June 1993, p. 4.
76 John Murray Brown, 'Azerbaijan in Caspian Sea Oilfields Deal', *Financial Times*, 2 November 1993, p. 8.
77 Karen Fossli, 'BP and Statoil's Joint Project in Azerbaijan May Cost 3 bn Dollars', *Financial Times*, 8 June 1993, p. 26.
78 Neil Buckley, 'Bringing Oil to Troubled Waters', *Financial Times*, 14 September 1992, p. 12.
79 Fuller, *Azerbaijan at the Crossroads*, p. 8.
80 Hunter, *Post-Soviet Transition*, pp. 95–7.
81 Ibid., p. 89.

82 Ronald G. Suny, 'Transcaucasia: Cultural Cohesion and Ethnic Revival in a Multinational Society', p. 231, in *The Nationalities Factor in Soviet Politics and Society*, ed. L. Hajda and M. Beissinger, Boulder, 1994.
83 *EIU Country Report*, 10 September 1995, 3rd quarter, pp. 29–30.
84 *EIU Country Report*, 4 June 1996, 2nd quarter, pp. 33–4.
85 *EIU Country Report*, 5 March 1996, 1st quarter, pp. 29–31.
86 Seck, *Oil and Gas Investments in Azerbaijan*, p. 6.
87 Ibid.
88 Ibid.
89 Ibid., pp. 51–2.
90 *EIU Country Report*, 6 November 1995, 4th quarter, p. 34.
91 Hunter, *Post-Soviet Transition*, p. 132. See also Swietochowski, *Russia and Azerbaijan*, p. 226.
92 'Moscow Rules', *The Economist*, 24 September 1994
93 *EIU Country Profile*, 6 March 1995, 1st quarter, p. 26.
94 Aidyn Mekhtiyev, 'Chernomyrdin and Kozyrev Argue Over Caspian Oil', *Nezavisimaya Gazeta*, 27 October 1994, p. 3.
95 Arif Useinov, 'To Whom Does the Caspian Shelf Belong?', *Rossiskaya Gazeta*, 11 June 1994, p. 17.
96 'Socar Section', *Azerbaijan International*, Vol. II, No. 3, Summer 1994, p. 19.
97 Steve Le Vine and Bruce Clark, 'Compromise Deal Today on Caspian Oil Route', *Financial Times*, 9 October 1995.
98 'Iranians Take Up the Offer on Shakh Deniz', *Nefte Compass*, 9 May 1996, p. 7.
99 Jonathan Aves, *Post-Soviet Transcaucasia*, London, 1993, p. 19.
100 Hunter, *Post-Soviet Transition*, pp. 131–2.
101 Fuller, *Azerbaijan at the Crossroads*, pp. 15–16.
102 Elmira Akhmedly, 'Istanbul has Special Relations with Baku', *Nezavisimaya Gazeta*, 15 December 1995, p. 3.
103 Betty Blair 'Presidential Interview with Heydar Aliev', *Azerbaijan International*, Summer 1996, Vol. 4, No. 6, p. 19.
104 Interview with Altaï Efendiyev, Councillor, Embassy of Azerbaijan, London.
105 Mekhman Gafarly, 'Russia Goes After Azerbaijani Oil Again', *Sevodnya*, 25 November 1993, p. 22.
106 *EIU Country Report*, 4 June 1996, 2nd quarter, p. 35.
107 *EIU Country Report*, 5 March 1996, 1st quarter, p. 24.
108 Nasser Sagheb and Masoud Javadi, 'Azerbaijan's "Contract of the Century" Finally Signed', *Azerbaijan International (SOCAR section)*, Vol. II, 4, Autumn 1994, p. 26. See also *EIU Country Report*, 10 November 1993, 4th quarter, p. 32.
109 'Will Azerbaijan Really Benefit from the Consortium Contract?', *Azerbaijan International (SOCAR section)*, Vol. III, 2, Summer 1995, p. 40.
110 Arif Useinov, 'Contract of the Century Presented for Signature', *Sevodnya*, 20 September 1994, p. 38
111 *EIU Country Report*, 10 September 1995, p. 30.
112 *EIU Country Profile 1995–96*, p. 57.
113 *EIU Country Report*, 6 March 1995, 1st quarter, p. 29.
114 *EIU Country Report*, 6 November 1995, 4th quarter, p. 38.
115 'Moscow rules', *The Economist*, 24 September 1994.

116 *EIU Country Report*, 6 March 1995, 1st quarter, p. 34.
117 *EIU Country Report*, 4 June 1996, 2nd quarter, p. 7.
118 Ibid., pp. 10–11, 25–6.
119 See for example Barbara Durr, 'Amoco in Soviet Oil Development Deal', *Financial Times*, 27 June 1991, p. 38 and Deborah Hargreaves, 'Western Oil Companies in Caspian Sea Project', *Financial Times*, 4 October 1991, p. 38.
120 Steve Le Vine, 'The Great Game Revisited: Russia, the West and Turkey are Jockeying for Baku's Oil Favours', *Financial Times*, 7 March 1994.
121 John Roberts, *Caspian Pipelines*, RIIA Former Soviet South Project Paper (1996), p. 2.
122 Ibid., pp. 3, 6–7.
123 'Historical Beginnings', *Azerbaijan International (SOCAR section)*, Vol. III, 2, summer 1995, p. 36.
124 Robert Corzine, 'Caspian Oil Outlook Rosy', *Financial Times*, 5 September 1995.
125 Forsythe, *The Politics of Oil*.
126 Joseph Stanislaw and Daniel Yergin, 'Oil: Reopening the Door', *Foreign Affairs*, Vol. 72, 4 (September/October 1993), p. 91.
127 Rosemarie Forsythe is a US diplomat now based in Brussels. She has played a key role in the establishment of relations between the United States and the Transcaucasian republics, especially Armenia and Azerbaijan. Daniel Yergin, of the Cambridge Energy Research Institute, has written profusely on oil politics and provides consultancy assistance to oil companies.
128 Parviz Mina, 'OPEC: The Difficult Choices it Faces in Days and Years Ahead', *Energy Compass*, 10 May 1996, p. 13. Roberts, *Caspian Pipelines*, p. 7. See also Stanislaw and Yergin, 'Reopening the Door', p. 92.
129 Stanislaw and Yergin, 'Reopening the Door', p. 82.
130 Robert Barylski, 'Russia, the West, and the Caspian Energy Hub', *Middle East Journal*, Vol. XLIX, 2 (Spring 1993), pp. 230–1.
131 Roberts, *Caspian Pipelines*, pp. 6–7
132 Ibid., p. 7.
133 Mina, 'OPEC: The Difficult Choices', pp. 11–14.
134 Dawisha and Parrott, *Russia and the New States of Eurasia*, p. 174.
135 Ibid., pp. 175–6.
136 Anthony Parsons, 'Foreword', p. xii in *From the Gulf to Central Asia*, ed. Ehteshami.
137 Sir Peter Ball, former ambassador of the United Kingdom to Russia, 'The Elections in Russia', speech at King's College, Cambridge, 30 April 1996.
138 See Dawisha and Parrott, *Russia and the New States*, pp. 60–9 for an excellent account of Russia's ethnic make-up. For an outdated though detailed analysis of Soviet demographic tendencies, see Hélène Carrère D'Encausse, *L'Empire éclaté*, Paris, 1978, especially pp. 53–108.
139 Konstantin Eggert, 'Russia in the Role of "Eurasian Gendarme"?', *Izvestia*, 7 August 1992, pp. 4–5.
140 Alexander Trenin, 'Russia's Security Interests and Policies in the Caucasus Region', in *Contested Borders in the Caucasus*, ed. Bruno Coppieters, Brussels, 1996, p. 91.
141 Hunter, *Post-Soviet Transition*, p. 123.

142 Ibid.
143 Ibid., pp. 94–5
144 Fuller, *Azerbaijan at the Crossroads*, p. 28.
145 Dewisha and Parrott, *Russia and the New States*, p. 224. For a detailed account see Elizabeth Fuller, *The Lezgin Campaign for Autonomy*, RFE/RL Research Report, Vol. I, 41 (16 October 1992).
146 Bruno Coppieters, 'The Caucasus as a Security Complex', in Coppieters (ed.), *Contested Borders in the Caucasus*.
147 See the concerns reflected by eight North Caucasus leaders in a statement addressed to Boris Yeltsin regarding the perils of Chechen terrorism. 'No Pardon for Gangsters', *Rossiiskaya Gazeta*, 13 January 1996.
148 Georgy Bovt, 'Moscow Explains the Boundaries of its Interests to its Neighbours', *Kommersant-Daily*, 15 February 1996, CDPP.
149 Roberts, *Caspian Pipelines*, p. 34.
150 For a thorough analysis, see Jeffrey D. McCausland, *The CFE Treaty: a Cold War Anachronism?*, Department of National Security and Strategy of the US Army War College paper, 20 March 1995.
151 A forthcoming paper published by the RIIA analyses in deep issues of demarcation in former Soviet Central Asia: Grigory Bondarevsky and Greg Englefield, *Boundary Issues in Central Asia*.
152 Dawisha and Parrott, *Russia and the New States*, p. 236.
153 Alexander Trenin, 'Russia's Security Interests and Policies in the Caucasus Region', p. 76 in *Contested Borders in the Caucasus*, ed. Coppieters.
154 G. Mirsky, *Trade and Investment Opportunities in the Russian Oil Industry*, paper presented at conference convened by the Royal Institute of International Affairs, the Centre for Foreign Investment and Privatisation and Petroleum Intelligence Weekly, London, 23–24 March 1995, Conference proceedings, p. 5.
155 Barbara Starr, 'CFE Countries Agree to Revise Russian Limits', *Jane's Defence Weekly*, 12 June 1996, p. 5.
156 See for example Henry Kissinger's views in *Diplomacy*, London, 1995.
157 'Azeri Interior Minister Discusses Security Issues with his Iranian Counterpart', *BBC Monitor*, 30 July 1996.
158 *EIU Country Report: Georgia, Armenia, Azerbaijan*, 5 March 1996, 1st quarter 1996, p. 34.
159 *EIU Country Report: Georgia, Armenia, Azerbaijan*, 4 June 1996, 2nd quarter, p. 35.
160 Andranik Migranyan, 'The Soviet Union has Gone Off in All Directions', *Megapolis-Express*, 28 October 1996, CDPP.
161 Hunter, *Post-Soviet Transition*, p. 96.
162 Aidyn Mekhtiyev, 'The Karabakh Problem has been Finally Internationalised', *Nezavisimaya Gazeta*, 8 April 1993, pp. 1, 3.
163 Aleksandra Lugovskaya, 'President Elchibey Does Not Believe in the CIS, Preferring Bilateral Agreements', *Izvestia*, 13 October 1992, p. 8.
164 'Radio Baku Asks for Holy War Against "Armenian infidels"', *Nezavisimaya Gazeta*, 11 June 1992.
165 Fuller, *Russian Strategy in the Transcaucasus*, p. 18.
166 *EIU Country Report: Georgia, Armenia, Azerbaijan*, 4 June 1996, 2nd quarter, p. 23.

167 Nikolai Burbyga and Albert Plutnik, 'In Essence, the Russian Army has to be Created from Scratch' (interview with Pavel Grachev), *Izvestia*, 1 June 1992, pp. 12–4.
168 Pavel Felgengauer, 'Russia Strengthens its Influence in the Transcaucasus', *Sevodnya*, 15 June 1994.
169 'Russian-Georgian accords', *Jane's Defence Weekly*, 17 April 1996, p. 21. See also Georgy Bovt, 'Moscow Explains the Boundaries of its Interests to its Neighbours', *Kommersant-Daily*, 15 February 1996.
170 For first-hand observations see Timothy Goltz, 'The Hidden Russian Hand', *Foreign Policy*, 92 (Autumn 1993), pp. 110–16. For a more cautious version see Fuller, *Russian Strategy in the Transcaucasus*, pp. 19–20.
171 Dawisha and Parrott, *Russia and the New States*, pp. 223–4. Fuller, *Azerbaijan at the Crossroads*, pp. 19–21.
172 Fuller, *Russian Strategy in the Transcaucasus*, p. 29.
173 *EIU Country Profile 1994–95*, p. 65.
174 Arif Useinov, 'Question of Russia's Leasing Gebele Radar Station Remains Open', *Sevodnya*, 5 May 1995, p. 19.
175 Hunter, *Post-Soviet Transition*, p. 123.
176 Aidyn Mekhtiev, 'Great Britain Promises to Support Geidar Aliyev', *Nezavisimaya Gazeta*, 2 March 1994, pp. 1, 3.
177 Baroness Cox, 'British Mercenaries for Azeri War', Letter to the editor, *The Independent*, 26 January 1994.
178 Robert Corzine, Steve Le Vine and John Lloyd, 'Moscow Still Holds Strings', *Financial Times*, 19 August 1994, p. 13. Though published much later, the letter was sent in April 1994.
179 Stephen Blank, *Energy, Economics and Security in Central Asia: Russia and its rivals*, Strategic Studies Institute, US Army War College, 10 May 1995. p. 5.
180 Blank, *Energy, Economics and Security*, p. 18.
181 Strobe Talbott, 'Promoting Democracy and Prosperity in Central Asia', address at the US–Central Asia Business Conference, Washington DC, 3 May 1994, US Department of State Dispatch, Vol. V, No. 19, 9 May 1994, p. 240.
182 'Just Too Horrible to Resist', *The Economist*, 9 September 1995, Vol. 336.
183 Steve Le Vine, 'US Stakes its Claim in Central Asia', *Financial Times*, 4 May 1995.
184 *Country Reports: Georgia, Armenia, Azerbaijan*, Economist Intelligence Unit, 2nd quarter 1995.
185 Forsythe, *The Politics of Oil*, p. 17.
186 Steve Le Vine and Bruce Clark, 'Compromise Deal Today on Caspian Oil Route', *Financial Times*, 9 October 1995.
187 Forsythe, *The Politics of Oil*, p. 18.
188 Interview with Elaine Holoboff, King's College London, 3 May 1996.
189 Blank, *Energy, Economics and Security*, p. 20.
190 Fuller, *Azerbaijan at the Crossroads*, pp. 13–5.
191 Forsythe, *The Politics of Oil*, pp. 21–3.
192 A group of experts at Moscow State University's Independent Institute of Social and Historical Problems and the Foros Foundation, 'The Caspian Intrigue', *Izvestia*, 19 October 1994.
193 Ibid.

194 Blank, *Energy, Economics and Security*, p. 18.
195 'Old Game, New Players', *The Economist*, 16 May 1992. See also Alexei Vassiliev, 'Turkey and Iran in Transcaucasia and Central Asia', in Ehteshami (ed.), *From the Gulf to Central Asia*.
196 Elmira Akhmedly, 'Istanbul has Special Relations with Baku', *Nezavisimaya Gazeta*, 15 December 1995, p. 3.
197 Roberts, *Caspian Pipelines*, pp. 41–4.
198 Goltz, 'The Hidden Russian Hand', pp. 100–1.
199 Interview with Elsan Aliev, BBC Central Asia Service, 30 July 1996.
200 Elizabeth Fuller, 'The "Near Abroad": Influence and Oil in Russian Diplomacy', *Transition*, 28 April 1995.
201 Ibid.
202 *EIU Country Report*, 4 June 1996, 2nd quarter, pp. 33–4.
203 Interview with Elsan Aliev, 30 July 1996. As no independent polls on presidential popularity are conducted in Azerbaijan, it is difficult to confirm these vague assessments.
204 Fyodor Tyunin, 'Russian Prosecutor General's Office Refuses to Extradite Ayaz Mutalibov to Azerbaijan', *Sevodnya*, 14 May 1996, pp. 16–17.
205 Ibid.
206 *EIU Country Report*, 4 June 1996, 2nd quarter, p. 35.
207 Georgy Bovt and Stanislav Tarasov, 'The Best Gift you can Give a Friend is the Head of his Enemy', *Kommersant-Daily*, 13 April 1996, p. 19.
208 'Russia Closes its Borders with Azerbaijan and Georgia', *Sevodnya*, 21 December 1994, p. 4.
209 Igor Korotchenko, 'The Storming of Grozny is Hardly Possible', *Nezavisimaya Gazeta*, 22 December 1994.
210 'Russia Closes its Borders', *Sevodnya*, 21 December 1994, p. 4.
211 *EIU Country Report*, 10 September 1995, 3rd quarter, p. 33.
212 *EIU Country Report*, 12 June 1995, 2nd quarter, p. 33.
213 *EIU Country Profile 1995–96: Georgia, Armenia, Azerbaijan*, p. 57.
214 *EIU Country Report*, 6 March 1995, 1st quarter, p. 28.
215 *EIU Country Report*, 6 November 1995, 4th quarter, p. 35.
216 Seck, *Oil and Gas Investments*, p. 28. See also Forsythe, *The Politics of Oil*, p. 34, and Gavan McDonell, *The Euro-Asian Corridor*, RIIA Post-Soviet Business Forum Paper (1995), p. 14.
217 For example, a Bulgarian journalist, who alleges to have close connections with intelligence services, claimed that Gorbachev and Shevardnadze were 'rewarded' by the German government for their decision to allow the collapse of the Berlin Wall (Interview with Alphonse Emanouiloff Max, 18 February 1995, Montevideo). Even if that were the case, no one would seriously consider the possibility that Gorbachev's policy towards Europe was driven by expectations of individual enrichment.
218 John Lloyd, 'The High-Wire Act Continues', *Financial Times*, 24 September 1994.
219 'Tilt to Armenia', *Azerbaijan International*, Summer 1995, Vol. IV, No. 2.
220 Cunningham, *Caspian Oil, An Antidote to the West's Energy Dependency on the Middle East, or an Economic Vietnam for the USA*, private report, 1995.
221 Steve Le Vine and Bruce Clark, 'Compromise deal on Caspian oil route', *Financial Times*, 9 October 1995.

222 Ibid.
223 See Rosemarie Forsythe for an account of views held by American officials. For an analysis of American government's officials' views, see John Roberts, *Caspian Pipelines*.
224 Steve Le Vine, 'US Stakes its Claim in Central Asia', *Financial Times*, 4 May 1995.
225 Andrei Kozyrev, 'Partnership or Cold Peace?', *Foreign Policy*, Summer 1995.
226 Jeffrey D. McCausland, *The CFE Treaty: a Cold War Anachronism?*, 20 March 1995.
227 Strobe Talbott, 'Promoting Democracy and Prosperity in Central Asia', address at the US–Central Asia Business Conference, Washington DC, 3 May 1994, US Department of State Dispatch, Vol. V, No. 19, 9 May 1994, p. 240.
228 Lev Klepatsky and Valery Pospelov, 'Manouevring Round the Caspian Sea', paper presented to the conference on the 'Legal Status of the Caspian Sea and Prospects for the Use of its Resources', Foreign Policy Foundation, Moscow, October 1995.
229 'Caspian Intrigue', by a group of experts at Moscow State University's Independent Institute of Social and Historical Problems and the Foros Foundation, *Izvestia*, 19 October 1994 (CDPP).
230 Fuller, 'The "Near Abroad"'.
231 'Turkish Concern over Russian Troop Levels', *Jane's Defence Weekly*, 1 May 1996, p. 9.
232 Barbara Starr, 'CFE Countries Agree to Revise Russian Limits', *Jane's Defence Weekly*, 12 June 1996, p. 5.
233 Elmira Amiraqizi, 'Russia's Foreign Policy Towards Azerbaijan', *Azerbaijan International*, Spring 1996, Vol. IV, No. 1.
234 See Boleslaw Boczek, 'NATO and the Former Warsaw Pact States', in *NATO in the Post-Cold War Era*, ed. S. Victor Papacosma and Mary Ann Heiss, Basingstoke, 1995.
235 Rob Sabhani, 'Russia Tests the US in Azerbaijan', *The Wall Street Journal*, 28 June 1994.
236 Steve Le Vine, 'Survey of Azerbaijan (2): the Great Game revisited', *Financial Times*, 7 March 1994.
237 *EIU Country Report: Georgia, Armenia, Azerbaijan*, 2nd quarter 1996.
238 'Iranians Take Up the Offer on Shakh Deniz', *Nefte Compass*, 9 May 1996.
239 For an account of the manipulative policies of the Soviet Union in Iranian Azerbaijan, see Simmonds, *Nationalism in the USSR and Eastern Europe*.
240 Alexei Vassilev, 'Turkey and Iran in Transcaucasia and Central Asia', p. 135 in *From the Gulf to Central Asia*, ed. Anoushiravan Ehteshami.
241 Hunter, *Post-Soviet Transition*.
242 'Will Azerbaijan Really Benefit from the Consortium Contract?', *Azerbaijan International*, Summer 1995, Vol. III, No. 2.
243 *EIU Country Profile 1995–96: Georgia, Armenia, Azerbaijan*. These are the latest statistics available provided by the European Bank for Reconstruction and Development (EBRD) and the World Bank.
244 Andrew Apostolou, 'The Problems of Creating Economies in Central Asia', p. 58 in *From the Gulf to Central Asia*, ed. Anoushiravan Ehteshami.

245 *EIU Country Report: Georgia, Armenia, Azerbaijan,* 2nd quarter, 1996.
246 An Azeri opposition newspaper, *Merdat,* has accused the Parliament speaker of having amassed a fortune of up to $1.5 billion from oil deals (interview with Elsan Aliev, BBC journalist, 30 July 1996). The *EIU Country Report* regularly covers this issue.
247 Mina, 'OPEC', p. 13.
248 Rob Sabhani, 'Russia Tests the US in Azerbaijan', *The Wall Street Journal,* 28 June 1994.

5
Private and National Interests in the Caspian Region*

Jean-Christophe Peuch

Eight years after the collapse of the Soviet Union, the newly independent states (NIS) of the Caspian Sea region have engaged in a lucrative cooperation with major oil corporations from all over the world. In Azerbaijan, the former Soviet republic with the most rapid development, oil projects involve more than twenty companies from twelve countries. They were worth about $30 billion at the end of 1997.[1] By contrast, Turkmenistan has lured only $600 million of Western investments in its oil and gas industry since 1991. One of the reasons put forward to explain this relatively low level is that the country was, until recently, pinning its hopes on Russia.[2] At odds with Moscow over transit fees for its natural gas shipments to Ukraine, Turkmenistan seems now determined to boost its cooperation with Western companies.[3]

True, Russia's biggest group, LUKoil, is part of several international consortia to develop oilfields in Azerbaijan and Kazakhstan.[4] But the presence of Russian private business in the Caspian basin remains well below one's expectations, given the historical and geographical links between Moscow and the Caspian region. This is due not only to the Western competition and the bad shape of the Russian economy, but also, and to a larger extent, to the fact that the political leadership has failed to push for the company's interests in the so-called 'near abroad'.

Unlike most Western countries, where private business can to a certain extent influence foreign policy, Russian companies have still to abide by what the political leadership considers its national interests.[5] As a consequence of the weakness of the Russian state, each ministry, each region, each administration, almost each individual has its own agenda. This is particularly true regarding the country's foreign policy. As we shall see, repeated disputes between ministries and a chronic lack of coordination among the country's leadership have prevented LUKoil and other Russian oil companies from developing a lucrative business around the Caspian Sea.

Despite its ambiguity, which sometimes gives it a rather chaotic character, American diplomacy is more strenuous than its Russian counterpart and has clear objectives. The Clinton administration and the US major oil corporations seem, in most cases, to act in unison. The White House and the State Department say they consider Transcaucasia and Central Asia as regions of vital interest to them. Anxious not to rely exclusively on the volatile Middle East for its oil and gas supplies, Washington claims that the Caspian area is essential in assuring the world's energy security.[6] It supports the oil-rich Azerbaijan and the tiny Transcaucasian state of Georgia which, although it has very small hydrocarbon reserves, is one of the most probable export routes for oil produced by American companies in the region. Although Washington's policy meets the interests of the major oil corporations on most of the issues, there is still one bone of contention: Iran.

Lost opportunities: Russia's foreign policy towards the Caspian states

The main trends of Russia's foreign policy are rooted in the country's former imperial status and in the military doctrine adopted in 1993. Six years after the collapse of the Soviet Union, Russia still considers itself a superpower surrounded by hostility. In 1997, the Russian Foreign Ministry saw as a top priority 'consolidating (Moscow's) role as a great power and one of the centres of the multi-polar world that is taking shape'.[7] Although the Kremlin denies it pursues a hegemonic or expansionist policy, it still considers 'territory' a synonym for 'power'. Hence the necessity to keep a military presence in Russia's former marches. Despite the ex-Soviet republics' formal independence, Moscow has army units and border guards in Tajikistan, Turkmenistan, Georgia,[8] Uzbekistan, Belarus, Armenia and Kyrgyzstan. It also has military facilities in the Ukraine, in Azerbaijan and in Kazakhstan. Of all the countries that make up the CIS, only Moldova has neither Russian soldiers nor Russian military installations on its soil.

Although the 1993 military doctrine claims that Russia does not regard any country to be its enemy, it stresses that the former frontiers of the Soviet Union are a continuing zone of security for Russia. This is particularly true concerning Transcaucasia and Central Asia, an area of traditional Russian expansion that goes back to the eighteenth and nineteenth centuries. According to a Russian foreign policy journal, 'the external borders of Central Asia are also a southern border of Russia'.[9] Chairing a Security Council meeting in August 1997, President Boris Yeltsin expressed his concern that the United States thought of Transcaucasia, a region Moscow still claims to be its legitimate backyard, as belonging to its sphere of interests.[10] As one top-ranking Russian Foreign Ministry official stated at approximately the same time, 'we are obliged to take appropriate actions to oppose attempts to elbow out Russia, to lock it within its borders, to infringe upon its legitimate interests in regions which include Transcaucasia'.[11] From a military point of view, Transcaucasia is of particular importance to Russia, for it is seen as a buffer zone to contain Turkey, a NATO member. Although they do not play a significant role in contemporary military strategies, buffer zones are still part of the conceptual tradition of Russian foreign and security policy.[12] For this reason, Moscow insists on having troops deployed along the Azerbaijan–Iran border, despite the 1990 CFCE Treaty on Conventional Forces in Europe.

For this reason also, during the years 1992–3, Russia has desperately tried to keep the former Soviet republics under its control by destabilising and ousting some of the most nationalist regimes that appeared in the region after the collapse of the empire. It therefore supported separatist movements in the republics that were most reluctant to join the CIS.[13] This is what happened in Tajikistan where Russia, acting through Uzbekistan, helped Imomali Rakhmonov seize power in 1992, forcing the country's democratic and Islamic leaders to take refuge in Afghanistan. This is what happened the same year in pro-Romanian Moldova, where Russia shipped arms and mercenaries to the Transdniester Russian-speaking separatists. This is also what happened in Azerbaijan in 1993, when the pro-Turkish, openly anti-Russian President Abulfaz Elchibey was overthrown by a military coup led by Suret Huseinov. The aim of the coup, plotted in Moscow, was to put former President Ayaz Mutalibov, the pro-Russian predecessor to Elchibey, back on the saddle. But Moscow's initial plans failed and the political events of June 1993 ended with former Politburo member Heydar Aliev seizing power.[14] Simultaneously, Russia unsuccessfully tried to force the CIS countries to join a new ruble zone created in 1993.

This interfering policy did not have the results Moscow was expecting. On the one hand, the CIS leaders have come to mistrust Russia and resist its attempts to recreate its former hegemony. On the other hand, those countries that had the biggest economic potential – Georgia and the hydrocarbon-rich republics of Azerbaijan, Kazakhstan and Turkmenistan – have embarked on a lucrative collaboration with the West, Turkey, China and Iran.

Russian foreign policy experts stress the need to put an end to what they call the US 'Drang Nach Osten'. Complaining that Moscow has suffered a threefold defeat since Azerbaijan granted the AIOC international consortium the right to develop Caspian oil deposits, some suggest the Kremlin should destabilise Georgia and Azerbaijan by encouraging the Lezghian, Talysh and Adzhar separatist movements.[15] Others say that Russia should use all possible means to prevent construction of the Baku–Ceyhan route. This includes 'political and economic pressure on Russia's neighbours, diplomatic struggle, information and psychological influence on ethnic Russians living beyond Russia's boundaries, support to national liberation movements in Transcaucasia and Middle East, the closing of navigation on the Volga–Don fluvial system, etc'.[16] Voices at the International Affairs committee of the State Duma, the Lower House of the Russian Parliament, call for the creation of an 'anti-Western' front in the CIS.[17]

Despite a formal alliance with Armenia and more fragile ties with Iran, Russia is today isolated and seems on the verge of being left out of the 'Great Game' that is taking place in its southern borderlands. Facing huge military losses against the Armenian separatists of its Nagorno-Karabakh enclave, Azerbaijan eventually joined the CIS in 1993. The following year, Aliev also agreed to renegotiate the terms of the 'deal of the century', letting LUKoil get a 10 per cent stake in AIOC to develop Azeri, Chirag and, later, Güneshli. But, for Moscow, this was a Pyrrhic victory. Following in Elchibey's footsteps, the new Azerbaijani President did not give up cooperation with the West and offered other deposits to European, American, Japanese and Middle Eastern companies. Simultaneously, Russia continued shipping tanks and other weapons to the Karabakh separatists, while officially co-sponsoring peace talks between Azerbaijan and Armenia.

In October 1997, an old pipeline running from Baku to the Russian Black Sea port of Novorrossisk was reopened, making Azerbaijan an independent oil exporter for the first time. But Aliev seems determined to ship further oil output to Western markets bypassing Russia. Along with the Baku–Ceyhan outlet, three other routes are currently under study. One sees the renovation of a 986 km (616 mile) pipeline between the Azeri capital and the Georgian port of Batumi, in the autonomous republic of Adzharia. The crude would then be shipped by tankers to the Turkish Black Sea port of Samsun and, from there, pumped through a pipeline to Ceyhan. Provided an agreement on the Kyapaz oilfield is reached,[18] Azerbaijan could also build an underwater connection to a proposed 1670 km (1040 mile) oil pipeline linking Turkmenistan to Pakistan. Finally, Iran recently suggested building a pipeline between Baku and Tabriz and connecting it to its national oil transport network.[19] Plans to export Azeri oil directly to Kazakhstan and Ukraine were also examined.

Anxious to break free from its dependence on Russian outlets for its natural gas exports, Turkmenistan envisages giant pipeline projects to Pakistan, India, China, Iran, Bulgaria and Turkey.[20] Turkmen President Saparmurad Niyazov is also considering ways to sell cheap natural gas to Germany, currently Europe's main importer of Russian gas.[21] For the same reasons as Turkmenistan, Kazakhstan – a country where LUKoil is also represented[22] – is looking at future pipelines to China, Turkey, Iran and Ukraine for its crude oil and/or natural gas output. Needless to say, all these routes would bypass Russia. True, a planned pipeline running from the Tengiz giant oilfield in western Kazakhstan to Novorrossisk exists and a final agreement on this was signed in May 1997 after five years of laborious negotiations. But the Caspian Pipeline Consortium (CPC) project is threatened by endless ownership disputes among its members and by the greediness of Russian regions and autonomous republics, which want high transit fees in return for allowing the pipeline to cross their territory.[23] Should this project fail, Russia would lose an estimated $33.9 billion revenue in transit fees and dividends.

In October 1997, Georgia, Ukraine, Azerbaijan and Moldova created an informal alignment known by its acronym: GUAM. Aimed at developing common energy transportation projects among its members, this group was perceived by decision-makers in Moscow as 'the first serious attempt to create an organised dissidence within the CIS'.[24] It appeared at the eve of the Chisinau Commonwealth summit, where Russia was severely chastised by its neighbours for having failed to transform the CIS into a genuine and viable common market. Another group, known as the Economic Cooperation Organization (ECO), is made up of Kazakhstan, Uzbekistan, Tajikistan, Kyrgyzstan, Turkmenistan, Iran, Pakistan, Turkey and Afghanistan. Chairing a meeting of the organisation, held in May 1998 in his former capital Almaty, Kazakh President Nursultan Nazarbayev mentioned three pipeline projects – one to Iran, one to Pakistan, and one under the Caspian Sea to Azerbaijan – as meeting Kazakhstan's 'strategic interests'. He qualified the CPC project as simply 'feasible'.[25] Finally, the TraCECA (Transport Corridor Europe-Caucasus-Asia) project, sponsored by the United States and the European Union, sees the creation of a major route for transportation of oil and other goods from Asia to Europe. Like other regional projects, it bypasses Russia.

The most common view among experts is that Moscow has pushed for the interests of its private oil companies in the Caspian region, particularly LUKoil's. Some energy specialists even speculate that the group should be considered a 'diplomatic flagship' for the rest of the Russian oil industry.[26] Others argue that LUKoil and Foreign Minister Yevgeny Primakov generally agree on what Russian diplomacy should be.[27] Nonetheless, recent history shows the opposite.

In June 1994, the Russian Foreign Ministry – then headed by Andrei Kozyrev – sent a note to the British Embassy in Baku, claiming that the treaties concluded between Russia and Persia in 1921 and between the Soviet Union and Iran in 1940 were still in force. This means, diplomats said, that the Caspian Sea should remain divided into two zones, regardless of the existence of three newly independent states (Azerbaijan, Turkmenistan, Kazakhstan) around the Sea. Claiming that the Caspian should be regarded as a lake and not as a sea, Moscow said that its resource development should be the responsibility of all riparian states and, therefore, should be developed in common. Azerbaijan objected that the treaties should not be binding on states that had not signed them. Clearly aimed at stalling the development of hydrocarbon fields in the Azerbaijani sector of the sea,[28] the Russian legal offensive came at a time when LUKoil, already granted a stake in the Chirag and Azeri projects, was negotiating the right to develop Güneshli and Kyapaz. It also came at a time when the Milli Meclis (parliament) in Baku had still to approve LUKoil's participation in the development of Azerbaijan's oil resources. The move was a complete surprise both for LUKoil and the Azerbaijani national oil company (SOCAR). The Russian group appealed to Fuel and Energy Minister Yuri Shafranik and Prime Minister Viktor Chernomyrdin. Also caught unawares by the diplomats' initiative, the head of government could do nothing but to deplore what he laconically called a 'lack of coordination' between two of his ministries.[29] It was not before 1996 – when Primakov succeeded Kozyrev – that the Foreign Ministry agreed to soften its stance on the Caspian legal status and say the dispute should be settled on a consensual basis. But this was not the end of trouble for LUKoil.

On 4 July, 1997, LUKoil, Rosneft and SOCAR signed a memorandum of understanding, which gave the two Russian companies the right to enter into a production-sharing agreement to explore and develop the Kyapaz-Serdar oil deposit.[30] The document was signed in Moscow by the then Russian Fuel and Energy Minister Boris Nemtsov and the Azeri

President. A month later, on 4 August, Rosneft unexpectedly said it would renounce the deal and, the following day, the Russian Foreign Ministry announced that LUKoil had also withdrawn from the competition. Two days later, on 7 August, Yeltsin welcomed Niyazov in the Kremlin and annulled the deal. Although LUKoil refused to comment on the Kremlin's decision, the Foreign Ministry said the company had supposedly promised not to start any new project in the Caspian basin without prior consultations with Russian diplomats.[31] The Russian President did not elaborate his decision to cancel the Kyapaz deal. But the Kremlin's U-turn came at a time when Gazprom was negotiating a stake in the CentGas consortium, leading contender to build a giant gas pipeline from Turkmenistan to Pakistan, and possibly to India. Although Ashgabat had already agreed to let Gazprom have 10 per cent in the deal, the Russian gas company reportedly wanted a bigger stake. It was also considering participating in the development of some of Turkmenistan's gas fields.[32]

Moreover, the company obstinately refused to compromise over transit fees and selling price for Turkmen gas supplies to Ukraine.[33] As a result, Gazprom's participation in CentGas was cancelled.

In early July 1998, Russia further alienated Turkmenistan by signing a separate deal with Kazakhstan on the Caspian Sea. Moscow and Astana agreed to divide the northern part of the sea-bed, while the Caspian waters will remain under common jurisdiction. If this agreement presents certain advantages for Moscow – it could stop further militarisation of the Caspian by preventing riparian states from deploying border guards in the middle of the sea – it could also have negative consequences for Russian strategic interests in the region. As soon as Russia announced it was close to an agreement with Kazakhstan already in April 1998, Ashgabat retaliated by promoting the so-called 'transCaspian' route to pump its future natural gas output to Azerbaijan, Georgia and Turkey through a $2.8 billion underwater pipeline. Along with Turkmenistan, Iran refused to endorse the legitimacy of the Russian–Kazakh treaty. There is also a risk that Iran, eager to develop its cooperation with Western oil companies and become a major route for oil and gas produced in Central Asia, might conclusively turn aside from its Russian ally. A 200 km (125 mile) gas pipeline running from the Turkmen Korpedzhe gas field, near Nebit-Dag, to the Iranian town of Kord Kuy was inaugurated on 29 December 1997.[34] Shortly after the separate agreement on the Caspian Sea was signed in Moscow, Teheran announced it had sealed with Turkmenistan a $25 million contract to drill four oilwells off Turkmenbashy (former Krasnovodsk) over the next eighteen months.[35]

But for LUKoil, Russian presence in the Caspian basin would be close to nil. The company, which started considering ambitious expansion plans outside Russia shortly after its creation in 1992, has succeeded where diplomats were inefficient and, it must be said, despite the professional diplomats. 'Oil corporations act . . . ahead of most others Russian political actors, therefore generating a new political system', LUKoil's spokesman wrote in 1997.[36] 'It is not the Russian government that defends the interests of the national companies on foreign markets but, on the contrary, the big firms that often make the life of the diplomats easier', echoed one Russian commentator.[37] The fact that LUKoil chairman Vagit Alekperov is a native Azerbaijani was perhaps instrumental in ensuring the group's successful negotiations with Baku. One thing is certain: the company is seeking profits where they are most accessible. Alekperov admitted recently that he found it more difficult to work in the former Soviet Union, particularly in Russia, than in other countries.[38]

The US search for stability and containment

The major US corporations showed interest in the vast Caspian hydrocarbon reserves immediately after the collapse of the Soviet Union. In Azerbaijan, negotiations on the 'deal of the century' started under Mutalibov, continued under Elchibey, and were successfully completed under Aliev. American oil companies working in Central Asia and Transcaucasia include Chevron, Pennzoil, Exxon, Mobil, Texaco, Amoco, Union Oil Company of California (Unocal), Enron, Schlumberger and Atlantic Richfield Company. Investments in those countries are expected to generate billions of dollars in oil services contracts. The United States is today strongly committed to backing up the interests of its companies working in the Caspian basin, as long as this support does not interfere with its domestic and international constraints.

It was a while before the United States, anxious not to alienate Moscow, gave its full support to American oil corporations. Clearly worried by the unpredictability of Russia's foreign policy, Washington was first anxious not to be seen as over-enthusiastic in its support of American oil companies whose activities in the region were obviously in line with some of the Transcaucasian and Central Asian states as opposed to official Russian policy. The presidents of Georgia, Kazakhstan and Turkmenistan were successively invited to Washington during the years 1997–8. These visits occasioned the signing of new oil deals with US companies. Washington's aim in the Caspian basin is twofold.

On the one hand, it wants to ensure for itself safe access to the underwater hydrocarbon reserves and, therefore, to protect US investments in the region. On the other hand, it wants to create some sort of 'neutral zone' bordering Russia, Iran, Afghanistan and China. Hence the necessity to provide peace and stability in an area which is considered of vital importance for US short-term strategic interests. As Deputy Secretary James Talbott said: 'If economic and political reform in the countries of the Caucasus and Central Asia does not succeed – if internal and cross-border conflicts simmer and flare – the region could become a breeding ground for terrorism, a hotbed of religious and political extremism, and a battleground for outright war. It would matter profoundly to the United States if that were to happen in an area that sits on as much as 200 billion barrels of oil. That is yet another reason why conflict resolution must be job number one for US policy in the region: it is both a prerequisite for and an accompaniment to energy development.'[39]

Along with Russia and France, the United States is a member of the so-called Minsk Group which, under the aegis of the Organisation for Security and Cooperation in Europe (OSCE), has laboured to find a peaceful solution to the conflict between Azerbaijan and its breakaway western enclave of Nagorno-Karabakh. Despite Elchibey's promises to gain a swift military victory against the Armenian separatists, the Azerbaijani national army suffered huge losses in 1992–3. By that time, Armenian forces, well-armed and well-equipped by Russia, had occupied up to 20 per cent of Azerbaijan's territory. Washington now insists that Armenian troops should withdraw from Azerbaijan in return for a greater autonomy. The proposed US plan also sees the deployment of international peacekeeping forces along the Lachin corridor, which links Karabakh to Armenia. Amidst protests from the Karabakh 'government', Armenian President Levon Ter-Petrosyan first signalled in September 1997 that he could agree to this plan.[40] Accused by his opponents, led by Prime Minister Robert Kocharyan, of pursuing a 'defeatist policy' that endangered the security of both Armenia and Nagorno-Karabakh, Ter-Petrosyan was forced to resign on 3 February 1998. A hard-liner on the Karabakh issue, Kocharyan won the early presidential election called a month later. No doubt the United States hopes that regional energy projects would help boost the peace process by forcing Armenia to break free from the trade embargo.[41] In September 1998, Armenian Prime Minister Armen Darbinyan went to Baku to attend an international conference devoted to the TraCECA project. Although he did not make any tangible progress towards resolving the conflict, representatives of the Minsk Group saw enough encouraging signs in this visit to start a new round of shuttle diplomacy between Yerevan, Baku and Stepanakert.[42]

Regardless of the human rights situation in Azerbaijan, Washington strongly supports Aliev's regime.[43] Until recently, the US administration, which has obligated more than $22 billion in overall assistance to the eight states of Transcaucasus and Central Asia, has seen its ability to provide assistance to Azerbaijan limited by Section 907 of the Freedom Support Act. This law, adopted in 1992 by the US Congress under pressure from the Armenian lobby in Washington, was initially meant to help Yerevan overcome Azerbaijan's embargo during the war in Nagorno-Karabakh. Under the pressure of the Azeri lobby in Washington,[44] the State Department and the White House eventually came to the conclusion that Section 907 hindered US energy diplomacy in the Caspian Sea region and, therefore, should be repealed.[45] In 1997, US Deputy State Secretary Talbott said times had changed and Section 907 was no longer necessary 'because it has made it impossible for (the United States) to provide the Azerbaijanis with assistance on elections, economic reforms, energy development, and in other areas where it is in our national interest to do so'.[46] For US companies, repealing Section 907 was seen as an essential step to boost Washington's interests in the region. According to C. D. Sabathier, president of Mobil Oil New exploration and Producing Ventures for the CIS and Caspian regions, providing Aliev's regime with financial assistance would help consolidate 'Azerbaijan's prosperous secular government' and, thus, protect US investments in this country.[47] Even before the House Appropriations Committee agreed to lift Section 907 in September 1998, Washington used the international financial institutions to leverage its economic assistance to Baku.[48] The United States wants export outlets for Azeri crude to be as diversified as possible. Speaking at a Caspian conference in November 1997, then Energy Secretary Federico Pena said his country welcomed the reopening of the Baku–Novorrossisk pipeline put into service a few days earlier. But he stressed that the Clinton administration would definitely prefer the Baku–Supsa–Ceyhan route as the main export corridor.[49] This route is also the preferred option for US companies working in Azerbaijan. 'This route, as far as Amoco is concerned, is the ideal route, if it can be made commercially viable, and we are consulting with all the parties concerned to try and find ways to bring that about,' Charles Pitman, chairman and president of Amoco-Eurasian Petroleum Company stated two days after Pena.[50]

Although Washington's policy coincides with the interests of the major oil companies on most issues, there is still one case of disagreement: Iran. Despite growing pressure from US oil companies to lift the embargo upon Teheran, the Clinton administration is still reluctant to soften its stance towards the Iranian regime. Although former Culture Minister Sayed Mohammad Khatami, a reputed moderate, won the presidential elections in May 1997, officials from the State Department keep saying that the Iran–Libya Sanctions Act (ILSA), adopted in 1996, is still necessary. Officially viewing Teheran and Tripoli as supporters of international terrorism, Washington has shaped the region into a system of 'dual containment', which has still to prove its efficiency.[51] Another reason US officials put forward is that Iran professes a fundamentalist Islam. But this has not prevented the White House from having political and economic relations with countries that obviously belong to one of those two categories (Syria, Saudi Arabia for example). The real reason behind the US policy towards Teheran is perhaps that the White House is reluctant to see Iran turn into a regional power which could pose a potential military threat to Israel and compete with Turkey in the Middle Eastern oil market.[52] Another concern for Washington could be the Iranian–Chinese military and nuclear partnership.[53] Fear of a potential Teheran–Beijing axis could explain why the Clinton administration initially said it would not oppose the Turkmenistan–Iran gas pipeline project before it changed its mind and started lobbying the so-called 'transCaspian' route.

The ILSA officially requires Washington to take action against non-US firms that invest $20 million or more a year in Iran's oil and gas sector. This was not the first US law to impose economic sanctions upon Iran. In January 1984, the Foreign Assistance Act severely limited business contacts between American and Iranian companies. For this reason, Conoco was forced to give up the multi-million dollar Sirri oil and gas project in January 1995, opening the way for France's Total to negotiate with Iran. Senators then started lobbying the US Congress to extend commercial restrictions to non-US firms and vote for a new legislation based on extra-territoriality.

When it was adopted, the ILSA clearly met the interests of US companies. Now things are quite different. Iran wants to be the main export corridor for Central Asian oil and gas. Turkmenistan and Kazakhstan, as well as foreign investors in the region, see Iran as the shortest and cheapest route to Europe and Asia.[54] The pro-Azeri lobby in Washington is trying to impress on the Clinton administration that the Iranian embargo is no longer profitable and insists that the ILSA should be repealed. 'American long-range interests in Eurasia would be better served by abandoning the existing US objections to closer Turkish-Iranian economic cooperation, especially in the construction of new pipelines from Azerbaijan and Turkmenistan', wrote Zbigniew Brzezinski, former Assistant to the US President Jimmy Carter for National Security Affairs, now an adviser to Amoco.[55] Meanwhile the ILSA has shown it was totally inefficient. In September 1997, Total, Gazprom and Malaysia's Petronas Dagang Bhd signed a $2 billion deal to develop the vast natural gas reserves of the South Pars deposit in southern Iran. Amidst protests from Russia and European countries, the White House has given up the idea of imposing sanctions on the signatories. Responsible for a projected gas pipeline running from Turkmenistan and Iran, the Anglo-Dutch group Royal Dutch/Shell decided to open an office in Teheran. It was soon followed by British Petroleum. Other possible projects in Iran include France's Elf Aquitaine and Italy's Agip.[56] Time is short for the American oil corporations willing to do business in the Caspian basin. Attending an oil conference in Dubai in 1998, Conoco's chief executive Archie Durham described the ILSA not only as being inefficient, but also as doing 'devastating harm' to US ties with its allies. Therefore, he said, his company would go ahead with its cooperation with Iran.[57]

The question is whether the United States will agree to adopt a softer stance on Iran and, consequently, meet the long-term interests of its major oil companies working in the Caspian area.[58] After Khatami first urged a cultural dialogue between the American and Iranian peoples in January 1998, the White House initially gave encouraging signs. In June 1998, US President Bill Clinton called for a 'genuine reconciliation' with Iran and said the country was changing for the better. Teheran responded by calling for deeds rather than words. The Iranian leadership wants the US to lift the freeze on its foreign assets, stop supporting the Iraq-based People's Mujahedeen opposition movement and 'publicly apologise to the Iranian nation for its 50 year long erroneous policy towards Iran'.[59] During his first visit to the United Nations headquarters in New York, in September 1998, Khatami said he also wanted Washington to stop trying to exclude his country from the export routes for Caspian hydrocarbons.[60] Still, the participation of State Secretary Madeleine Albright and Iranian Foreign Minister Kamal Kharrazi in an eight-nation meeting on Afghanistan that took place in parallel to this visit was one of the highest level contacts between the two countries since they broke off diplomatic relations in 1979. In the meantime, European oil companies are taking advantage of the official absence of the major US companies from the Iranian market to negotiate lucrative projects with Teheran. Washington's policy towards Iran puts American companies 'in a distinct competitive disadvantage in those parts of the world where energy companies are allowed'.[61]

Although not part of the Caspian basin, Afghanistan is a striking example of symbiosis of interests between the US administration and private oil corporations. This country is a required export route for Turkmen gas to the East. Led by US Unocal, the CentGas consortium[62] sees the construction of a 1271 km (790 mile) pipeline from the Dauletabad gas field in south-eastern Turkmenistan to Karachi and Multan in Pakistan, with a possible extension to India. Unocal is also a contender for another giant project, which envisages an oil pipeline from the Chardzhou Turkmen deposit to Pakistan, roughly parallel to the CentGas project. Despite the war in Afghanistan, the CentGas project is still on – at least on paper – and Niyazov would like to see this export route completed by the year 2000. The Taleban fundamentalists, who controlled three-quarters of the Afghan territory by the end of 1998, have given their go-ahead to the project, although they still have not signed an official agreement with the consortium leadership.[63]

During the 1980s the United States armed, equipped and trained some of the most fanatic Sunni Islamic groups of the Afghan resistance against the Soviet army. Among them were fighters of a group headed by Osama Bin Laden, the Saudi-born millionnaire seen today in Washington as the man who masterminded recent attacks on US embassies in Kenya and Tanzania.[64] Those groups were controlled by Pakistani secret services and funded by Saudi Arabia. For Washington, this logistic support was seen as an essential element of its containment policy towards Iran and the Soviet Union. No wonder then that the State Department welcomed the fall of Kabul in the hands of the Taleban in September 1996 as a 'positive step'.[65] Washington saw in the victory of the Islamic students a means to further contain the Iranian Shiite influence in the region. It was also seen as opening the way to the creation of a centralised government in Afghanistan, a prerequisite to the CentGas project, in which Pakistan and Saudi Arabia are also represented. Unocal is said to have provided the Taleban with 'humanitarian aid', notably in the form of fax machines.[66] The company's board also expressed support to the Taleban forces shortly after they gained control over the Afghan capital. 'If the Taleban lead to stability and international recognition, then it is positive. I understand Pakistan has already recognized the (Taleban) government. If the USA follows, it will lead the way to international lending agencies coming in', stated one of Unocal's top executives.[67] The Clinton administration has refused to recognise the new

Afghan leadership, officially because of its poor human rights record and its widespread opium production. Nonetheless, a Taleban delegation met with State Department officials in Washington in December 1997. At the end of the meeting, organised at the instigation of Unocal, the United States confirmed its support to the CentGas project and stressed the need to put an end to the civil war.[68] When Iran, which supports the Shiite faction in the anti-Taleban coalition, started building up forces on its eastern border and threatened to retaliate for the alleged massacre of Shiite Muslims in the Afghan towns of Mazar-i-Sharif and Bamiyan, the US administration urged all Afghanistan's neighbours – especially Pakistan, the Taleban's key regional supporter – not to intervene militarily. The United States, Pakistan and Unocal obviously hope the Sunni fundamentalists would eventually gain control over the totality of Afghanistan.[69]

Conclusion

Looking retrospectively at Russia's foreign policy towards the Caspian states, one is surprised to note that the interests of oil companies were of little concern to the Kremlin. Obviously private business is not perceived by the Russian political leadership as a potential auxiliary for foreign policy. Nor is oil considered as a possible source of revenues for the country's ailing economy.[70] It is merely a tool in the hands of diplomats eager to maintain Russia's hegemony on its former marches. True, the appointment of financial tycoon Boris Berezovsky at the head of the CIS executive secretariat, in April 1998, first signalled a change in Russia's policy towards its neighbours. A champion of economic integration through private capital,[71] Berezovsky is said to lobby Caspian states, countries where privatisation is still to come, to give access to Russian companies owned by the so-called 'oligarchs'. He reportedly acts as a go-between in a proposed Ukraine–AIOC–Azerbaijan triangular deal.[72] But the financial crisis that hit Russia in the summer of 1998 may well prevent for some time private banks from developing ambitious projects in the 'near abroad'.[73] Russia could have acted wisely by developing new projects, alone or with foreign companies working around the Caspian. Instead of relying on its oil corporations, it has chosen to block initiatives and stall progress in the area. Russia has missed an opportunity to play a significant role in the development of the Caspian resources. Commenting on the Kremlin's support to Iraq in late 1997, one leading Russian newspaper complained that, instead of dealing with oil and gas projects, Moscow was playing 'the geopolitical games of a decade ago, as if (it) was still a superpower'. 'As a rule its victories in this sphere are dubious and the losses suffered by Russian companies are considerable', it added.[74] As we see, this is also true for the Caspian region.

Unlike their Russian counterparts, which have to abide by the neo-imperial trend of Kremlin diplomacy, private oil companies in the United States have a certain degree of influence over Washington's diplomacy. Even if this influence should not be exaggerated, it has already brought some results. Not so long ago, US companies part of AIOC were said to be somehow frustrated by their government's policy towards Azerbaijan. They urged the Clinton administration to invite the Azerbaijani president to Washington and to lift Section 907 of the Freedom Support Act.[75] No doubt the Congress decision to repeal the law will open the way for Aliev's visit, if he wins the October 1998 presidential elections. As for Iran, constant pressures from US private oil corporations have already convinced the White House to soften its stance towards this country. Washington is certainly aware that refusing dialogue would strengthen Khatami's conservative foes within the Iranian leadership. It would also stimulate the nuclear cooperation between Teheran and Moscow, and between Teheran and Beijing. Finally, it would deprive US private oil companies of another lucrative market in the region.

Notes

* This is a revised version of an article previously published in *The Fletcher Forum of World Affairs*, Vol. 2, No. 2, Summer/Fall 1998.

1 Expected investments in 1998 were targeted at $9 billion in new contracts, *Reuters*, 19 May 1998.

2 *Russkii Telegraf*, 13 March 1998.

3 Turkmen officials claimed they expected up to $951 million in 1998 from Western countries, partly in the form of loans, *Interfax*, 23 January 1998.

4 The company has already invested $145 million in Azerbaijan and was planning to pour in another $90 million in 1998.

5 The first attempt to define what Russia's national interests should be was made only in December 1997. See 'Kontseptsiya natsional'noi bezopasnosti Rossiiskoi Federatsii', *Diplomaticheskii Vestnik*, No. 2, February 1998.

6 'The United States considers the Caspian area a major, important area for America's national security, but also for the world,' the new Energy Secretary Bill Richardson was recently quoted as saying. *Reuters*, 14 September 1998.

7 'Foreign Policy of Russia in 1996 and 1997', *International Affairs*, No. 2, 1997. This policy paper was published in Washington and prepared by a group of experts from the Russian Foreign Ministry.

8 In June 1998, Moscow and Tbilisi signed an agreement handing over the protection of the Georgian border to Georgian soldiers. The withdrawal of Russian troops should be completed in 1999. 'Gruzii rossiiskie pogranichniki bol'she ne nuzhny', *Segodnya*, 2 July 1998.

9 Sergei Razov, 'New Developments in Central Asia', *International Affairs*, No. 3, 1997.
10 *Reuters*, 20 August 1997.
11 A. Zaitsev, 'Russia and Transcaucasia', *International Affairs*, Vol. 43, No. 5, 1997.
12 Roland Goetz, 'Political Spheres of Interest in the Southern Caucasus and in Central Asia', *Aussen Politik*, Vol. 48, No. 3, 1997.
13 Support to separatist movements for diplomatic purposes is a recurrent trend in Russia's foreign policy throughout history. See John P. LeDonne, *The Russian Empire and the World (1700–1917). The Geopolitics of Expansion and Containment*, New York: Oxford University Press, 1997.
14 Rasul Guliyev, 'Pravleniye Geydara Aliyeva zakontchitsya v etom godu', *Moskovskie Novosti*, 21–28 June 1998. For a detailed description of the coup, see Elizabeth Fuller, 'Azerbaijan's June Revolution', *RFE/RL Research Report*, Vol. 2, No. 32, 13 August 1993. Huseinov eventually fled to Russia and was not handed over to the Azerbaijani authorities before March 1997.
15 'SNG: Nachalo ili konets istorii?' *Nezavisimaya Gazeta*, 26 March 1997. Although this report is anonymous, it is commonly believed that its authors are Andronik Migranyan, a former adviser to Soviet Presidents Mikhail Gorbachev and Boris Yeltsin, and Konstantin Zatulin, a former member of the Lower House of the Russian Parliament, now a close associate to Moscow Mayor Yuri Luzhkov.
16 'Kaspiiskii global'nyi pas'yans i rossiiskie interesy', *NG-Sodruzhestvo*, No. 4, 1998, supplement to *Nezavisimaya Gazeta*, 22 April 1998. This report was prepared by experts from the Institute of CIS countries, a think-tank headed by Zatulin.
17 See, for example, Alexei Mitrofanov, 'Russia's New Geopolitics', and Alexei Podberyozkin, 'Russia's New Path', both translated from Russian, *Strengthening Democratic Institutions Project* (John F. Kennedy School of Government, Harvard University, July 1998). Mitrofanov is a prominent member of the far-right Liberal Democratic Party (LDPR). Podberyozkin is a close associate of Communist leader Gennadii Zyuganov.
18 Azerbaijan and Turkmenistan both claim ownership rights over the Kyapaz (Serdar, in Turkmen) offshore oil deposit.
19 *Reuters*, 13 August 1998.
20 About 85 per cent of Turkmen gas exports go to European markets through Russia.
21 'Gazprom toropitsya v Turtsiyu', *Ekspert*, 8 September 1997.
22 The Russian company is part of the Karachaganak onshore gas project and is a member of the international consortium granted development rights over the Tengiz offshore oilfield. It also has a 50 per cent stake in the Kumkol deposit.
23 ''Trio' igralo na trube', *Novoye Vremya*, No. 37, 1997; 'Kogda potechet Kazakhstanskaya neft'?' *Kompaniya*, 19 March 1998.
24 Andrei Zagorsky, Vice-Rector of the Moscow State Institute of International Relations (MGIMO). Author interview, 7 July 1998.
25 *Reuters*, 11 May 1998.
26 Yevgeny Khartukov, general director of the Moscow International Center for Petroleum Business Studies, quoted in *Reuters*, 15 December 1997.

27 Yakov Pappe, 'Neftyanaya i gazovaya diplomatiya Rossii', *Pro et Contra*, Vol. 2, No. 3, summer 1997.

28 As the president of Caspian Energy Consulting, also an adviser to US Amoco, recalls, 'Russian officials have come into the (AIOC) offices in London and threatened the consortium, saying, "You are working here illegally"'. S. Rob Sobhani, 'The United States, Iran, Russia, and Turkey: the Struggle for Azerbaijan', *Demokratizatsiya*, Vol. 6, No. 1, winter 1998.

29 *Reuters*, 12 October 1994.

30 The field is located 104 km (65 miles) from the Turkmen coast and 184 km (115 miles) from Azerbaijan's littoral. Known as Promezhutochnoye under the Soviet Union, it was renamed Serdar ('The Leader') in 1991 in honour of the Turkmen president.

31 'Chernyi peredel Kaspiya', *Ekspert*, 11 August 1997.

32 *Interfax*, 30 January 1998; 'Turkmeniya perekryla gaz Gazpromu', *Kommersant*, 6 February 1998.

33 Gas supplies to Ukraine came to an halt on 25 March 1997, leaving the Turkmen economy on the verge of paralysis. Turkmen gas exports through Russia totalled 25 billion cubic metres (bcm) in 1996, down from an average 90 bcm a year under the Soviet times. This sharp decline is due to high transit fees imposed by Gazprom, which regularly diverts gas from European countries to insolvent former Soviet republics.

34 Iran would eventually receive 12 bcm a year of Turkmen gas.

35 *Reuters*, 16 August 1998. Iran and Turkmenistan are also linked by an oil swap agreement similar to the one that was signed in 1996 by Teheran and Astana.

36 Alexander Vasilenko, 'Rossiiskie neftyanye kompanii i politika v perekhodnyi period', Moscow, *Lesar*, 1997, quoted in Yakov Pappe, op. cit.

37 'Gosdep SshA ugrozhayet Gazpromu', *Nezavisimaya Gazeta*, 17 October 1997.

38 'Neftyanoi "sprut" Vagit Alekperov', *Argumenty i Fakty*, No. 50, December 1997.

39 US Deputy Secretary James Talbott, 'A Farewell to Flashman: American Policy in the Caucasus and Central Asia', Address at the Johns Hopkins School of Advanced International Studies, Baltimore, Maryland, 21 July 1997, *US Department of State Dispatch*, Vol. 8, No. 6, July 1997.

40 V. G. Mitayev, 'Karabakhskii konflikt v kontekste mezhdunarodnykh otnoshenij', in *Armenija: problemy nezavisimogo razvitija*, Russian Institute for Strategic Studies (Moscow, 1998).

41 The State Department wishes Armenia would eventually join the GUAM.

42 *Reuters*, 16 September 1998.

43 In February 1998, the Milli Meclis abolished the death penalty at Aliev's request. The move was obviously motivated by Azerbaijan's desire to join the Council of Europe, which has coaxed prospective members to eliminate the death penalty within three years after their admission. There are currently more than 100 convicts on death row in Azerbaijani jails.

44 This lobby is made up of former top US officials, many of whom now work as consultants to oil companies involved in the Caspian development. Among them are former National Security Advisers Zbigniew Brzezinski and Brent Scowcroft; former White House Chief of Staff John Sununu; former Secretary of Defense Richard Cheney; former Secretary of State James A. Baker; former Secretary of Treasury Lloyd Bentsen; former Deputy Energy Secretary William

White; and former Assistant Secretary of Defense Richard Perle. Douglas Blum, 'Sustainable Development and the New Oil Boom: Cooperative and Competitive Outcomes in the Caspian Sea', *Program on New Approaches to Russian Security,* Working Paper Series No. 4, Davis Center for Russian Studies, Harvard University, May 1998.

45 Meeting with Aliev in early 1998, Texaco's Senior Vice-President Robert Black pleaded his company could lead lobbying efforts in Washington to back aid to Azerbaijan. *Intercon,* 13 February 1998.

46 James Talbott, op. cit.

47 See Ilkham Aliev, 'Azerbaijan: The New Source of Energy of the 21st Century', *Strengthening Democratic Institutions Project, Caucasus and the Caspian Seminar Series,* John F. Kennedy School of Government, Harvard University, 21 November 1997.

48 In December 1997, the International Monetary Fund (IMF) approved a loan worth $64 million to support economic reforms in Azerbaijan.

49 US Energy Federico Pena, 'Remarks at US–Russian Business Council Conference Regarding the Caspian Sea', Washington, DC, *Federal News Service,* 19 November 1997.

50 Ilkham Aliyev, op. cit. Amoco, which holds a 17.01 per cent stake in AIOC, now says projected costs should be reduced considerably.

51 See Michael Barry, 'Washington-Téhéran: De l'endiguement à l'enlisement', *Politique Internationale,* No. 76, summer, 1997.

52 'We oppose transportation of (Caspian) oil through Iran. It is bad for us and for other littoral states. We do not want to see Iran acquire a dominant position on the world energy market', one top State Department official stated in early 1998. Deputy to US Ambassador to the NIS countries Victoria Nulan, *US–Russian Relations Now that the Honeymoon is Over,* talk delivered at the Davis Center for Russian Studies, Harvard University, 6 February 1998.

53 Teheran and Beijing have signed several agreements on military and nuclear cooperation. In September 1997 China said it could participate in the construction of an oil pipeline between Kazakhstan and Iran.

54 Experts generally agree that Caspian hydrocarbon reserves could be brought to those markets through Iran at one-third of the cost and in one-third of the project time of any alternative route, including Russia. *Reuters,* 9 November 1997.

55 Zbigniew Brzezinski, 'A Geostrategy for Eurasia', *Foreign Affairs* Vol. 76, No. 5, September–October 1997.

56 *Reuters,* 3 April 1998, quoting the French daily newspaper *Le Monde.*

57 *Reuters,* 16 March 1998.

58 American companies are not only interested in investing in Iranian oil and gas fields. A lift of the US ban would boost pipeline projects in the region. In April 1998, Mobil asked the US government permission to ship crude to northern Iran from the company's oilfields in neighbouring countries (presumably Kazakhstan) and swap it for Iranian oil that would be shipped from a southern port. In the absence of pipelines, such a move would make easier for Mobil to get its oil out of the Caspian region.

59 'Bill Clinton veut une "véritable réconciliation" avec l'Iran', *Le Monde,* 20 June 1998.

60 'Iranian Dismisses All Hope For Now of Political Thaw', *The New York Times*, 23 September 1998.
61 Richard Matzke, President of Chevron Overseas Petroleum Inc., quoted in *Reuters*, 31 January 1998.
62 Unocal – which controls about 10 per cent of AIOC – has a 54.11 per cent stake in the consortium. Other participants include the Turkmen Ministry of Oil and Gas Industry (7%), Saudi Arabia's Delta Gas Pipeline Company Ltd (15%), South Korea's Hyundai (5.56%), Japan's Indonesia Petroleum Ltd (INPEX) and CIECO TransAsia Gas Ltd (7.22% each) and Pakistan's Crescent Steel and Allied Products (3.89%).
63 'Unocal Calls a Halt to Caspian Pipeline After Afghan Raids', *The Wall Street Journal*, 21 August 1998.
64 *Reuters*, 27 August 1998, quoting an interview given in April 1995 by Bin Laden to the French daily newspaper *France Soir*.
65 Olivier Roy, 'Faut-il diaboliser l'Iran?', *Politique Internationale*, No. 78, winter 1997–8.
66 *Index on Censorship*, Vol. 26, No. 4, 1997.
67 *Pipeline News*, No. 33, 12–18 October 1996.
68 *Reuters*, 8 December 1997.
69 Pakistani officials have denied the US air strikes on Bin Laden's Afghan base in August 1998 would durably affect the CentGas project. *Reuters*, 21 August 1998.
70 One possible explanation is that, in the view of Russia's political leaders, the country has sufficient oil reserves of its own, although new fields lie in inhospitable regions with no immediate access to export routes. Russia is self-sufficient in oil and it sells about half of its output to other countries.
71 'It is high time to undertake decisive steps to build a genuine Commonwealth of Independent States. Private capital is the only force capable of strengthening the CIS', he stated the day he was appointed. *Itar-Tass*, 29 April 1998.
72 In May 1998, Ukraine said it was considering buying a 0.5 per cent stake in AIOC in the hope of guaranteed oil shipments from Azerbaijan. Russian bankers could lend Kiev money in return for shares in the Odessa and Lisichansk oil refineries. 'AOZT Sodruzhestvo Nezavisimykh Gosudarstv', *Kommersant-Vlast*', 12 May 1998.
73 At least two of the banks hit by the crisis – Vladimir Gusinsky's Most Group and Alexander Smolensky's SBS-Agro – were considering development plans in Azerbaijan.
74 'Ministerstvo strannykh del', *Kommersant-Weekly*, 2 December 1997.
75 As one oil executive put it, inviting Aliev to Washington 'would be a clear signal to Russia and Iran that we value our relationship with Azerbaijan and that Azerbaijan is a partner'. S. Rob Sobhani, op. cit.

6

The Nagorno-Karabakh Conflict, Caspian Oil and Regional Powers

Kamer Kasim

The end of the Cold War has changed the dynamics of international relations and marked the end of the era of bipolarity. One of the important consequences of the end of the Cold War is the increasing role of the regional powers in world politics. As a result, regional powers got more actively involved in regional events. This phenomenon has been clearly seen in the Caspian region, which suddenly became an area of competition for the three regional powers, namely Turkey, Russia and Iran.[1] The emergence of the new independent states with valuable resources intensified the competition. Some even talked about the revival of the nineteenth century's 'Great Game' with different actors.[2] Today's struggle for Caspian oil is a mixture of security, geopolitical and economic games. In fact, the competition includes states as well as multinational companies that want to influence the region and benefit from the economic opportunities. The construction of the pipelines to transport oil and natural gas from the Caspian region to the world market is a major area of competition.

Rivalry among the regional powers with mostly conflicting interests became the main theme in the Caspian region. Rivalry focused on Azerbaijan for two main reasons: the Azeris' ethnic ties with the two regional powers, and Azerbaijan's strategic position. The Azeris are of Turkic origin and their language is the closest one to Turkish of all other Turkic republics' languages. For this reason, Azerbaijan shares strong ethnic and cultural affinity with Turkey. Azerbaijan is also the geographical gateway to Central Asia for Turkey. Thus, it has a central position in Turkey's foreign policy towards the region.[3] For historical and political reasons, Iran sees newly independent Azerbaijan as a threat. Twelve million Azeris live in Iran, which is more than those living in Azerbaijan. This may cause tension between Iran and Azerbaijan. Unless and until Iran emerges from its economic and political isolation, it will not welcome a prosperous, secular Azerbaijan on its northern border.[4] Azerbaijan has also got strategic importance for Russia, because of the Caspian oil and its border with Iran.

Azerbaijan's oil resources put it at the centre of attention, both worldwide and regionally. With the independence of Azerbaijan, multinational oil companies rushed to take part in the exploitation of Azerbaijan's oil. For Azerbaijan, Caspian oil is the main source of hard currency which is necessary for future investment and development.[5]

In this chapter I will evaluate the role of the regional powers as well as the US as a superpower in the competition. Because of its strategic importance and key role in the relations among the regional powers, Azerbaijan will be the focus. First, the Nagorno-Karabakh conflict will be dealt with, because of its importance for all regional countries and its effect on the stability of the region.

Nagorno-Karabakh conflict and Russian foreign policy

Azerbaijan's oil resources and competition over the transportation of oil caused the involvement of regional countries in the conflict. For at least three reasons, the Nagorno-Karabakh conflict is of vital importance with regard to the future role of each regional power and the shaping of their policies. Firstly, the conflict showed that, despite the shrinking of its role, Russia will continue to exert influence even by using military power regardless of international criticism. The Nagorno-Karabakh conflict also indicated the Russian ability to overthrow governments that follow foreign policy against the Russian national interest. Secondly, it indicated Turkey's inability to influence the region and its unwillingness to engage in military confrontation. However, it also showed Turkey's ability to use diplomatic channels. Thirdly, as a country isolated by the West and without any regional allies, Iran has almost no room for manoeuvre; also, contrary to its revolutionary rhetoric, Iranian policy in the region was more like that of a nation-state.[6]

Russia's struggle for regional dominance and Azerbaijan's war with the Armenians concerned all countries in the region and caused instability.[7] The conflict in the largely Armenian-populated province of Azerbaijan began in 1988. It became a large-scale war in 1991, with the Armenians demanding independence from Azerbaijan. On 2 September 1991, the Armenians declared Nagorno-Karabakh a Republic, and, shortly after, the Nagorno-Karabakh conflict was internationalised with the Russian and Armenian demand for the involvement of CSCE and a UN peacekeeping force. Azerbaijan rejected the deployment of a peacekeeping force, but allowed a CSCE mission to visit Nagorno-Karabakh.[8] Officially, Russia supported the CSCE mission to find a peaceful solution to the conflict. But it is widely believed that Russia supported the Armenian separatists of Nagorno-Karabakh in order to bring Azerbaijan into the Commonwealth of Independent States (CIS). The Russian troops located in Stepanakent even participated in the massacres of Azeri civilians in Khojaly, a town in Nagorno-Karabakh, and delivered weapons to the Armenian militias.[9] To understand Russian involvement in the conflict, we need to evaluate Russia's national interests in the region. Firstly, Russia considers the region its sphere of influence. Although the oil and natural gas sources of the Caspian region are not very important for Russia, since it has such reserves in its own territory, Russia wants to control the transportation of the Caspian oil as a lever to preserve or strengthen its influence in the region. For Russia, the region is also important in terms of security. According to the Russian leadership, the defence of the region is crucial for the defence of Russia. Russia is concerned about the rise of strong nationalist movements in the former Soviet republics for two reasons: firstly, Russia has a substantial number of minorities that are linked with the Caucasus and Central Asian republics. In this context, the Turkic minorities of Russia are particularly important, because dissatisfaction of the Turkic minorities could encourage autonomous republics, such as Tataristan, Baskirdistan and Yakutistan, to seek independence.[10] Secondly, 10 million Russians live in Central Asia. Although the number of Russians is relatively small in other countries, in Kazahkistan, ethnic Russians constitute 38 per cent of the total population.[11] The Russian government feels responsible for their situation in the new republics. This adds an ethnic dimension to the Russian foreign policy. With the Eurasianist influence on Russian foreign policy-making, Russia put the region as a priority for the Russian national interest.[12]

The Nagorno-Karabakh conflict affected Azerbaijan's domestic stability and made it vulnerable to Russian influence. The Armenian militias' success on the battlefield weakened the Azeri governments. The first change in the government came after the fall of Shusha, the last town under the control of Azerbaijan in Nagorno-Karabakh. President Mutalibov resigned, and Popular Front leader Elchibey was elected President in June 1992. With Elchibey's presidency Azerbaijan took radical steps to make significant changes in its foreign policy. Azerbaijan refused to join the CIS and called for the withdrawal of all Russian troops.[13] Elchibey turned to the West for support and refused to have anything to do with Russia. His Pan-Turkist ideas made Iran and Russia suspicious. Elchibey's government signed an accord with Turkey to build a pipeline from Baku to Ceyhan, to transport Caspian oil to the international market, which was incompatible with the Russian national interests.[14] As a result, he was forced out of office by a Russian-backed coup. Azerbaijan's continued failure on the battlefield also weakened Elchibey's government. Although at the beginning of his presidency Azerbaijan launched some successful military advances towards the Armenians, such as recapturing Agdere and some parts of the Lachin corridor, the Armenian militias later captured Kelbajar, the Azeri town separating Armenia from Karabakh in March 1993. By July 1993, Azerbaijan lost Mardakert and Agdam. After the retired member of the former Soviet politbureau Haidar Aliev became president, Azerbaijan joined the CIS. Then Russia evaluated the seizure of Nagorno-Karabakh as a violation of international law and condemned it. However, Russia later tried to use the Nagorno-Karabakh conflict to enable Russian troops to return to Azerbaijan. Russia proposed a so-called peacekeeping force to be stationed inside Azerbaijan. But Aliev refused to agree to the return of Russian troops to Azerbaijan. For the first time in 1996, at the OSCE meeting in Lisbon, Russia backed Azerbaijan's position regarding the Nagorno-Karabakh dispute. The Russian delegation stated that the principle of territorial integrity should take precedence over the right of self-determination. But Russia did not put pressure on Armenia to make concessions in the Nagorno-Karabakh dispute.[15]

The international community tried to find a solution to the conflict. Russia, Turkey and the US initiated a joint plan of peaceful settlement in Karabakh, immediately supported by Azerbaijan. Although Armenia described the joint plan as a positive step, it refused to approve it. Peace talks re-opened under the CSCE peace plan in December 1993. Azerbaijan described the plan as pro-Armenian and rejected it. Azerbaijan and Armenia signed a ceasefire agreement without a mediator in 1994, and the war which killed over 15 000 people ended. It was the first serious ethnic conflict on former Soviet territory. Although a ceasefire stopped the fighting, negotiations for a resolution of the conflict have not produced results. Twenty per cent of Azerbaijan's territory is still under Armenian occupation and many refugees live in squalid conditions.[16]

Turkey and Azerbaijan

Turkey is another regional power that wants to exert influence in the region. Turkey sees its regional role as a way to revive its strategic importance, which was undermined with the collapse of the Soviet Union, in the eyes of the West. As a country which depends on energy imports, one of the major aims of Turkey is to diversify its sources of supply and to be host of the transportation of Caspian oil to the world market. Turkey's geopolitical position and the Turkic character of five of the new republics increased Turkey's regional role and forced it to take more responsibilities in regional events. In fact, the independence of the Caucasus and Central Asian republics was considered one of the most important events by the Turkish foreign policy-makers. Turkey considers itself one of the major regional powers with relative military and economic strength. With the encouragement of the United States, Turkey presented itself as a model of development for the Caucasian and Central Asian states, at least officially. But Turkey had to compete with Russia and to some extent with Iran. In many ways Turkey and Russia have conflicting national interests. For this reason, Turkey is considered a geopolitical rival in the Caucasus and Central Asia by Russia, which also regards Turkey as a 'spearhead' for the West, particularly the US. In fact, Turkey has been relying on the support of the West, particularly of the US in its foreign policy towards the region. The US also saw Turkey's influence in the region as a counterbalance to that of Iran and Russia. Turkey hoped that the emergence of the new republics would boost Turkey's claim for full membership in the EU. The Turkish elite started to talk of Turkey as being a 'bridge' between Europe and the Caucasian and Central Asian Republics. However, as Lorca correctly pointed out 'The so-called "bridge theory" was also used during the negotiations for Spain's entrance in to the EEC with respect to Latin America. Spain has had privileged cultural, historical and economic ties there. However, experience has shown that Europe does not need Spain for dealing with Latin America.'[17]

Turkey gave special importance to the Turkic republics of the Caucasus and Central Asia. Because of its proximity and strategic position, cultural closeness made Azerbaijan more special for Turkey's foreign policy towards the Caucasus and Central Asia. Even before the collapse of the USSR, Turkey had developed economic ties and other contacts with Azerbaijan. After the independence of Azerbaijan, relations between the two countries were promoted by exchange of visits, and agreements on many cultural and economic levels. In September 1991, an Azerbaijani Consulate was opened in Trabzon. At the beginning of 1992, Turkish television programmes were received in Azerbaijan. Turkish President Ozal visited Azerbaijan in the Autumn of 1992. During his visit negotiations resulted in the treaty on friendship, cooperation, and good-neighbourliness, and in more than two dozen agreements on collaboration in economic issues, trade and culture.[18]

Parallel to cooperation with Azerbaijan as a whole, Turkey also collaborates with the autonomous republic of Nakhicvan. On 25 March 1992, during the official visit of Heydar Aliev, former chairman of the Nakhicvan National Assembly, a protocol on bilateral cooperation was signed in Ankara that provided for a $100 million Turkish loan for Nakhicvan. Turkey undertook to admit 100 students from Nakhicvan to its colleges and universities annually, connect the autonomous republic to its television and telephone networks, and establish regular railway and air traffic with Azerbaijan.[19]

Although all Azerbaijani leaders agree on the need for close contacts with Turkey and support the 'Turkish model of development', during Elchibey's presidency Azerbaijan's view of Turkey as a model to admire reached its zenith. But after Aliev took power, at least at the beginning of his presidency, relations between Turkey and Azerbaijan cooled down. Firstly, contrary to Elchibey's pro-Turkish stand, Aliev adopted a more balanced approach towards the regional powers. Although he did not allow Russian troops on Azeri territory, Azerbaijan became a member of the CIS. Secondly, one of the unsuccessful coup attempts against Aliev was linked with some officials from Turkey, which caused tension in their relations.[20] In addition, Azerbaijan's disappointment with Turkey's foreign policy towards the Nagorno-Karabakh conflict caused relations to deteriorate. Before the independence of Azerbaijan, Turkey evaluated the Nagorno-Karabakh crisis as an internal affair of the Soviet Union. But when the crisis spread through Nakhicvan, with which Turkey shares a common border, the situation reached a level that could not be ignored by the Turkish government. The town of Sadarak was besieged by Armenian militias. Parliament in the autonomous Republic of Nakhicvan decided that 'Nakhicvan should declare its independence from the USSR and unite with Turkey in order to save their lives'.[21] The Turkish government felt strong popular pressure to join the battle on Azerbaijan's side. After the independence of Azerbaijan, public pressure for military support to Azerbaijan increased. Due to the fact that the Nagorno-Karabakh conflict became a conflict between two independent states, namely Azerbaijan and Armenia, it could no longer be described as an 'internal dispute'. Although 1600 Turkish military experts were sent to Azerbaijan, Turkey generally maintained an even-handed policy towards the conflict and resisted the temptation and pressure to intervene. Turkish authorities worried that siding with

Azerbaijan would jeopardise Turkey's relations with the US, because of the existence of an Armenian lobby there. The presence of Russian soldiers at the border between Turkey and Armenia increased the probability of a Turkish–Russian conflict, which was another reason why Turkey decided not to intervene.[22] Given the fact that Turkish–Russian trade accounted for 90 per cent of trade between Turkey and the CIS countries, worth US $2 billion, and the hard currency earned by Turkish companies in Russia is increasingly important for the Turkish economy, Turkey needs to keep its relations with Russia at a somewhat decent level for its own interests. For this reason Turkey could not enter into a direct confrontation with Russia.[23]

Turkish foreign policy aimed at mobilising international forums to condemn Armenian acts. For Turkey, it was important to prevent the Nagorno-Karabakh conflict from being defined as a Christian–Muslim confrontation or an Arab–Israeli conflict of the Caucasus. Another important objective of Turkey was to prevent international recognition of any territorial gains of Armenia.[24] At the same time, Turkey tried to find a compromise between Azerbaijan and Armenia. But trying to find a compromise was not an easy task. Turkey made a US-backed proposal, which included the transfer of an Armenian-controlled land bridge between Azerbaijan and Nakhicvan to Azerbaijani control, while leaving a part of Nagorno-Karabakh under Armenian control. Armenia did not accept this proposal, because it would loosen its ties with Iran. Azerbaijan did not accept it because Azerbaijan would thus lose the Nagorno-Karabakh region.[25] Turkey also followed policy based on support for relatively moderate politicians in Armenia. After the resignation of the hawkish Armenian Foreign Minister Hovanesian, Turkey even sold electricity to Armenia and allowed humanitarian aid to pass through its territory. Turkey hoped this policy would strengthen Prime Minister Ter-Petrosyan against strong nationalist Dashnak opposition and eventually Armenia would come to an agreement with Azerbaijan. But Turkey's policy was seen by the Azeris as a 'stab in the back', which greatly disappointed them. Azerbaijan understood that Turkey would not sacrifice its international prestige and its security for the sake of 'Turkic brotherhood'. On the other hand, Turkey is still the only country that can be counted on as an ally against the Armenians. Turkey is also the only country that constantly expressed its support for Azerbaijan, which is really important, considering the fact that Azerbaijan has almost no support from outside. In the international arena, Turkey has tried to explain and promote the Azeri view of the conflict. In fact, Azerbaijan never officially asked Turkey to intervene in the conflict. The main support Azerbaijan wanted from Turkey was to try to use its Western alliance contacts to show Azerbaijan's side of the story to the world.[26] Given the fact that Azerbaijan's relations with Russia and Iran remain tense, Turkey's support has vital importance for Azerbaijan. And Turkey will remain its closest ally.

Iran and Azerbaijan

With the independence of the Caucasian and Central Asian republics, Iran also joined in the competition. Like Turkey and Russia, Iran wants to exploit economic opportunities in the region. Like Turkey, Iran has close historical and cultural links with the regional states, particularly with Azerbaijan. For Iran, the new states in Central Asia and the Caucasus were a means of escaping a geographic isolation imposed on it by the West. Thus, one of the central objectives of the Iranian foreign policy towards the region is to break its isolation through the partnership of the new states of the former Soviet Union. To reach this objective, Iran tried to increase trade with the new republics and Iranian officials considered that the revival of the Silk Road was vital for restoring Iran's status in international trade.[27] The existence of rich oil and natural gas sources in the Caucasus and Central Asia provides opportunities for Iran, involving modernisation or expansion of oil and natural gas refineries. This is why it actively lobbied to transport the Caspian oil through its territory.

For Iran, Azerbaijan is important in the sense that Iran has a substantial number of Azeri minorities. Russia invaded northern Azerbaijan, while southern Azerbaijan remained part of Iran. With the independence of Azerbaijan, the Azeris living in both countries are in a position to increase contacts.[28] Iran had mixed reactions towards the independence of Azerbaijan. On the one hand, close relations with Azerbaijan could help Iran get out of its isolation and enable it to exert influence over Azerbaijan. On the other hand, Iran does not want to see a strong nationalist Azerbaijan stirred by pan-Turkism. This could induce irredentist feelings among its Azeri minority. In fact, during Elchibey's presidency relations between the two countries were cool. Elchibey's demand for cultural autonomy for the Azeris living in Iran, as well as his statements about unification of what he called 'north and south Azerbaijan', disturbed Iran.[29]

Even after Elchibey stopped being in power, Iran had concerns about independent Azerbaijan. Iran does not want to see prosperous Azerbaijan on its northern border. However, Iran tried unsuccessfully to find a peaceful solution to the Nagorno-Karabakh conflict which disrupted Iranian trade with Armenia, Azerbaijan and Georgia. Because of this conflict, the railway service between Iran and Transcaucasia was shut down. On 8 May 1992, Iran brought together the Armenian and Azeri presidents and an agreement was signed in Teheran. According to the agreement, within one week a ceasefire would come into effect, the blockade of Armenia would be lifted, international observers would be admitted into the area and prisoners would be exchanged. However, the next day the Armenian militias captured Shusha and continued their attacks. Following Armenian advances, Azerbaijani refugees rushed to the Iranian border creating a big refugee problem for Iran.[30]

Iran's antoganistic relations with the West serve as a disincentive for the new republics, which seek access to Western aid and investment. However, the biggest obstacle for Iran is the US effort to prevent and/or decrease the Iranian influence in the region. Thus, Iran can only play a limited role in the region.

Finding a safe way to carry Caspian oil to the world market occupied centre stage in the discussions about Caspian oil. Because the Caspian states are landlocked, oil must pass through other countries before reaching the market. For this reason, the main competition among the regional powers evolved around taking part in the transportation of the oil. Turkey, Russia and Iran wanted Caspian oil to pass through their own territory. Turkey came up with the Baku–Ceyhan pipeline project. Russia wanted the oil to be shipped from Novorrossisk. Iran wanted a pipeline to be built at the Persian Gulf and oil to be shipped from an Iranian port. Although some specialists argued that this was the cheapest way to carry Caspian oil to the world market, the Iranian option faced strong opposition from the US. If positive signs continue to come from moderate President Mohammad Khatami, the US restrictions against Iran could gradually be lifted. But for the time being, it seems that the US objection made the Iranian route impossible.

The United States opposes the reimposition of Russian control over former Soviet states by force or intimidation. Also one of the main objectives of American foreign policy is to contain Iran. For this reason, since the independence of the Caucasian and Central Asian states, the US urged these states not to follow the Iranian example. The US sees its objectives in the region as promoting the economic independence and autonomy of the former Soviet republics from Russia, and ensuring that Caspian oil does not come under the sole control of Russia. This is also in the interest of American companies, which are keenly interested in gaining a share in the exploitation of the petroleum and the other mineral resources of the region, and in developing export markets for American goods.[31]

Although the US supports the total independence of the former Soviet republics from Moscow, a policy requiring support for territorial integrity of the new independent states, the United States foreign policy towards the Nagorno-Karabakh conflict, which posed a direct threat to the territorial integrity of Azerbaijan, was not in favour of Azerbaijan. Under the influence of the Armenian lobby, the US Congress passed the Freedom Support Act (Section 907), preventing the US government from sending aid to Azerbaijan.[32] On the other hand, after Israel, Armenia has constantly been the highest per capita recipient of US foreign aid. Despite the fact that the Congress passed the Freedom Support Act, the State Department has tried to pursue a more balanced policy. Both the Bush and the Clinton administrations have repeatedly tried to lift the Freedom Support Act's restriction on Azerbaijan. In January 1996, the US Congress gave President Clinton the right to suspend the effectiveness of the Freedom Support Act Section 907, in case he decides on the inadequacy of the non-governmental US assistance to refugees and Internally Displaced Persons (IDPs) in Azerbaijan. This piece of news was accepted in Azerbaijan as the beginning of an improvement in US–Azerbaijani relations. The frequent visits of US senators and congressmen to Azerbaijan, as well as the personal contacts with the leaders of Azerbaijan aimed at obtaining objective information about the economic and political situation in the country, prove the growing interest of the US Congress in the situation in Azerbaijan, and, undoubtedly, have a positive impact on the process of decision-making in the legislative framework. During his visit to the United States, the Azerbaijani President Heydar Aliev expressed his fervent hope that, thanks to Bill Clinton's efforts, Section 907 which hampers the development of bilateral economic relations would be abolished soon. During the talks, the two presidents agreed on the necessity to abrogate Section 907. In Heydar Aliev's opinion, the cancellation of Section 907 would first of all alleviate the sufferings of one million refugees in Azerbaijan, pointing out the importance of relations between the United States and Azerbaijan for the security and prosperity in the Caucasus region. During President Heydar Aliev's visit, four oil contracts, including a joint statement and a number of agreements pertaining to further strengthening of US–Azeri relations, were signed, and President Bill Clinton stated that Azerbaijan had achieved great upheavals in its struggle with difficulties on the way to independence, and the United States will support Azerbaijan in further pursuing this course.[33] Contrary to the rhetoric, President Heydar Aliev's official visit to the United States failed to achieve the desired goal.

Azerbaijan hopes that Caspian oil will strengthen its hand in its relations with the United States, since the US companies have a great role in the development of Caspian oil. The US government is actively involved in the debate about the transportation of main oil from the Caspian to the world market. The US administration supports a multi-variant system of Caspian oil deliveries to the world markets, but believes that the main export pipeline must pass along the Baku–Ceyhan route via Georgia. This was announced by the US Secretary of State's adviser on the new independent states Steven Sestanovich and the Secretary of State's assistant on Europe and Canada, Mark Grossmann, during the hearings at the Congress. Grossman stated that 'We assume the economically approved corridor East–West must consist of Baku–Ceyhan oil pipeline, parallel gas pipeline to be spanned to the Turkish market as well as Transcaspian gas and oil pipelines.'[34] However, many US officials acknowledged that the pipeline decisions are commercially driven. They will be determined by the companies involved in pipeline projects. Even some US advisers expressed their doubts about the Baku–Ceyhan route. For example, Ross Wilson, a special adviser for CIS countries, stated on behalf of the US State Department that 'There will not be any commitment to Baku–Ceyhan [the route of the MEP] in 1998. There is just no way... It would be crazy for AIOC to commit itself firmly to Baku–Ceyhan that soon, with so much uncertainty.'[35]

The US is generally very determined in its opposition to the pipelines extending to and through Iran. Mark Grossman stated that 'US opposition to building a pipeline through Iran has not changed. We will continue to oppose such lines and to support alternate non-Iranian routes for the export of Caspian energy resources.'[36] But recently this policy has been questioned by some specialists. Former US White House national security adviser Zbigniew Brzezinski says American efforts to isolate Iran and keep Caspian oil pipelines out of that country could push Teheran into a collaboration with Russia to exclude Western presence from the region. Brzezinski stated that if the US wants a stable Persian Gulf and Central Asian region, 'some gradual accommodation is in the mutual interest of both countries'.[37] There may be softening of the US policy towards Iran, depending on Iranian President Khatemi's *rapprochement* with the West. But it would be unrealistic to expect sharp changes in the US policy towards Iran.

Conclusion

The regional countries and the United States recognise the importance of Caspian oil resources in contributing to the economic prosperity, energy security and stability of the region. These resources will be an important addition to world oil and gas supplies and require secure access routes to world markets. Major export pipeline(s) from the Caspian will accordingly contribute to the secure delivery of an important new source of world energy supplies. Development of Caspian energy supplies will support stable world energy markets. Whichever route is chosen for the main oil, it will continue to be an area for rivalry and it will definitely occupy centre-stage in the Turkish, Russian and Iranian foreign policies. Russia's return to the region became a reality, but its future foreign policy orientation remains uncertain. Russia is benefiting from the state of 'frozen instability' in the Caspian region, which effectively denies independence and economic development to the states in the region, and Russian policy aims at placing Moscow in a position of exclusive control over all future pipelines in the region. Turkey will not abandon its interest in the region, for it has strong cultural and economic ties with the regional countries. Instead, it will continue to pursue a pro-Western foreign policy. Iran has a limited role because of its isolation by the West, but if with its moderate president Iran reaches a compromise with the US, Iran may still play a vital role in regional economic cooperation. The US and its allies have paramount interest in ensuring that the Caucasian states as well as Central Asian countries maintain their independence and remain mostly secular and reasonably pro-Western. The future of the Caspian region will depend on the commitment of the governments to strengthen modern political and economic institutions. If Russia challenges the West with a policy of destabilisation of the region, tension and hostile alignments will emerge in the region. In addition to cooperation among the regional powers, finding solution to the conflicts among the regional countries is the key to the stability in the region. The Nagorno-Karabakh crisis and Azeri–Armenian relations will continue to challenge the stability of the region, unless the US and regional powers actively put pressure on the new Armenian Prime Minister Kocharyan, who seems to be very close to nationalist Dashnak policies, risking a renewal of the conflict between Azeris and Armenians.[38]

Notes

1 Roland Goetz, 'Political Spheres of Interest in the Southern Caucasus and in Central Asia', *Ausen Politik*, 1998, p. 262.

2 Stuart Parrott, 'Central Asia: Powers Replay Great Game', *RFE/RL*, 3 February 1998.
3 Philip Robins, 'Between Sentiment and Self-Interest: Turkey's Policy Towards Azerbaijan and the Central Asian States', *Middle East Journal*, Vol. 47, No. 4, p. 597.
4 C. Frederick, 'The Great (Oil) Game', *Journal of Commerce*, 22 April 1998.
5 S. Levine, 'Moscow Pressures its Neighbors to Share their Oil and Gas Revenues', *The Washington Post*, 18 March 1994.
6 H. Yusuf, 'State Interests vs the Umma: Iranian Policy in Central Asia', *Middle East Journal*, Vol. 50, winter, p. 80.
7 B. Keller, 'Did Moscow Incite Azerbaijanis? Some See a Plot', *The New York Times*, 19 February 1990.
8 E. Fuller, 'Nagorno-Karabakh: Internal Conflict Becomes International', *RFE/RL*, 13 March 1992.
9 R. S. Tabrizi, 'Azerbaijan and Armenian Conflict and Coexistence', in A. Ehteshami (ed.), *From the Gulf to Central Asia: Players in the New Great Game*, University of Exeter Press, 1994.
10 J. W. R. Lepingwell, 'Russian Military and Security Policy in the Near Abroad', *Survival*, Vol. 36, No. 3, p. 75.
11 M. Klatt, 'Russians in the Near Abroad', *RFE/RL*, 19 August 1994, p. 33.
12 M. Meshabi, 'Russian Foreign Policy and Security in Central Asia and the Caucasus', *Central Asian Survey*, Vol. 12, No. 2, p. 188.
13 W. W. Maggs, 'Armenia and Azerbaijan: Looking Toward the Middle East', *Current History Journal*, 1995, Vol. 92, No. 570, p. 8.
14 Stephen, Blank, 'Energy and Security in Transcaucasia', 1994, US Army War College, p. 7.
15 R. Freedman, 'Russia and Azerbaijan: Are Relations Beginning to Improve?', *Caspian Crossroads*, Vol. 2, No. 4, Spring.
16 P. Goble, 'Caucasus: Analysis from Washington: Armenia–Azerbaijan Conflict Risks Reignition', *RFE/RL*, 8 May 1998.
17 A. V. Lorca, 'Turkey: the Door to Central Asia', *Eurasian Studies*, Vol. 2, No. 3, p. 63.
18 A. Vassiliev, 'Turkey and Iran in Transcaucasia and Central Asia', in Ehteshami (ed.), *From the Gulf To Central Asia*.
19 E. Fuller, *Azerbaijan at the Crossroads*, Royal Institute of International Affairs, 1994, p. 15.
20 M. A. Birand, 'Aliyev'i Artik Rahat Birakin', *Sabah*, 14 February 1998.
21 FBIS-WEU, 'Nakhichevan Said Wants to Unite', 25 January 1990, p. 28.
22 D. Pipes, 'The Event of Our Era: Former Soviet Muslim Republics', in Michael Mandelbaum (ed.), *Central Asia and The World*, The Council of Foreign Relations, 1994, pp. 47–94.
23 A. Ehteshami and E. Murph, 'The Non-Arab Middle East States and the Caucasian and Central Asian Republics: Turkey', *International Relations*, Vol. 11, No. 6, 1993, pp. 513–34. According to Turkish Ministry of Foreign Affairs, the non-registered trade between Turkey and Russia reached around $10 billion in 1997. http://www.mfa.gov,tr/Grup/Russian.htm.
24 K. Kirisci, 'The End of the Cold War and Changes in the Foreign Policy Behaviour', *Dis Politika*, 1993, Vol. 18, pp. 14–15.

25 P. Goble, 'Coping with the Nagorno-Karabakh Crisis', *Fletcher Forum of World Affairs,* 1992, Vol. 16, pp. 19–26.
26 S. E. Cornell, 'Turkey and the Conflict in Nagorno-Karabakh: a Delicate Balance', *Middle Eastern Studies,* 1998, Vol. 34, No. 1, January, pp. 57–9.
27 E. Herzig, *Iran and the Former Soviet South,* The Royal Institute of International Affairs, 1995.
28 G. Fuller, *Turkey Faces East: New Orientations Toward the Middle East and the Old Soviet Union,* Rand, Santa Monica, 1992, p. 54.
29 D. Pipes, 'The Event of Our Era: Former Soviet Muslim Republics', in Michael Mandelbaum, *Central Asia and the World,* Council of Foreign Relations, 1994, p. 61.
30 G. M. Winrow, 'Azerbaijan and Iran', in Alvin Rubinstein and Oles M. Smolansky (eds), *Regional Power Rivalries in the New Eurasia,* M. E. Sharpe, 1995.
31 L. Hamilton, 'Caspian and the US', *Journal of Commerce,* 19 July 1998.
32 S. E. Cornell, 'Turkey and the Conflict in Nagorno-Karabakh: a Delicate Balance', *Middle Eastern Studies,* Vol. 34, No. 1, January 1998, p. 57.
33 *Azernews International Independent Newspaper,* No. 8 (08), 23–30 July 1997, p. 1.
34 Quoted from *Turkistan Newsletter,* 13–15 July 1998. http://www.euronet.nl/users/sota/turkistan.htm.
35 U. Akinci, 'Baku–Ceyhan Pipeline is not Possible in 1998', *Turkish Daily News,* 19 March 1998.
36 Quoted from *Turkistan Newsletter,* 13–15 July 1998. http://www.euronet.nl/users/sota/turkistan.htm.
37 R. Lyle, 'Caspian: Brzezinski Cautions Against Isolating Iran from Pipeline', *RFE/RL,* 9 July 1998.
38 P. Goble, 'Caucasus: Analysis from Washington: Armenian–Azerbaijani Conflict Risks Reignition', *RFE/RL,* 8 May 1998.

7

The Russians, Chechens and the Black Gold: a Geo-economic Explanation for the Chechen War

Andrew Towner

On the morning of 20 December 1994 Russians awoke to newspaper claims that a 'regiment of the Taman motor rifle division is [was] to be sent to Chechnya'.[1] This news marked the manifestation of a new chapter in bilateral relations between the ailing superpower and the upstart republic, signifying the continuation of a century-long struggle. Freaks of geography have forced upon the Caucasus states a strategic importance which transcends their borders. To the east and west, the area is framed by the Black and Caspian Seas respectively, whilst the northern border is formed by the Kuban and Kuma rivers, the southern border is provided by the Kura river. The region lies at the crossroads between Asia and Europe, a confluence for traders and merchants; to the Europeans it provided vital access to the fabled riches of the Orient, to the merchants from the East it provided a gateway to the markets of Europe.

Geography has determined to a large extent the eventful history of the Caucasus, which is dominated by competing empires, many of which have swept through all or part of the region without regard for indigenous people. Greeks, Romans, Byzantine, Arab and Mongol conquerors dominated early Caucasian history before surrendering to the emergent power of the Russian, Persian and Ottoman empires. In the baggage of these new powers were the seeds of later religious conflict. By the mid-nineteenth century Russia had assumed position of regional great power, gaining control over a patchwork of ethnic groups, more than '42 peoples speaking distinct languages with more than 100 dialects',[2] riven by cultural, religious and historical differences with few unifying factors, except inbred solidarity against invasion.

Hostility, combat, vengeance and revenge were essential ingredients necessary for the survival of any individual. 'The more severed heads [that] dangled from his [the] saddlebow',[3] the better as a reflection of his status within the tribe wherein warriors were thought to sleep with their 'kindjals'.[4] The reputation of these dervishes led to a degree of autonomy, leading observers to view aggression against them as actions bordering on insanity. An oft-repeated Persian dictum illustrated the potency of their reputation: 'when the Shah is a fool he attacks the north Caucasus'. The Russians foolishly disregarded this and became embroiled in a bloody conflict, believing the Caucasus would provide a gateway to the riches of the south. As a result of the bloody campaigns that followed, the Caucasus gained a special place in the collective psyche of Russians. Exotic tales of inaccessible cultures banished the ennui from the oppressive claustrophobia of the St Petersburg court, becoming an essential ingredient of Russian culture and literature, portrayed by literatary luminaries such as Pushkin, Lermontov and the young Tolstoy. The Chechen Imam Shamyl and his fanatically religious Murids held the Russians at bay for 30 years, until their inevitable defeat. As the fire of war departed the glowing embers of enmity remained to be stoked from time to time. Stalin attempted to ethnically cleanse the region by ordering the mass deportation of the Chechen people for traitorous acts, as he viewed them as 'tools of the Nazi invaders',[5] an act which became seared into the collective consciousness of the Chechen people, hardening their collective memory, increasing their need to avenge themselves.

Vengeance came in the form of the war against the 'infidel invader'. The war was marked by its ferocity, leaving casualties between 30 000 and 50 000 and the total destruction of two-thirds of Chechnya. The causes of this war are more complicated than pure revenge. Amongst the causes normally cited are: Russian reluctance to relinquish political control of Chechnya, Russian concern at the proximity of an Islamic nation to their vulnerable southern border, security worries which reflected Russian paranoia over state security emanating from the fact that Russia has always been a land-based empire of disparate colonies. Moscow was concerned by the belief that its former Great Game opposition, Turkey and Iran, would attempt to undermine its hegemonic position. Many of the previous causes could be defined as geopolitical; it is the author's belief that the primary cause of the Chechen war was geo-economics. This equates with the statement that 'Moscow's tenacious attempt to hold on to Chechnya was largely determined by the territory's control of a strategic pipeline; its murky intrigues in Transcuacasia are similarly motivated',[6] to maintain political influence at the heart of the hydrocarbon-producing Caspian Sea states.

Geo-economics, it may be argued, has supplanted geopolitics as the motivation for world events, switching from ideological conflicts to the quest for economic superiority and the assurance of a constant supply of necessary resources. Amongst these resources, oil is the most important, providing the lubrication for all developed economies. There are other conflicts that could be identified as motivated by geo-economics. N. Riasanovsky believes that Russian aggression towards Turkey can be explained by examining the economic requirements of Russia, such as the need to protect grain trade through the Black Sea or to obtain markets in the Near East.[7] Commentators also view the recent Gulf war as being a conflict motivated through the economic prudence of securing future supplies of energy resources.

Since the 1991 collapse of the Soviet Union, the independent states of the Caspian–Caucasus region have achieved full economic autonomy. To maintain this autonomy the states have sought new resources, chief amongst which are the massive hydrocarbon resources. During the late 1970s and 1980s the Soviet Union was blighted by economic stagnation. Due to Moscow's lack of interest in the oilfields of Azerbaijan,[8] this permitted independent Azeri exploration, leading to a recurrence of perennial problems and a lack of financial resources. Once again the problem was solved by re-admitting the same companies that had been forced out under the Bolsheviks. The second oil rush began in 1991 with Western investors flocking to the area, drawn by the unprecedented reserves of 'the most sought after new oil province'.[9] A further reason for their arrival was the message it sent to Moscow that they wanted to deal with the newly independent state instead of the leviathan of Russian officialdom.

Within the Caucasus, most states view the oil industry as beneficial; Azerbaijan has access to the majority of resources and believes oil will provide sufficient funds to alter the state's destiny. Azeri political orientation has gradually shifted away from Russia, as President Aliev resents 'big brother', perceiving Russia as a neighbour greedy for further resources. Georgia has few of her own resources; its importance is due to its strategic location. The Black Sea port provides an outlet to European markets. Economic security would be guaranteed from revenue accrued from transit fees. At present the existing Baku–Grozny–Novorrossisk bisects the state, giving an importance to the state disproportionate to Chechnya's size. Chechnya also has proven reserves of 60 million tonnes. Commentators believed 'the Republic's oil reserves, created the illusion that Chechnya's wealth was misappropriated by Moscow'. Many therefore accepted the corollary; that once Chechnya had its own national government it would, as Dudayev put it, 'become a second Kuwait'.[10]

Within inter-state relations, oil has become the key ingredient. Azerbaijan's utilisation of oil as an economic and political tool during the Nagorno-Karabakh conflict illustrates the offensive potency of oil. September 1991 saw Azerbaijani officials halt the flow of oil to Armenia, reducing energy supplies by 90 per cent. An official declared 'the pipeline will not be reopened unless the Armenians comply with our political demands'.[11] Despite the counterproductive result of this action, it illustrates the importance of oil in a separate sphere to economics, by reducing an opponent's military capability. Production of oil has already begun in the Azeri fields following the signing of the 'contract of the century' in September of 1994 between a consortium of multinational oil companies and the Azerbaijani oil company SOCAR, worth an estimated $8 billion. Amongst the consortium is the Russian state oil company LUKoil, holding a 10 per cent share. The motivation behind this expedient act appears to be a 'political and economic measure',[12] to attempt to preclude Russian state activity from Azerbaijani affairs.

The prospects of regional economic security appear relatively feasible, but prospects for regional security are dependent upon the extent of Russia's desire to manifest her influence within the region.

Oil: a cause of the Chechen war?

Recent events in Chechnya and the wider area of the Caspian–Caucasus region have shown great preoccupation with the economic viability of restructuring the formerly economically depressed region. Plans for economic redevelopment are based around potentially huge earnings accrued from hydrocarbon developments. Akimov believes 'the Caspian Sea basin, particularly its energy resources is the focus of a huge debate between the countries surrounding it'.[13] Akimov's beliefs can be regarded as out of date, as the region's oil has now transcended debate to its present position as principal motivation for regional events.

This section will focus on a single event: the outbreak of the Chechen war of 1994–6, whilst attempting to reinforce the author's belief that the war was a manifestation of Moscow's desire to retain regional geo-economic influence. Chechnya's geo-economic significance is closely related to the distribution of oil, as Grozny represents an important refining centre closely linked with the production of specialised lubricants for the aviation industry. More importantly, it represents the mid-point in the Baku–Novorrossisk pipeline. Within this final section, the primary aspect will reflect upon the significance of pipelines attempting to validate the statement that pipelines represent the most pertinent of 'political symbols'.[14] Contained within the examination will be a discussion detailing the geo-economic significance of the prospective pipelines to the states, followed by a commentary on the detrimental effects of political instability upon the region. Contained within this investigation will be an analysis of the importance of Grozny's pipeline, which will assist in the exploration of Russia's geo-economic goals, which the author believes played an integral role in Moscow's decision to invade Chechnya. Contained within the latter half of the section will be an investigation into alternative causes offered by commentators, to explain the origins of the bloody war, with an assessment of the validity of the causes, followed by an examination of the possible future implications for both Russia and Chechnya.

The statement that pipelines represent 'political symbols' forms the foundation of an exploration of the causes of the Chechen war being related to Moscow's desire to maintain geo-economic influence. However, one must explain what the pipelines symbolise. This can be accomplished by dividing the examination into two parts: political significance and geo-economic relevance. Politically, pipelines are symbolically significant at two levels. At the state level they represent economic security, attained through the provision of transit fees. A further beneficial effect of pipeline possession is revenue accrued from supplementary industries, enabling burgeoning states to sustain economic growth across all sectors. Commentators believe, 'Because [the] oil economy has an immense infrastructure, many service industries will be involved'.[15] Thus states involved accrue vast incomes, whilst gaining necessary infrastructure improvements and radical modernisation of their service sectors, an area largely ignored under Communism. As a by-product of the oil industry, states foresee vast economic progression guaranteeing future financial and therefore political stability, whilst disassociating themselves from the current Russian economic malaise.

Secondly, pipelines illustrate political stability, as wealthy oil companies are unwilling to sacrifice vast sums of money on projects that may be disrupted by political uncertainty stemming from internal problems or external pressures, for 'political problems make large investments risky and unprofitable'.[16] In order to facilitate investment, political stability must be iron-clad. Political stability also brings forth further opportunities for further foreign investment, therefore demonstrating the importance of stability to promote external recognition and economic investment.

At a geo-economic level, pipelines are doubly symbolic. Primarily they represent states having control of resources, as any state with a pipeline transiting it has a capability to shut down supply; therefore, oil can be viewed as a geo-economic weapon. An example of this is the Nagorno-Karabakh struggle. A further significance of pipelines is their regional importance, due to their physical presence. A state with a pipeline automatically assumes disproportionate importance. The governments of foreign investors increase levels of political interest, in order to protect investments. Pipelines provide obvious targets for acts of sabotage and terrorism from dissatisfied political groups or envious neighbours. Furthermore they provide tangible evidence of inter-state links in a similar way to roads, demonstrating a collective unity between all states involved. As Isa Bisaev[17] said, 'this road [linking Chechnya and Georgia] has strategic importance for Chechnya'.[18] His statement emphasises the psychological importance of pipelines in representing physical links dispelling isolation, also stressing the state's control of resources. This may be viewed as the motivation behind Turkish attempts to promote an alternative pipeline route. It could be argued that Turkish campaigning was motivated by a geo-economic desire to exhibit a brotherly affinity with the states of the Caspian–Caucasus region, whilst demonstrating Turkey's geopolitical ambitions to prove herself an integral player in the rapidly developing re-run of the Great Game.

The second factor which exhibits the geo-economic significance of oil pipelines is the legal or illegal access it permits to resources. An example of this occurred during the Dudayev[19] period. 'Oil was being siphoned from the Chechen pipelines and stolen.'[20] This act provided the perpetrators with free oil whilst demonstrating the advantageous position that states in control of a pipeline find themselves in. Access to resources provides individual states with further geo-economic recognition, as they instantly become important. The degree of trust placed in them by the international oil conglomerates reflects the belief that states will not engage in such illegal siphoning, thus leaving states which actively stop such acts in a better position than those states who are unable or unwilling to halt the unscrupulous activity.

One may conclude that as 'political symbols' pipelines are prestigious symbols denoting a state ambition and signifying geo-economic importance. With reference to the states of the Caspian–Caucasus region, the variety of prospective routes illustrates a means of fulfilling the ambitions of states, in as much as they demonstrate a governmental willingness to promote regional stability at the internal level and intra-state levels. The pipelines promise a level of economic stability[21] which commentators believe 'will definitely have a noticeable effect on social and economic life in the region'.[22] On the other hand, the pipelines, and the wealth that comes with them, could cause regional friction between those states with money and those without.[23]

The following section will provide an examination of how these illustrations of geo-economic importance apply to the causes of war between Chechnya and Russia. This will be achieved by discussing firstly the Russian position, before continuing to examine the Chechen position.

It can be argued that Russia's geo-economic reasons for the invasion of Chechnya are two: the need to control resources and the desire to have access to hydrocarbon resources. At the control level, 'the decision by Moscow to send its military forces into the republic of Chechnya was motivated by a desire to secure control over its oil industry'.[24] A clarification should be made; Russian forces were not concerned with the indiginous oil industry, but with the more tangible 'political symbols' of the pipelines. The pipeline from Baku to Novorrossisk bisects Chechnya for 160 km. For the Moscow government the loss of such a physical symbol of influence equated with disaster. Their concerns revolved around the supposition that the Western-dominated oil consortium would be unwilling to utilise a route that traversed such a sensitive area as newly independent Chechnya, therefore reducing the possibility of the Russian pipeline route being selected (a huge loss of financial revenue for Moscow). The initial investment by the Western oil companies necessitated a westward flow for the oil. Moscow viewed this as advantageous for two reasons.

Firstly, their monopoly of the already existing pipeline increased the possibility of attracting Western investment to update and expand it. Secondly, the utilisation of the existing pipeline exhibited Moscow's willingness to become involved in the region's economic fortune, projecting geo-economic security. The invasion of Chechnya may also be viewed in geo-economic terms as a device to propel Russia back to its previous position at the heart of the hydrocarbon producing area, through the provision of a ready-built pipeline. Moscow viewed events as an opportunity to re-assert flagging regional influence, whilst re-establishing influence over Azerbaijan and Georgia. For the fledgling Chechen state the pipeline similarly represented control over their own destiny, providing valuable funds to reverse decades of Soviet neglect. It was the belief in Chechnya that Moscow had misappropriated wealth owed to them. Assuming control over the pipeline, they believed, would finance redevelopment, whilst vastly multiplying their geo-economic influence putting them on a par with Georgia, which also sought to gain a pipeline.

The second geo-economic cause for Moscow's action can be linked to its desire to maintain a quiescent Chechnya, in order to improve the Russian economic situation, despite Akimov's assertion that the 'necessary reconstruction of Novorrossisk's port facilities will contribute to high transport costs'.[25] However, the Russian leadership knew that the potential gains from the pacification of Chechnya were more valuable than if it surrendered its geo-economic interest. At a financial level, the vast wealth accrued through transit fees would more than justify necessary investments in improving facilities at Novorrossisk. It would also finance work necessary to 'upgrade or replace [the existing pipeline] to cope with the expected increase in output'.[26] Following large investments, residual capital could be employed extricating Russia from its economic quagmire. Thus one may concur with Galaev when he states that 'If Russia were to impose its preferred export route upon Azerbaijan i.e. through Chechnya . . . then the Chechen pipelines obviously had to be placed under Russian control.'[27] In order to accomplish this, the solution necessitated the pacification of the independent Chechen state and a reimposition of a pro-Russian government, which could only be achieved through conflict. From a Chechen perspective, the oil symbolised an economic opportunity to extricate themselves from their situation.

A further benefit of imposing Moscow's control over the republic's oil infrastructure would be dramatically increased geo-economic influence attained through a rise in regional profile. Russian regional influence, following the collapse of the Soviet Union in 1991, had not recovered, leaving Moscow with little input into regional events. Despite a piecemeal 10 per cent share in the 'deal of the century', Russian political and military influence was based too far from the region to manifest any control. The subjugation of Chechnya would facilitate closer contact with the area, allowing Moscow to increase influence in two ways: firstly by curtailing the growing influence of Turkey and Iran, and secondly by restricting the influence of the Western oil companies and their governments, through Moscow's demonstration of its determination to reinforce its position as an important player in Caspian–Caucasian affairs.

Another benefit of a successful little war in Chechnya would have been the increased prestige that would boost national morale, following the deep-seated national psychological shock after the momentous events of the late 1980s and early 1990s. At a geo-economic level, it would demonstrate the importance which Moscow accorded to the region, therefore emphasising Russian willingness to commit themselves to a region and demonstrating to other powers an ability and need to control geo-economic positions.

One can see the degree of importance the Russians attributed to the problem of Chechnya. To them, the conquest of an errant republic represented an opportunity to reassert geo-economic control, so one could argue that geo-economic goals were an integral motivation behind the origins of the Russian–Chechen war. However, in order to achieve their goal, the Russian government needed to gain stability, necessary to facilitate approval for the pipeline routes from the consortium of Western oil companies that provided necessary investment. They believed stability was possible if achieved through invasion. It would be naive, though, to believe that geo-economic aims provided the sole cause for invasion.

It is difficult to argue that one definite cause led to military hostility. Two other causes can be linked to the 1991 declaration of independence, which can be seen as a cause itself. The other important causes are: first, the security dilemma incorporating the problems associated with religion, and second, the effects of the deep-seated political enmity that exists between the two peoples stemming from perceived historical injustices.

To examine the importance of the declaration of independence as a cause of war, one must first examine the state of Chechnya during Soviet rule. As an autonomous republic of the Soviet Union, Chechnya received less political freedom than other areas. The national significance of the oil industry led to strict industrial control to maintain specialist aviation supplies. Economists based in Moscow dominated the entire industry. Communist power in Chechnya was held by the First Secretary of the Communist Party, a role traditionally held by a Russian, which was symbolic of Moscow's mistrust of Chechens. The treatment of Chechens constitutes an example of the backwardness of the Soviet nationalities policies.

One may see the timing of Dudayev's decision to proclaim independence as crucial to the future of his state, for he struck at a momentous moment in Soviet history, just as the coup of 1991 occurred. 'There was little Boris Yeltsin could do to prevent them, for the only reliable pro-Moscow force in Chechnya were the Communists, who were Yeltsin's main political foes.'[28] Initially, Yeltsin supported the calls for independence, because he viewed the act as strengthening his own hand in the fight against Communism, whilst demonstrating his democratic credentials. For some commentators Chechnya's declaration to secede from the voluntary union they had joined in 1922 'was the faultline down which the Soviet Union eventually cracked apart'.[29] It represented the crucial area which differentiated the plans of Gorbachev (to maintain the Communist union) and Yeltsin (who saw the future without the union but with the states of the FSU forming an economic and military bloc). After initial Russian support, opinions changed and Chechen independence became a problematic area. It could be argued that the alteration of opinions was a reaction to the speed and ease with which the symbols of Communism were dismantled and the rate at which the new state legitimised itself through elections. Real enmity has afflicted relations since 1991, stemming from the loss of Red Army power in Chechnya. If one examines Russian attitudes to Chechnya the conflict seems unavoidable, with Moscow's lack of recognition fuelling Chechen resolve for complete independence. Thus Russian intransigence escalated the problem, leading to mutual enmity and mistrust, setting both sides on a route to war.

Mistrust was mutual. Dudayev's post-independence actions did little to placate Moscow's fears. His relationship with Ruslan Khasbulatov[30] greatly irked Moscow, as did his decision not to return the Grozny KGB building. At a high-level meeting of the Supreme Soviet in Moscow an ultimatum calling for the disarmament of Chechen gangs was produced. The ultimatum can be read as an implicit declaration of war, as no state had succeeded in peacefully disarming the Chechens in 200 years. The physical result was the arrival of 600 Russian Interior Ministry troops at a nearby airbase. Thus one may sum up by saying that through Russian insensitivity and Chechen stubbornness both sides moved closer to war. The actions prove two points: firstly, that Russia was willing to utilise force to pursue its geo-economic goals; secondly, that the psychological effect that force had on the Chechens galvanised them into one body behind Dudayev, willing to fight and die as their forefathers had.

The Chechen situation dogged Yeltsin's first Russian government, illustrating many flaws in both policy and execution. To both the Russian government and the population, Chechnya represented a bandit state prospering under criminal leadership. To shellshocked Russia, military Chechnya seemed to be an opportunity to regain lost prestige. The Kremlin intrigues are well known, with ideas of *realpolitik* played out daily, to fortify or undermine individual political positions. With reference to Chechnya, 'a small victorious war' was seen as a miracle cure to banish re-election concerns, deflecting the population from domestic woes to bask in the glory of a successful military campaign. Evidence of this belief can be witnessed in the attitudes of significant governmental figures, such as Mikhail Barsukov:[31] 'Stalin sorted the Chechens in two weeks. What are we afraid of?'[32] Also in the flippant comments of Pavel Grachev[33] 'that whoever takes Dudayev's palace will get three stars'.[34] The war was to be originally initiated from within, by the Moscow-backed anti-Dudayev opposition. Summer 1994 marked an alteration in Moscow's policy, switching from direct conflict to open support of the opposition. However, one may view this shift in policy as a result of political intrigue. Galaev believes the switch constituted a wider policy to halt Khasbulatov ascendancy to a decisive position empowering him to alter events. To Yeltsin's government he represented a worse spectre than Dudayev. 'So dreaded was this scenario that rumours surfaced in Moscow that Yeltsin was contemplating a deal with Dudayev at Khasbulatov's expense.'[35] The result of Moscow's support of the Chechen opposition was the attempted coup of 26 November 1994, which ended in unmitigated disaster. The captured Russian troops demonstrated to the Chechens that the attempted coup was an act of state-sponsored terrorism, a fact which further vindicated Dudayev's claim that there was no opposition to him. The military success appears to vindicate the opinion of Yury Golotyuk that 'it looks like the republic has begun a countdown of the final hours before a major bloodletting'.[36] From a Russian perspective, the abortive coup was truly catastrophic, illustrating, firstly, the glaring problems of their armed forces, and secondly, an inability to achieve goals. A further problem revealed was the power vacuum that paralysed Russian government following President Yeltsin's health problems, leaving cabinet ministers to view the war as an opportunity to score political points against each another.

A possibility for an alternative cause of the Chechen war was that it would provide a solution to Russia's southern security dilemma. Dudayev orchestrated the 1992 withdrawal of the Russian army through an agreement with Yeltsin. The Russian security dilemma was two-fold; their departure had effectively marked the end of Russian dominance, as they had no recognisable regional force to maintain influence. Secondly, desertion left the North Caucasus military district arsenals at Dudayev's mercy. The Russian Ministry of Defence responded by seeking a meeting with the Chechen leadership to resolve their 'uncertain and perilous position[s], it seems they reluctantly struck a deal with Dudayev, leaving large quantities of weapons'.[37] The remaining weapons provided the nucleus of the Chechen army and formed the stock for the pre-war arms dealers who plied their trade in Grozny. Such a large amount of freely available military hardware hardened Moscow's perceptions that Chechnya was a bandit state dominated by the Mafia, creating an economic free-trade zone, jeopardising Russian security through an abundance of weapons. Moscow's security dilemma can be viewed as an important cause of the fateful Chechen invasion, due to the perceived lawlessness and the close proximity of Chechnya. Therefore an invasion of Chechnya could be seen to represent a policing measure designed to eradicate the den of thieves.

Also involved in Moscow's considerations would have been the perilous position of the ethnic Russian population living in Chechnya, who dominated the lucrative positions in the oil industry. The perceived security dilemma was further exacerbated by the religious demographics of Chechnya. When assessing the problems associated with Russia's security dilemma, it is important to understand the level of paranoia prevalent in Russian society concerning their security. One may hypothesise that this is the by-product of Russia constituting a land-based empire open to attack through thousands of kilometres of border. Tied in with the fact that Russians prefer to guard their own borders instead of trusting security to third parties, the need to gain control of Chechnya to allay Russian paranoia suggests the importance of the security dilemma as another possible cause of the Chechen war.

Islam has long served to alienate Chechnya from Russia. As a result, the Soviet authorities sought to crush Islam and replace it through Russification. The expulsion of Russia cleared the path for an Islamic renaissance, wholeheartedly supported by neighbouring Muslim states, which had succeeded 'in admitting a number of Muslim states of the former USSR to the Organisation for Economic Co-operation'.[38] From the Russian perspective any alteration in Chechen influence presented problems, the most pertinent being the switch in polarity from north to south. Any attempt to subjugate an Islamic nation could provoke sympathy amongst Islamic nations and the native Islamic minority in Russia, possibly causing assistance to be granted. Of further concern to Moscow was the possibility of a *jihad*. The depth of this concern can be discerned if one examines examples of previous attempts to subjugate Islamic nations. During the Afghan war the fundamentalist opposition (Mujahadeen) mounted fierce resistance to the Red Army, eventually forcing withdrawal. The Soviet Ministry of Defence was unprepared for the strength of the resistance, a resistance motivated by Muslim fundamentalists. Chechnya presented similar obstacles, having a highly motivated Islamic population willing to pay any price for the expulsion of the 'infidel invader', in a similar manner to their forefathers led by Shamyl, who 'would never surrender: he fought for Allah and freedom'.[39] Thus one may conclude that the religious problem further exacerbated Russian paranoia over their security dilemma.

A further cause of the war can be found in the long history of enmity between the two nations. Throughout their collective histories there are many significant events which illustrate enmity, and contribute to their mutual mistrust. The examination of historical factors will take place in chronological order. Commentators believe that the roots of the present struggle can be found in the eighteenth century. In many ways the war of the nineteenth century can be regarded as similar to the recent war. The Russian military relied upon its numerical superiority, believing 'that the sheer size of their force (40 000 troops) would be sufficient to scare off Dudayev and his "gangs"'.[40] Their wrong assumption echoes that of their military forebears, as both underestimated the strength and quality of the opposing forces. The first great Chechen leader, Iman Shamyl, utilised tactics of guerrilla warfare to assist in the destruction of the Tsarist forces. 'Shamyl had all the advantages of the guerrilla commander: speed, surprise and closeness to the land.'[41] Despite such advantages, his resistance proved futile, and he was captured in 1859, ending six decades of struggle. A further similarity between the two conflicts was the motivation. Imperialist Russia was in an expansionist phase, wishing to increase regional geopolitical control, whilst the Chechens were fighting for autonomy. In essence, one may examine the recent war as a mere continuation of the former struggle, as neither side completely achieved its original aims. Throughout the Soviet period Communist control in Chechnya was never complete, but punctuated by occasional revolts and events, which appeared to strengthen the Chechen sense of homogeneity.

The event that strengthened national identity was Stalin's decision to deport the entire population of Chechnya to Kazakhstan. The deportations added to Chechnya's sense of historical grievance whilst acting 'as an important but often forgotten factor behind the four-year stand-off'.[42] During the deportation an estimated 100 000 Chechens died. Despite the commonly held view that Stalin's crude attempt at ethnic cleansing was a success, revisionist opinion may judge his decision differently. Commentators believe the period in exile left deep scars across a new generation, making them more willing to achieve their goals. The validity of this opinion is reinforced if one reflects on the products of this generation: Khasbulatov, Dudayev, Maskhadov and all Chechens born before 1957 (the date signifying their rehabilitation). For the nationalist Dudayev the atrocities of the deportations acted as an essential ingredient of his anti-Russian stance.

However, the years following the rehabilitation demonstrated that the obedience of the Chechens had altered little, as they constituted a group highly dissatisfied with Communist rule. Examples of their displeasure include protests and demonstrations. 'February 1973 [saw] one of the largest demonstrations of the Brezhnev years take place in Grozny',[43] over a territorial dispute. Other grievances included Russian chauvinism and the lack of educational opportunity, effectively turning Chechens into second-class citizens. These problems were compounded by allegations of economic misappropriation. The result of the disturbances was the tangible hardening of an anti-Chechen feeling that has clouded relations ever since. It may be argued that a further cause of bilateral antagonism was the Chechen Mafia. As organised crime constitutes a notoriously difficult phenomenon to substantiate accurately, it is necessary to rely on circumstantial evidence. However, Chechnya's criminal power was obvious to the citizens of Russia who witnessed the Chechens grow rich from protection rackets, theft, prostitution and drugs rings. The shadowy godfathers were products of the rootless deportation generation; their brutality and ferocity may be interpreted as a reaction to their upbringing. Indeed, many Russians perceive the agony of deportation as providing the impetus for criminal gangs, especially when coupled with the importance of the clan structure within Chechen society. In his monumental catalogue of Soviet injustice, Solzhenitsyn comments that the deported Chechens took positions in which they were able to fulfil 'their passion for thieving', adding 'they were capable of rustling cattle, robbing a house, or sometimes taking what they wanted by force'.[44] After the collapse of Communism, they took advantage of the situation. Journalistic reports of pre-war Grozny depict a den of thieves, an arena for them to display their wealth. Thus they gave Moscow further justification for the war, for it could claim that as a result of victory the problems of organised crime would disappear, restoring law and order.

Thus one could argue that history has been used by both sides. To the nationalist Chechen ideology 'history is utilised to instill and reinforce the collective memory of the past',[45] despite the history comprising a catalogue of failures. The events demonstrate that Russia, in whichever incarnation, has acted as the aggressor. From this collection of historical examples, one may say that states' attitudes to one another have changed little in three centuries, which demonstrates the validity of the claim that historical events provide essential causes for the outbreak of the Chechen war.

To conclude this section on the causes of the Chechen war, one cannot say that any one cause was responsible for initiating events. At an individual level the causes amount to little more than hypotheses. Yet together they represent a reasonable explanation. It is estimated that the conflict cost 50 000 Russian and Chechen lives, including civilian casualties. Indeed, the horrors of the Chechen war are not yet fully understood. One may argue that this is the fault of Western governments and media which did little to publicise the war and the atrocities carried out by both sides in the name of victory, from the bombing of Chechen villagers by Russian forces to the hostages taken by the Chechens. The financial and psychological cost of the war may never be known, but the estimates for the cost of rebuilding Grozny run into billions of dollars. However, one fact is certain: until a definitive peace is reached this will represent another entry in the collective catalogue of injustice to the Chechens. To Russia it will represent their darkest military hour, their mighty army humbled by 'gangsters'. The desperation felt at the situation is evident in the views of one conscript: 'Mistake? This is more than a mistake, it's stupid, it's a disaster, it's a complete fucking shambles. We've lost an enormous number of men for no reason at all.'[46] At a political level the same strong language could be used. The detrimental geopolitical effects include a growth in confidence by states of the Southern Caucasus and Central Asia in the pursuance of policies unpopular to Moscow, in the fields of energy transportation and military cooperation. The former threat of Russian force is now perceived as a joke. Yet the war was caused by all factors. 'Russia invaded Chechnya out of a mixture of frustration, anger and humiliation resulting from the 26 November 1994 blunder. Far-reaching considerations of strategy, geo-economics and domestic politics were secondary.'[47]

Notes

1 M. A. Smith, *A Chronology of the Chechen Conflict,* Conflict Studies Research Centre, June 1995, p. 16.
2 B. Gokay, 'Chechens Make Fearsome Enemies – Historical Background of Russia's Agelong Fight in Chechnya', *Cambridge Review of International Affairs,* 1994/1995, pp. 80–8.
3 L. Blanch, *The Sabres of Paradise,* New York, 1984, p. 1.
4 Kindjals – wickedly pointed sharp daggers passed down through families. The essential part of any warrior's armoury.
5 R. Kangas, 'Remembering the 1944 Chechen Deportation', in A. Digaev (ed.), www.amina.com/chechens/article/deport.html.
6 *The Times,* 12 March 1998, p. 23.
7 N. Riasanovsky, *A History of Russia,* Oxford, 1993, p. 337.
8 *Dispatches,* BBC 2, 21 March 1998.

9 Chairman of Ramco Oil.
10 M. Galaev, *The Chechen Crisis: Background and Future Implications*, Conflict Studies Research Centre, June 1995, pp. 2 and 17.
11 Azeri official, *Reuters*, 15 November 1991.
12 *Dispatches*, BBC 2, 21 March 1998.
13 A. Akimov, 'Oil and Gas in the Caspian Sea Region: an Overview of Co-operation and Conflict', http://www.intr.net./cpss/casian/akim.txt.p.1.
14 B. Gokay, 'Caspian Uncertainties: Regional Rivalries and Pipelines', *Perceptions*, March–May 1998, p. 12.
15 Ibid., p. 18.
16 Akimov, 'Oil and Gas in the Caspian Sea Region', p. 4.
17 Isa Bisaev, an adviser to the current Chechen president Aslan Maskhadov.
18 Isa Bisaev, an excerpt taken from 'Putting Business First', *War Report*, December–January 1997, p. 17.
19 Dhozhkar Dudayev, leader of the breakaway Chechen republic. An ex-Red Army bomber commander and member of the nomenkultura nationalists. He assumed the presidency to facilitate independence, succeeding only in leading the state to war.
20 C. Gall and T. De Wall, *Chechnya – A Small Victorious War*, London, 1997, p. 128.
21 Economic stability is of course dependent upon the global price and demand for oil being kept sufficiently high to justify the expenses accrued from exploiting the oil.
22 Gokay, 'Caspian Uncertainties', p. 18.
23 R. E. Ebel, 'The History and Politics of Chechen Oil', http://www.amina.com/chechens/article/oil-op.html., p. 1.
24 Ibid., p. 2.
25 A. Akimov, 'Oil and Gas in the Caspian Sea', p. 4.
26 Gokay, 'Caspian Uncertainties', p. 12.
27 Galaev, *The Chechen Crisis*, p. 7.
28 Ibid., p. 17.
29 Gall and De Waal, *Chechnya*, p. 89.
30 Ruslan Khasbulatov, Speaker of the Russian Federation's Supreme Soviet. He featured as Yeltsin's principal political foe and Russia's second famous Chechen. His relations with Dudayev strengthened anti-Chechen feelings through allegations of collusion.
31 Mikhail Barsukov, Chief of Russia's counter-intelligence service.
32 Gall and De Waal, *Chechnya*, p. xii.
33 Pavel Grachev, President Yeltsin's Defence Minister.
34 Sergie Yushenko, excerpt from an interview from 29 October 1996, cited in Gall and De Waal, *Chechnya*, p. 13.
35 Galaev, *The Chechen Crisis*, p. 6.
36 Y. Golotyuk, 6 August 1994, p. 3, cited in *The Current Digest of the Post Soviet Press*, Vol. 46, No. 31, 31 August 1994.
37 M. Galaev, *The Chechen Crisis*, p. 17.
38 A. Vasilyev, *Izvestia*, 10 March 1992, p. 6, cited in *The Current Digest of the Post Soviet Press*. Vol. 44, No. 10, 8 April 1992, p. 1.
39 L. Blanch, *The Sabres of Paradise*, New York, 1960, p. 188.
40 Galaev, *The Chechen Crisis*, p. 7.

41 Gall and De Waal, *Chechnya*, p. 46.
42 R. Kangus, 'Remembering the 1944 Chechen Deportations', http://amina.com/chechens/article/deport.html, p. 1.
43 Gall and De Waal, *Chechnya*, p. 78.
44 A. I. Solzhenitsyn, *The Gulag Archipelago*, Vol. 3, New York, 1973, p. 402.
45 Galaev, *The Chechen Crisis*, p. 2.
46 A. Lievan, 'Beyond the Victory', *War Report*, February–March 1998, p. 78.
47 Galaev, *The Chechen Crisis*, p. 7.

Select Bibliography

Newpapers, magazines and newswires

'Russia Drills Less Oil, OPEC Keeps It Cheap', *Economist*, 8 June 1985, p. 65.

'Fact Sheet on Declarations of Independence', *Radio Liberty Report USSR*, No. 45, pp. 23–5 and No. 46, p. 23, 1990.

'Armenia Elects Nationalist as Head of Parliament', *Reuters*, 4 August 1990.

'Azerbaijan Taking its Capitalism a Single Spoonful at a Time', *Chicago Tribune*, 20 August 1990.

'Azerbaijan; Was Might Right', *Economist*, 29 September 1990.

'Statoil, BP, Aim to Develop Soviet Caspian Oilfield', *Reuters*, 23 October 1990.

'Azerbaijan Invites Foreign Firms to Develop Oil', *Reuters* (Money Report), 15 September 1991.

'Azerbaijan Blasts Gorbachev Initiative on Karabakh', *Reuters* (Money Report), 20 September 1991.

'Tehran Cautious over Soviet Break-up; Iran Delays Recognition of Muslim Republics to avoid Antagonising Moscow', *Middle East Economic Digest*, Vol. 35, No. 37, p. 12, 20 September 1991.

'Armenia, Azerbaijan Sign Accord over Territory', *Reuters*, 23 September 1991.

'Amoco Subsidiary Names Five Western Partners in Azeri Oilfield Project in Azerbaijan Sector of Caspian Sea, USSR', *PR Newswire*, 27 September 1991.

'Soviet Republics Ready to Initial Economic Deal', *Reuters*, 1 October 1991.

'Azerbaijan Cut Gas Line, Plans Attack–Armenia', *Reuters*, 5 November 1991.

'World Wire: Energy Crunch Slows Armenia', *Wall Street Journal*, 11 November 1991.

'Fuel Blocade of Armenia Creates Bread Shortages', *Reuters*, 15 November 1991.

'Turkey Aims to Revive Ancient Silk Road Ties', *MidEast Markets*, 18 November 1991.

'Yerevan: Gas Blockade is Expected to be Broken at Midnight', *Isvestia*, No. 274, p. 1 (from *SovDataDiaLine*), 18 November 1991.

'Copter Crash Kills 20 on Armenia-Azeri Peace Bid', *Reuters*, 20 November 1991.

'Two More Dead in Soviet Transcaucasia Unrest', *Reuters*, 24 November 1991.

'Gorbachev Seeks Neutral Zone in Caucasus', *Reuters*, 25 November 1991.

'Armenia Receives Gas Through Georgia', *Izvestia*, No. 286, p. 2 (from *SovDataDiaLine*), 3 December 1991.

'The Changing Union', *Financial Times*, 13 December 1991.

'Life after Gorbachev', *Economist*, 3 January 1992.

'Russia, Azerbaijan Seek IMF, World Bank Membership', *Bureau of National Affairs (BNA) International Trade Daily*, 8 January 1992.

'Azerbaijan Still Hopes for Amoco Deal', *Financial Times*, 10 January 1992.

'The Killing Mountains', *Economist*, 18 January 1992.

'Azerbaijan Wants Gas; Azerbaijan's Natural Gas Supplies; News', *Middle East Business Weekly*, Vol. 36, No. 34, p. 13, 28 August 1992.

'Between America and Europe: Oil Rich Azerbaijan Seeks Close Ties With America', *Megapolis-Express* [*Russian Press Digest*], No. 38, p. 22, 23 September 1992.

'Pressure Grows on Azerbaijan Leader to Quit', *New York Times*, Section A, p. 3, 23 June 1993.

'Economic Cooperation Organisation Summit: Relations Between Azerbaijan and Iran', *BBC Summary of World Broadcasts* (source: Islamic Republic News Agency, Iran), 8 July 1993.

'Azerbaijan Looks to Russia for Help', *UPI*, 5 September 1993.

'Correcting Mistakes: Azerbaijan is Changing its Policy in Regard to Russia', *Pravda*, [*Russian Press Digest*], p. 1, 8 September 1993.

'Karabakh Conflict Internationalized', *Obschaya Gazeta* [*Russian Press Digest*], p. 2, 4 February 1994.

'"Breakthrough" in Armenian and Azerbaijan Peace Talks', *Deutsche Presse Agentur*, 9 September 1994.

'Azerbaijan Signs Contract with Western Oil Consortium', *Izvestia* [*Russian Press Digest*], p. 2, 21 September 1994.

'Hand of Moscow Waving Kerchief From Wharf', *Izvestia* [*Russian Press Digest*], p. 4, 5 November 1994.

'Azerbaijan Ratifies Multi-Billion Dollar Oil Deal', *Deutsche Presse-Agentur*, 15 November 1994.

'Exxon to Acquire Interest in Azerbaijan Project', *Univresal News Services*, 3 April 1995.

'Geidar Aliev Discovers that He Was Slave', *Pravda* [*Russian Press Digest*], p. 1, 6 July 1995.

'Ramco Energy Says Caspian Most Sought After Oil Province', *Extel Examiner*, 5 September 1995.

'He Wants to be President, Not Khan: Former President of Azerbaijan Ayaz Mutalibov has Chances of Regaining Lost Power, Say Analysts', *Obschaya Gazeta* [*Russian Press Digest*], p. 5, 7 September 1995.

'Oil Giants Seen Favouring Dual Azerbaijan Pipeline', *Reuters* (Money Report), 8 October 1995.

'Focus–Azeri Oil Export Struggle Ends', *Reuters* (Money Report), 9 October 1995.

'Russian Threat Will Not Stop Azerbaijan Oil Ops in Caspian: Industry Source', *AFX News*, 3 November 1995.

'Geidar Aliev Hopes to Attract Western Capital to the Economy of Azerbaijan', *Segodnya*, p. 7 [source: *Russian Press Digest*], 30 November 1995.

'Getting Azerbaijan's Oil to the International Market: the Turkish Perspective', *Azerbaijan International*, 3/3, Autumn 1995, pp. 54–7.

'Turkish President Begins Two-Day Visit to Azerbaijan', *Deutsche Presse-Agentur*, 7 December 1995.

'Demirel reiterates support for Azerbaijan over Nagorny-Karabakh', *Deutsche Presse-Agentur*, 8 December 1995.

'Chechen War Compels Azerbaijan to Look for Parteners Outside the CIS', *Literaturnaya Gazeta* [*Russian Press Digest*], p. 2, 17 April 1996.

'Iranian Azeris Protest Arrest of Religious Leaders in Azerbaijan', *Agence France Presse*, 28 May 1996.

'Caspian International Petroleum Company Formed for Exploration, Development of Karabakh Project', *PR Newswire*, 10 June 1996.

'Geidar Aliyev is Critical About Porter Amendment to Nagorny- Karabakh', *Segodnya* [*Russian Press Digest*], p. 7, 14 June 1996.

'Exxon/Socar Sign Memorandum of Understanding on Two Caspian Sea Exploration Blocks', *PR Newswire*, 6 June 1996.

Note on Russian sources

The main source for the above information from Russian-speaking sources is the *Russian Press Digest*. The copyright belongs to Russica Information Inc., RusDataDiaLine.

Other information from Russian and FSU sources (*Interfax, Turan, Azerbaycan Radio, Yerevan SNARK* etc.) comes from the Foreign Broadcast Information Service, *Daily Report-Central Eurasia* (formerly FBIS-SOV), for the research period September–December 1994 and September–October 1995 (Chapter 5).

McDonald, Paul. *The Oil Markets of the Pacific Rim: into the 1990s*. A Financial Times Management Report, London: Financial Times Business Information, 1990.

Country Profile: Georgia, Armenia, Azerbaijan. 1995–1996. London: The Economist Intelligence Unit, 1996.

'Energy Map of the World (1996)', *Petroleum Economist Map Series*, No. 2, 5th.

'Gas in the CIS, 1996', a special report, *Petroleum Economist*, 1996.

'Oil and Gas Guide to the FSU', 4th edn, CIS Technical and Publishing Institute, London, 1995.

Books and journal articles

Akiner, Shirin. *Islamic Peoples of the Soviet Union*. London: Kegan Paul International, 1983.

Aves, Jonathan. *Post-Soviet Transcaucasia*. Post Soviet Business Forum Paper, London, Royal Institute of International Affairs, 1993.

Aves, Jonathan. *Georgia: From Chaos to Stability*. Former Soviet South Project, RIIA, 1996.

Aydin, Turan. 'Russia's Petroleum and Natural Gas Policy'. *Eurasian Studies*, 1/4 (Winter 1995), 40–62.

Baranovsky, Vladimir. 'Post-Soviet Conflict Heritage and Risks'. *Stockholm International Peace Research Institute Yearbook 1993: World Armaments and Disarmament*. Oxford, Oxford University Press, 1993, 131–58.

Barnet, J. *Middle East Oil and the Energy Crisis*. Joe Stork, New York, 1975.

Benningsen, Alexander. 'Pan-Turkism and Pan-Islamism in History and Today'. *Central Asian Survey*, 3/3 (1985).

Blank, Stephen. 'Energy, Economics and Security in Central Asia: Russia and its Rivals'. *Central Asian Survey*, 14/3 (1995), 373–406, and 'Central Asia, South Asia and Asian Security', *Eurasian Studies*.

Bremmer, Ian and Taras, Ray (eds). *Nations and Politics in the Soviet Successor States*. Cambridge, Cambridge University Press, 1993.

'Conflict Developments on the Territory of the Former Soviet Union'. *SIPRI Yearbook 1994*, 169–203.

Croissant, M. and Aras, B. (eds). *Oil and Geopolitics in the Caspian Sea Region*, Westport, Praeger, 1999.

Dadrian, Vahakn N. 'Nationalism in Soviet Armenia – a Case Study of Ethnocentrism', in George W. Simmonds (ed.), *Nationalism in the USSR and Eastern Europe*. Papers and Proceedings of the Symposium held at the University of Detroit on 3–4 October 1975, Detroit, Michigan, University of Detroit Press.

Dawisha, Karen and Parrott, Bruce. *Russia and the New States of Eurasia: the Politics of Upheaval*. Cambridge, Cambridge University Press, 1995.

Demirhan, Ali A. 'Economic Cooperation on the Silk Road'. *Eurasian Studies*, 2/1 (Spring 1995), 75–87.

Dragadze, Tamara. 'Azerbaijanis', in Graham Smith (ed.), *The Nationalities Question in the Soviet Union*. London, Longman, 1990, 163–79.

Dudwick, Nora. 'Armenia: the Nation Awakens', in Ian Bremmer and Ray Taras (eds.), *Nations and Politics in the Soviet Successor States*. Cambridge, Cambridge University Press, 1993, 261–87.

Flakierski, Henryk. *Income Inequalities in the Former Soviet Union and its Republics*. Armonk, New York, M. E. Sharpe, 1993.

Forsythe, Rosemarie.*The Politics of Oil in the Caucasus and Central Asia*. Adelphi Paper 300, London, IISS, 1996.

Fuller, Elisabeth. *Azerbaijan at the Crossroads*. PSBF Paper, London, RIIA, March 1994.'Transcaucasia: Ethnic Strife Threatens Democratisation'. *RFE/RL Research Report*, 2/1, 1 January, 17–24.

Fuller, Graham E. and Lasser, Ian O. 'Turkey's New Geopolitics from the Balkans to Western China'. *RAND Study*, Boulder,Westview Press, 1993.

Gökay, Bülent. 'Turkish Settlement and the Caucasus, 1918–1920'. Special Issue: *Turkey Identity, Democracy, Politics*. *Middle Eastern Studies*, 32/2, April 1996, 45–76.

Gökay, Bülent and Langhorne, Richard. *Turkey and the New States of the Caucasus and Central Asia*. Wilton Park Paper 111, London, HMSO, January 1996.

Goldenberg, Suzanne. *Pride of Small Nations: the Caucasus and the Post-Soviet Disorder*. London, Zed Books, 1994.

Hegaard, Steven E. 'Nationalism in Azerbaidzhan in the Era of Brezhnev', in George W. Simmonds (ed.), *Nationalism in the USSR and Eastern Europe*. Detroit, Michigan, University of Detroit Press, 1975, 188–99.

Henze, Paul B. 'Georgia and Armenia Troubled Independence'. *Eurasian Studies*, 2/2 (Summer 1995), 25–35.

Hill, Fiona. 'Russia's Tinderbox', in *Report on Conflict in the North Caucasus and its Implications for the Future of the Russian Federation*. Strengthening Democratic Institutions Project, Cambridge, Massachussets, Harvard University, John F. Kennedy School of Government, September 1995.

Hill, Fiona and Jewett, Pamela. 'Confederation of Peoples of the Caucasus', in *Report on Ethnic Conflict in the Russian Federation and Transcaucasia*. SDI Project, Cambridge MA, John F. Kennedy School of Government, July 1993.

Hunter, Shireen. 'Azerbaijan: Search for Identity and New Partners', in *Nations and Politics*, 225–60.

Ilhan, Suat. 'Geopolitic Developments and the Turkish World'. *Eurasian Studies*.

Kaiser, Robert J. *The Geography of Nationalism in Russia and the USSR*. Princeton, Princeton University Press, 1994.

Karklins, Rasma. *Ethnic Relations in the USSR: the Perspective from Below*. Boston, Allen & Unwin, 1986.

Kennedy, Paul. *The Rise and Fall of Great Powers: Economic Change and Military Conflict from 1500 to 2000*. London, Fontana Press, 1989.

Kuliev, Fuad. 'Prospects for Foreign Investment in the Azerbaijan Oil Industry'. *Oil and Gas Guide to the FSU*, CIS Technical Publishing Institute, 4th edn, London, 1995.

Kuliyev, Ragip. 'General Problems of Implementation of Economic Reforms in Azerbaijan'. *Eurasian Studies*, 1/3 (Fall 1994), 45–53.

Landgren, Signe. 'Post-Soviet Threats to Security'. *SIPRI Yearbook 1992: World Armaments and Disarmament*. Oxford, Oxford University Press, 1992.

Lane, David. *Soviet Economy and Society*. Oxford, Basil Blackwell, 1985.

Lane, David (ed.). *Russia in Flux: the Political and Social Consequences of Reform*. Aldershot, Edward Elgar Publishing Limited, 1992.

Lermontov, Mikhail. *A Hero of our Time*, trans. Paul Foote. London, Penguin Books, 1966.

Martin, Rob. *Inter-Ethnic Conflict in Soviet Azerbaijan*. Thames Paper, The School of Social Sciences at Thames Polytechnic, London, 1990.

Mesbahi, Mohiaddin (ed.). *Central Asia and the Caucasus after the Soviet Union: Domestic and International Dynamics*. Gainsville, Florida, University Press of Florida, 1994.

Mesbahi, Mohiaddin. 'Russian Foreign Policy and Security in Central Asia and the Caucasus'. *Central Asian Survey*, 12/2 (1993), 181–215.

Motyl, Alexander J. *Sovietology, Rationality, Nationality: Coming to Grips with Nationalism in the USSR*. New York, Columbia University Press, 1990.

Naumkin, Vitaly V. (ed.). *Central Asia and Transcaucasia*. Westport, CT, Greenwood Press, 1994.

Nichol, James. 'Azerbaijan', in James Curtis (ed.), *Armenia, Azerbaijan, and Georgia Country Studies*, Library of Congress, Federal Research Division, Washington, 1995.

Nissman, David. *The Soviet Union and Iranian Azerbaijan: the Use of Nationalism for Political Penetration*. Boulder, Westview, 1987.

Nissman, David. 'Kurds, Russians, and the Pipeline'. *Eurasian Studies*, 2/1 (Spring 1995).

Odell, Peter R. *Oil and World Power*, 5th edn, Penguin Books, 1979.

Ögötçü, Mehmet. 'Eurasian Energy Prospects: Need for a Long-Term Western Strategy'. *Eurasian Studies*, 1/3 (Fall 1994), 61–99.

Papava, Vladimir. 'The Georgian Economy: Problems of Reform'. *Eurasian Studies*, 2/2 (Summer 1995), 52–62.

Rakowska-Harmstone, Teresa. 'The Study of Ethnic Politics in the USSR', in George W. Simmonds (ed.), *Nationalism in the USSR and Eastern Europe*, Detroit, Michigan, University of Detroit Press, 1975, 20–36.

Rarhr, Alexander. '"Atlanticists" versus "Eurasians" in Russian Foreign Policy'. *Radio Free Europe/Radio Liberty Research Report*, 1/22, 29 May 1992, 17–22.

Reed, Robert G. III and Fereidun Fesharski (eds). *The Oil Market in the 1990s: Challenges for the New Era*. Boulder, Westview, Special Studies in International Economics and Business, 1989.

Roberts, John. *Caspian Pipelines*. A Former Soviet South Project, London, RIIA, 1996.

Sayigh, Yezid. *Confronting the 1990s: Security in the Developing Countries*. Adelphi Paper 251, London, Brassey's, for the International Institute for Strategic Studies, 1990.

Shakoor, Abdul. 'Central Asia: the US Interest-Perception and its Security Policies', *Eurasian Studies*, 2/2 (Summer 1995), 14–24.

Stern, Jonathan P. *Oil and Gas in the Former Soviet Union: the Changing Foreign Investment Agenda*. PSBF Paper, London, RIIA, July 1993.

Suny, R. G. (ed.). *Transcaucasia: Nationalism and Social Change (Essays in the History of Armenia, Azerbaijan and Georgia)*. Ann Arbor, University of Michigan, 1983.

Swietochowski, Tadeusz. *Russian Azerbaijan, 1905–1920: the Shaping of National Identity in a Muslim Community*. New York, Cambridge University Press, 1985.

Swietochowski, Tadeusz. *Russia and Azerbaijan: a Borderland in Transition*. New York, Columbia University Press, 1995.

Wheelwright, Ted. *Oil and World Politics: From Rockefeller to the Gulf War*. Sydney, Australia, Left Book Club, 1991.

Yergin, Daniel. *The Prize: the Epic Quest for Oil, Money and Power*. London, Simon and Schuster, 1991.

'The Geopolitics of Oil in Central Asia', in *Cosmos*, Vol. 1, No. 2, Institute of International Relations, Athens, August 1995 and 'Pipeline Politics: Trans-Balkan Pipeline, the Most Important Greek Post Cold War Strategic Move?', Vol. 1, No. 1, May 1995.

Unpublished papers

Herzig, Edmund. 'The Post-Soviet Foreign Policies of Armenia and Azerbaijan', from the Seminar on 'Security and Foreign Policy in Central Asia and the Caucasus', Institute for Political and International Studies, Teheran, 14–16 January 1996.

Myrianthis, Michael L. 'Oleaginous Geopolitics in South-West Asia and the Burgas–Alexandroupolis Oil Pipeline'. The paper is based on seminar material, presented by the author, at the Institute of International Relations of the Panteion University, Athens, 31 May 1995.

Index